WINNING AT MATH

Your Guide to Learning Mathematics Through Successful Study Skills

SIXTH EDITION

Paul D. Nolting, Ph.D.
Learning Specialist

Academic Success Press, Inc.
FLORIDA

This book is dedicated to my son, Eric, to my wife, Kim, and to the memory of my good friend Bill Thomas. It is also dedicated to the thousands of students who are having difficulty learning mathematics and the instructors who are teaching them.

Winning at Math:
Your Guide to Learning Mathematics
Through Successful Study Skills
(Sixth Edition)
by Paul D. Nolting, Ph.D.
New, Expanded and Revised Sixth Edition, 2014
Copyright © 2014 by Paul D. Nolting, Ph.D.
ISBN-13: 978-0-940287-63-6
Published by Academic Success Press, Inc.
Editor: Daniel Crown
Assistant Editor: Kimberly Nolting
Photo Credits: Unless otherwise noted, all photos and clipart are reproduced
with the permission of
Fotosearch.com and ClipArt.com.

Printed in the United States of America.

Contents

Preface

College students have a complicated relationship with mathematics. Some love math's ironclad logic and ceaseless challenges. Others hold a special kind of hatred for the subject—the medieval sort usually reserved for murderous rogues, vengeful witches and bilious plagues.

While students are allowed to feel any way they want about math, the necessity of the subject is beyond debate. Simply put, students *must* pass math to graduate college. In fact, some colleges and universities require students to take and pass up to four math classes to graduate. Too many students are intimidated by math because they have a poor high school math background, have test anxiety or are returning to school for the first time in many years. Even these students, however, understand that, like it or not, thriving in their math courses leads to more career options and better paying jobs.

For this reason, students want assistance to help them become successful in math; they want tips and procedures they can easily implement to help improve their grades. Many of these students believe tutoring will fix any and all problems. In reality, this is only one part of the equation. Before a student can thrive in math, he or she must reduce anxiety, learn math-specific study skills and adopt a series of effective test-taking strategies.

Winning at Math is the only math-specific study skills book to offer statistical evidence demonstrating an improvement in students' ability to learn math and to make better grades. The math study skills, anxiety reduction techniques and test-taking procedures provided in *Winning at Math* are based on learning specialist Dr. Paul D. Nolting's 30 years of research. This research has concentrated on students who have difficulty learning math at colleges and universities throughout the United States. The *Winning at Math* techniques are equally as effective for students who are taking math for the first time as they are for those who have previously failed math. In fact, evidence also suggests the book leads to improvement in other non-math courses as well.

The sixth edition of *Winning at Math* is of special interest to a new group of students. These new students may have a learning style that does not mesh well with the way math is traditionally taught, they may have a disability, or they may have to take a non-traditional math course such as a distance learning course or an Emporium model course.

These students face additional challenges to be successful in math and graduate. In almost every case, these students must become better independent learners. This text provides research-based, practical suggestions to this new group of students and courses. The text also has a special website that features additional information and surveys built to improve student success, which can be found at www.AcademicSuccess.com. These suggestions, of course, also improve the success of all students in the areas of mathematics learning and grades.

No matter who you are, the skills in this book can work for you!

Introduction

Learning math requires a different set of learning skills, testing skills and anxiety reduction techniques than those used in other courses. That is why general study skills courses or freshman seminar courses are not typically successful in improving math grades. For this reason, many students make "A's" and "B's" in all other courses but have difficulty passing math. By using the suggested study procedures in Winning at Math, you will be able to improve your math grades by developing an individualized math success plan.

The format of the sixth edition of *Winning at Math* has been revised to make it easier to read. First of all, the book is printed in color. Second, it contains even more proven math study skills techniques than ever before. Third, it focuses on different types of math courses, including online courses and Emporium model courses.

As always, this edition of *Winning at Math* includes Web-based support in the form of the revised Math Study Skills Evaluation, Learning Modality Inventory and online homework. The chapter on reading and homework has been expanded to include more strategies for online reading and homework. The math anxiety section focuses on how students develop math anxiety and how to decrease the anxiety with an online "How to Reduce Text Anxiety" track. The last chapter focuses on student motivation, including an expanded productive persistence section that has students complete a blueprint called "My Math Success Plan," which helps them create an individualized plan for math success.

Other chapters also include new information. Some of the new topics include:

- Reshaping a student's math attitude
- Understanding the different types of math courses
- The more math courses you take, the more money you make
- Developing "My Math Success Plan"
- Understanding how post-traumatic stress disorder affects learning
- Coping with post-traumatic stress disorder
- Effectively using today's new study environment
- Emporium model classroom learning strategies
- How to develop an online study group
- Using an electronic study schedule
- How to take smartphone notes
- How to take online notes
- How to read online textbooks and understand the material
- How to read a single section of an online textbook
- How to use a virtual study buddy to improve learning
- Communicating with your instructor online
- How to take online homework notes
- How to get help from your instructor in his or her office
- Assessing test-taking methods

- Ten steps to computer-based tests
- Applying student productive persistence

Other chapters in the sixth edition have expanded information about many important topics. These topics include:

- More interactive student learning assessments
- How learning math is different from other courses
- Math is the only socially acceptable course to fail
- More sample math profile sheets
- Expanded Winning at Math Student Resource website
- Improved understanding definitions of test anxiety
- Online math autobiography
- Expanded test anxiety myths
- Expanded section on how students learn
- Expanded section on using math learning styles
- Expanded section on math memory techniques
- Expanded taking classroom notes
- Expanded reading classroom texts
- Expanded doing textbook homework
- Expanded doing online homework
- Expanded section on using metacognition
- Expanded section on taking classroom tests
- Expanded section on Ten Steps to Taking a Math Test
- Expanded section on Six Test-Taking Errors
- A new advanced color-coded note-taking system
- Additional strategies on Taking Control of Math

Winning at Math helps you become successful in mathematics by teaching you how to study it on your own, as part of a traditional math course or modular course, and by helping you establish an independent study program through a math or learning resource center. Also, by going to www.AcademicSuccess.com and clicking on the "Winning at Math Student Resources" button—using "Wam" as the username and "Student" as the password—you can access the Math Study Skills Evaluation, Math Learning Modality Inventory, How to Reduce Test Anxiety CD, online homework tools and other resources.

Acknowledgments

Craig Hardesty, Ed.D., is the Dean of Academic Affairs at Hillsborough Community College, South Shore Campus in Ruskin, Florida. Dr. Hardesty previously worked as a math instructor for 18 years, teaching at several different community colleges. He taught courses ranging from Pre-Algebra to Differential Equations and is considered an expert in teaching developmental math. He still teaches math online as an adjunct. He has received a number of recognitions including an Outstanding HCC Faculty Award (2007), a National Institute for Staff and Organizational Development Award (2010), and a Catalyst Award in Exemplary Online Course Design from Blackboard (2011). At his own campus, he designed a curriculum that included teaching math study skills in developmental math courses, which greatly improved the success of the courses. He has also consulted with a number of other colleges on mathematics issues and improving student success. One of these consultations helped result in the institution receiving a national award for Quality Enhancement Plan of the Year, which focused on improving the school's performance in Intermediate Algebra. He served as a college mentor for the National Math Summit held in conjunction with the American Mathematical Association of Two-Year Colleges annual conference in 2013, helping other college faculty develop their own Math Success Plan for College Innovation. His favorite phrase, "Students don't care how much you know until they know how much you care," says a great deal about his passion for student success. Dr. Hardesty wrote the "Communicating with Your Instructor" section of this text. He also contributed additional math study skills suggestions pertaining to online homework and taking online tests.

Nathan Kurtz, M.S., M.E., is currently the Assistant Chair of Teaching and Learning in the Department of Mathematics at Glendale Community College (GCC) in Glendale, Arizona, which is part of the Maricopa Community College District and one of the top five largest mathematics departments in the nation. He also taught at the University of Colorado Denver (UCD) for six years. Nathan has been teaching mathematics for 10 years in traditional, online, and hybrid settings. He has taught courses from pre-Algebra through the Calculus sequence, as well as upper division and graduate level mathematics courses at both GCC and UCD. Nathan has won awards for his quality of teaching, dedication to his students, and his innovative instructional methods.

Nathan is dedicated to quality instruction, inclusion and exploration of technology with instruction, and non-traditional education such as hybrid, flipped, and online classroom environments. Nathan is dedicated to being a change agent and has the ability to see beyond the classroom and the need to help colleges redesign their math curriculum. He has conducted math success research by reading articles and by attending training conferences. Nathan recently attended the first National Math Summit held in conjunction with the American Mathematical Association of Two-Year Colleges annual conference, where he obtain information on course redesign. Using the information gained at this conference, Nathan has implemented strategic plans for his mathematics department to help increase retention, instructional quality, curriculum, and success rates of several of the mathematics courses that his department offers. He knows in order to improve math learning there needs to be a team approach of improving curriculum, instruction, and teaching students to become improved math learners. There needs to be direct instruction to students to improve their math study skills.

Recently, Nathan sponsored a Maricopa Community College District conference consisting of all ten colleges in the Phoenix area to improve the curriculum design for classroom and online courses. The main emphasis of the conference was on how to improve student learning in classroom and online course success by teaching students math learning skills and redesigning curriculum. His contribution to the Winning at Math text, along with study skills suggestions, was developing an advanced note-taking system. This advanced note-taking system is color-coded, precise, and divided into three sections. It is an excellent note-taking system, especially for visual learners. Nathan is also now training his faculty to model this system on the board as well as through technology, such as tablets and screen projectors, in order to train students to use the note-taking system to improve their learning and grades. Nathan is using the team approach to improve student learning and so can you.

James (Jay) Martin, M.S., is a Professor of Mathematics at Wake Technical Community College in Raleigh, North Carolina. Jay has been teaching mathematics for 29 years. He has been a member of AMATYC for over 20 years and has been a major figure at the national conference, conducting annual presentations and serving on the conference committee. Jay was awarded 1996 Instructor of the Year at Wake Tech and has co-authored the text "Instructors Resource Guide to Technical Mathematics with Calculus." Jay mainly teaches college transfer mathematics courses such as Statistics, Pre-Calculus and Calculus.

Jay is considered one of the most dedicated instructors at his college and spends countless hours helping his students. He believes that students and instructors can work together in and outside the classroom to become successful. For example, one of Jay's proudest moments came when one of his students, Shahid, who came back to college after 20 years and started in developmental math, credited Jay with his success in obtaining a BS in Mechanical Engineering.

Another career-changing moment came when he realized that even his Pre-Calculus students did not have good math study skills. With this in mind, he taught his Pre-Calculus students math study skills, time management, test-taking skills and set up a prerequisite review system that utilized many resources at his school. His students' success rate soon went from 42% to 57%.

I would like to thank Jay for editing the Winning at Math text, making recommendations, and contributing his online homework experimental data. The homework experiment is part of the "Do Not Fall Behind" and "Watch out for Shortcuts" sections.

How Learning Math is Different and Why It Pays Off

1

In Chapter 1
You will learn these concepts:

✓ The factors and characteristics that contribute to success in math classes

✓ How a student's affective characteristics influence success in a math class

✓ How to determine your best learning style

Reshaping Your Attitude Toward Math

It's no secret math is not a popular subject these days. Not that this is anything new. From the moment man first began counting on his fingers, math has been the ultimate love or hate subject—even among the greatest minds in history. For every math-centric thinker like Pythagoras or Isaac Newton, there is at least one contrarian like Augustine of Hippo, a 5th-century philosopher who once claimed that mathematicians had made a covenant with the devil "to darken the spirit" and "confine man in the bonds of Hell."

While most modern math students may not take their disdain for the subject quite as far as jolly-old-Augustine, the fact remains that many view math differently than they do other courses. According to a recent poll conducted by Amplicate.com, nearly 86 percent of high school students claim to "hate" algebra. The same data shows that geometry is by far the most reviled subject for students under the age of eighteen—this despite the fact that many of these same students claim to enjoy school and look forward to attending their other classes.

If you are a college student, and the previous description rings a bell, you need to remember two things. First, there is nothing wrong with disliking math. Second, plenty of students who hate math pass it anyway. A negative math attitude is only dangerous if it becomes the basis for bad behavior. If a negative math attitude leads to poor class attendance, poor concentration and poor study skills, however, then you have more than a bad attitude—you have a problem.

The key to combating a bad math attitude is to develop a persistent attitude. Persistence, perhaps more than any other behavior, is absolutely crucial to success—not only in terms of passing math and graduating from college, but also in determining one's ability to thrive in the outside world. As former U.S. President Calvin Coolidge once wrote: "Nothing in this world can take the place of persistence. Talent will not; nothing is more common than unsuccessful people with talent. Genius will not; unrewarded genius is almost a proverb. Persistence and determination alone are omnipotent. The slogan 'press on' has solved and always will solve the problems of the human race."

In other words, even the smartest, most capable student cannot succeed in college without the ability to learn from failure and adversity. In the same way, those who struggle with school—or specifically math—are just as capable of success, so long as they "press on" through their problems.

By coupling a positive, tenacious attitude with proper study and test-taking skills, you are entirely capable of rising above any challenge college might throw at you—big or small. If you see math as one of these challenges, that is perfectly okay. The key is to remain persistent. Don't give up. Remember, the harder the challenge, the greater the reward.

Opinions about mathematics are all over the map. Even the greatest minds this planet has ever known can't come to a consensus.

Mathematics is like checkers in being suitable for the young, not too difficult, amusing, and without peril to the state.
—Plato

Do not worry about your difficulties in Mathematics. I can assure you mine are still greater.
— Albert Einstein

God used beautiful mathematics in creating the world.
—Paul Dirac

Mathematicians have made a covenant with the devil to darken the spirit and to confine man in the bonds of hell.
—Augustine of Hippo

?

What do you think about math?

Taking the Math Study Skills Evaluation

Math courses are not like other college courses. Most college courses only require you to read, understand and recall subject material to pass a class. To pass math, however, an extra step is needed; you must use the information you have learned to correctly solve math problems. This may sound like common sense, but this fourth step is a true game changer. It means the general study skills you use in other classes are insufficient for math.

To get better grades in math, you need to learn math-specific study skills. These skills help you build confidence and achieve better grades. They also help you reduce your math-based anxiety—especially during your first college math course. This book not only covers these study skills, but also allows you to custom build your own study plan by addressing your unique strengths and challenges.

Before learning what study strategies work best for you, however, it is first important to take the Math Study Skills Evaluation. To access the MSSE, visit AcademicSuccess. com—Student Resources and enter "WAM" for the username and "Student" for the password. This program determines exactly what you know about how to study for math and helps you determine what material in this book will help you improve success in your current or future math course. The MSSE involves answering a series of questions about your basic study behaviors. It does not contain any math equations or questions. Your answers result in an overall score between 0 and 100. When you finish, you will receive a results sheet, which presents information on the basic areas of this text you already understand, as well as those areas on which you can improve.

Your overall score and accompanying advice will look something like this:

Sally College, the overall result of your evaluation is a score of 47. A score of 70 and below means you need to improve your math study skills and this could be the main reason you are having difficulty learning math.

You will also receive specific results on one of many subjects:

You have a score of 48 in Memory and Learning, which measures your understanding of learning styles and the learning process, as well as your ability to develop a useful learning plan. You need to read and study chapters 2 and 5.

If your results seem low, do not worry! This low score may explain your poor math grades, and you now know exactly what you need to work on! If you have spent your entire academic life using inefficient study skills, this is likely the source of your problems with math. The skills you'll read about in this book directly address this problem.

Activity 1.1 Math Study Skills Evaluation Results

Student Name_____   Date_____

Advisor Name_____   Email_____

Overall result_____
A score of 79 and below means you need to improve your math study skills, and this could be the main reason you have had difficulty learning math.

Study Effectively_____, which measures how well you understand that studying for math differs from studying from other subjects. It also measures your effective use of study goals, reading/homework systems, study tools, and motivation. The reference chapters are 1 and 9.

Memory and Learning_____, which measures what you know about learning styles, the learning process, as well as developing a learning plan and memory strategies. The reference chapters are 2 and 5 .

Reading and Homework_____, which measures how well you understand a course's syllabus and what you know about developing reading and homework strategies to improve math learning. The reference chapter is 7.

Classroom Learning_____, which measures the ability to develop listening strategies, note-taking systems as well as the ability to ask questions. The reference chapter is 6.

Test Anxiety and Test Taking_____, which measures how well you understand the effects of test anxiety, how to reduce test anxiety, how to take tests and how to analyze test results. The reference chapters are 3 and 9.

Based on your scores and a discussion with your advisor, list from most important to least important the order of the chapters in this text you most need to read:

Chapter___,
Chapter___,
Chapter___,
Chapter___,
Chapter___,
Chapter___,
Chapter___,
Chapter___,
Chapter___,

I will complete reading these chapters by this date: _____

How Learning Math Is Different

To learn and thrive in your math courses, it is important to understand the basic elements of the learning process. Math courses require you to do four things:

1. Understand the material,
2. Process the material,
3. Apply what you have learned to correctly solve a problem, and
4. Remember everything you have already learned to learn new material.

These four tasks help you master the math you must learn. If you do not complete one of the tasks, you will not complete the others. In other words, in order to successfully complete math problems, you must actively engage with the topics you are studying in real time. This is not true in most other courses.

Example: Political science courses require you to learn about politics and public service, but your instructor will not make you run for governor to pass the course. In math, however, you must be able to correctly solve problems. When you learn about factoring techniques, for example, you must solve numerous factoring problems in order to pass a test.

Math as Sequential Learning

Another way math differs from other subjects is its sequential learning pattern. This means that the material you learn on one day is used the next day and the next day and so forth.

Example: Learning math is like building a house. Houses are built from the ground up: you build the foundation first, then the walls, then the roof. Math is the same way. It must be learned in a specific order. You cannot learn complex problems without first learning simple ones.

Unlike other subjects, you cannot forget important material after a math test. Each chapter in a math book is a foundation block for the next chapter. All building blocks must be included to successfully learn math. This building-block approach to learning math is the reason why it is difficult to catch up when you get behind. You can't skip information in one chapter to hurry up and get caught up in the next chapter. To succeed in math, each previous chapter has to be completely understood before continuing to the next chapter.

Sequential learning also affects studying for math tests. If you understand Chapter 1 and 2 but do not understand Chapter 3, you will not understand Chapter 4. When your test time approaches, you end up trying to teach yourself too many concepts while studying for the test when you should be reviewing and practicing. This makes it highly likely your results won't represent the best you can do.

Now that you understand how learning math is a building experience, what should you do if you have already fallen behind?

1. *Don't get anxious.* Stay calm.

2. *If your college* has a diagnostic math inventory in the tutoring center or math lab, take it to see what math concepts you have forgotten, and ask your instructor where you can go to relearn these math concepts.

3. *Take the time* to follow through. Many students give up too easily, or they think they will catch up a little at a time. Don't give up. The energy you put into your class at the beginning of the session will be more productive than energy put into class at the end of the session when you try to learn everything during the last week before the final exam.

4. *Study and really* learn the math; don't practice mimicking it.

5. *When it is time* to register for the next session, register immediately so you will be able to get into the math class you need. Why do all this? Because, again, math is sequential!

Math as a Sequential Course

Now that you understand the "building block" nature of math, think about your math history.

- What are your previous math grades?
- How well did you do on the math placement test at your college?
- How long has it been since you took a math course?

- When you look at your math history, are there times when you did not take math?

These questions are important because if you allow too much time to pass between different math courses, you may forget important math concepts you need in a future class. In other words, your foundation might require a few repairs. This means that it is incredibly important to take a math placement test before enrolling for any college-level math course.

Math placement test scores are determined by how well you have learned previous math and whether the sequence in which you took your previous courses has helped you build a strong foundation. If you barely score high enough to be placed into a math course, then you will have gaps in your knowledge base. Learning problems then occur when new math material is based on one of these gaps.

In addition to considering how well you place into a course, the age of the placement test score must also be considered. Placement test scores are designed to measure your current math knowledge and are best used immediately.

Example: While a student can maintain success by taking U.S. History I and then waiting a year to take U.S. History II, taking Beginning Algebra and then taking Intermediate Algebra a year later decreases his or her course success rate by 20%, according to Miami Dade College research.

Other research indicates that even skipping one session greatly decreases math course success rates. The same problem has also been documented at Rutgers University where students were allowed to take their developmental courses whenever they wanted. Many of these students took developmental courses during their freshman years then waited to finish their math courses as seniors. This caused major problems as the students forgot everything they learned and still needed over a year of math courses to graduate. After conducting this research, the university implemented a policy requiring students to continuously enroll in their math courses to improve their course success rate.

College math courses should be taken in order, from the fall session to the spring session. If possible, avoid taking math from the spring to fall sessions. It is easy to forget important concepts over summer break. Summer math courses are also a good idea, unless the sessions are very short. Extended summer sessions, which typically last between 10 and 12 weeks, are preferable to waiting three months to take another course. If you cannot take summer math courses, make sure to review the last chapter in your last math course to refresh your math memory during your vacation. If you do not have your text, consider visiting math websites, such as www.purplemath.com. This will better prepare you to make a good grade in your next math course.

Math as a Thinking Subject

In a math class, you have to think from the minute the instructor begins talking. Note-taking is challenging because you have to think about the math as your instructor explains a problem, all while writing the information down in your notes. In most cases, you are not just copying down facts. This could cause problems in note taking because you are concentrating on understanding the explanation while also trying to write down each problem step.

Also, students must think when reading the math textbook, which is why it takes longer than reading other texts. Remember when we said math is sequential?

Math is a series of steps and combinations of rules and properties; math students have to think between each step, remembering the rules and properties they have learned throughout their entire collegiate careers. When reading a math textbook, take time to think how each new concept connects with the previous one. This slows the reading process down significantly.

Since math is a thinking subject, what should you do?

1. *Reserve much more* time to read a chapter or complete your homework.
2. *During the evenings* or days when you don't have time to complete the entire homework assignment, at least review your notes and do a couple of problems to keep the information in your brain.
3. *You need to learn* how to think like a math instructor. This means you need to think in a step-by-step way to solve problems, writing down each step of the problem without skipping steps until the problem is solved.

Math as a Speed Subject

In most cases, math is taught faster than your other subjects. Math instructors have a certain amount of material to cover each session. They have to finish certain chapters because the next math course is based on the information taught in their courses. In many cases, math departments give a common final exam to gauge your readiness for your next course.

Another way math is a speed subject is that most math tests are timed, and many students fear they will run out of time. THIS CAUSES PANIC AND FEAR! What makes me curious is, if students feel like they don't have enough time to complete the math test, why are most of them gone before the test time is over? Sure, students who have learned the math thoroughly may complete the test early. That makes sense. Some students leave, however, because they either don't know the material, want to leave the anxious environment, or carelessly work through the test.

So, since speed is an issue in learning math, what should you do?

First, to use an analogy, start a daily workout program to stay in shape. Review, review, review as you learn and digest new material.

Second, practice doing problems within a time constraint. This prepares your for upcoming tests.

The Differences Between High School and College Math

Math, as a college-level course, is almost two to three times as difficult as high school-level math courses. There are many reasons for the increased difficulty: course class-time, the amount of material covered, the length of a course, and the grading system, among others. College math instruction for the fall and spring sessions is usually three hours per week; high school math instruction is usually provided five hours per week. What is learned in one year of high school math is learned in one session of college math. Simply put, in college, students receive less instructional time per week and instructors cover twice the material per course. As a result, most of the learning occurs outside of the college classroom.

During orientation sessions, I often ask students how much time they used to spend studying for math in high school. Without fail, most answer that they'd studied between one and five hours. Others tell me that they had paid attention in class, barely studied at all and still managed to pass. This method DOES NOT WORK in college. In order to succeed in a college-level math course, you must study at least 10 hours per week. This sounds like a lot, but when broken down into one or two hour study sessions, the time is not so intimidating.

Course-Grading System

While in high school, if you make a borderline D/F in a math course, your teacher might give you a "D," and you may continue to the next course. However, in some college math courses, a "D" is not considered a passing grade, or, if a "D" is made, the course will not count toward graduation. College instructors are more likely to give the grade of "N" (no grade), "W" (withdrawal), or "F" for barely knowing the material. This is because the instructors know students are unable to pass the next course if they have learned only a part of the curriculum. Also, in most high schools, you may graduate by passing one to three math courses. Some college programs require four math courses, and students must make at least a "C" in all of them to graduate.

What should you not expect in a college math course? First, since math is not as subjective as English, do not expect to talk a math instructor into extra work to earn a better grade. Second, in college, there are no "daily work" grades—though you still have to do your homework. Don't expect to do well without doing the homework even though it is not collected. Third, test scores may be the only grades that count toward your final grade. Therefore, do not assume you will be able to "make up" for a bad test score.

Your First Math Test is Much More Important

Making a high grade on your first major college math test is more important than making a high grade on the first major test in other college subjects. The first major math test is the easiest and, most often, is the one that students are least prepared for.

Beginning college students often feel that the first major math test is mainly a review and they can make a "B" or "C" without much study. These students are overlooking an excellent opportunity to make an "A" on the easiest test of the session. At the end of the session, these students sometimes do not pass the math course or do not make an "A" because of their first major test grade. In other words, the first test score was not high enough to "pull up" a low test score on one of the remaining major tests. Studying hard for the first major college math test and getting an "A" offers you several advantages:

- *A high first test score* compensates for a low score on a more difficult fourth or fifth math test, especially if all major tests are equal in the final grade calculations.

- *A high first test score* provides assurance that you have learned the basic math skills required to pass a course. This means you will not have to spend time relearning the misunderstood material covered on the first major test while learning new material for the next one.

- *A high first test score* motivates you to do well. Improved motivation causes you to increase your math study time, which allows you to master new material.

- *A high first test score* improves your confidence. With more confidence, you are more likely to work harder on difficult math homework assignments, which will increase your chances of doing well in your course.

What happens if after all your studying, you still make a low score on your first math test? You can still use this test experience to help you improve your next grade or to help determine if you are in the right math course.

Your first math test, no matter what you make on it, can be used as a diagnostic test. Your teacher can review your test with you to see which type of math problems you got right and which ones you need to learn how to solve. It may be that you missed only a few concepts that caused the low score, and you can learn how to do these problems by getting help from the teacher, a learning resource center or the math lab. However, you need to learn how to do these problems immediately so that you don't fall behind in your course.

In some cases, students guess well on the math placement test or enroll in their next math course after being out of college for several years. Some of these students don't do well on their first test because they have forgotten most of the required concepts or did not know the material in the first place. I have seen hundreds of these students over the years. If they make below a 50 on their first test, I suggest that it might be a good idea to drop back to a lower level math course. Even beyond the first week of drop and add, many colleges/universities still let you drop to a lower math class after the first major test.

Dropping back to a lower level math course and passing it is the smartest move. These students typically go on to become more successful in future courses.

Self-Learning

As mentioned earlier in this section, college math courses require students to learn a great deal of information outside of class. Luckily, modern math students have more tools at their disposal than ever before. Over the course of this text, we will introduce you to numerous supplementary tools that will help you learn complex mathematical concepts. Some of these resources are physical locations on your campus, others are Web-based research tools.

Putting Math Into Perspective

One way to change the way you learn math is to compare it to one of your favorite hobbies or extracurricular activities. The following activities all relate to math in fundamental ways.

Math as a Puzzle

Have you ever tried to put a puzzle together with one or more of the pieces missing? It becomes very frustrating, especially if you think all the parts are there and, after hours and hours of work, you realize you won't be able to finish. Puzzles are fickle that way. Each piece is crucial. If even a single piece is missing, you are left with an incomplete picture. This is also true when you are halfway through solving a math problem and find out you do not know or have forgotten the rules for the next step. In order to solve math problems, you need to understand all the rules. In other subjects, you may forget some of the rules and still pass a test. In math, however, not knowing or forgetting one major concept often causes you to miss problems.

Math as a Foreign Language

Another way to properly study math is to treat it as a foreign language. Like a foreign language, math has unfamiliar vocabulary words, which must be put in sentences called expressions or equations. Understanding and solving a math equation is similar to speaking and understanding a sentence in a foreign language. When read or spoken aloud, mathematical symbols are translated into words and sentences. Math sentences use symbols (spoken words), such as:

"=" (for which you say, "equals"),
"-" (for which you say, "less"), and
"a" (for which you say, "unknown").

If you do not understand these symbols, you are in serious trouble. This is best illustrated by the experiences of a student named Charlie, whom I once worked with. While preparing for a math test, Charlie memorized how to work every type of problem his teacher had covered in the previous weeks. Despite his efforts, he still failed. When I went over the test with him, I asked him how to factor a polynomial. He asked me, "What is a polynomial?" I then asked him what a monomial was, and he did not know. I talked to his tutor and the rest of the tutor session was spent learning the language of mathematics by developing vocabulary notecards so he could understand what we were talking about. He had the ability to do math but could not understand the language. Learning how to speak math as a language is key to success. With this in mind, to stay fluent in a foreign language, you need to use it every day. Math is no different. If you want to retain your ability to speak and read mathematics, you must practice every single day.

So, now that you know math is like a foreign language, what should you do?

1. *Start a vocabulary* list in the back of your notebook. Include the definitions and examples the instructor uses in class. Writing this vocabulary list helps you study too!

2. *Preview the chapter* before class in order to identify vocabulary words that you will hear in class. You don't have to understand all of them while previewing the chapter, but familiarize yourself with the words. This will help you improve taking notes in class.

3. *Practice saying* the vocabulary words out loud. Get comfortable with the words, their meanings, and how they connect with one another.

Math as a Sport

Learning math is similar to learning to play a sport such as basketball, track or football. In order to find success, you must actively practice. You can listen and watch your coach all day, but unless you practice those skills yourself, you will not learn and probably won't even get into the game or meet.

For example, in basketball, the way to improve your free-throw percentage is to watch and understand the correct shooting form and then to actively practice the shots. If you simply listen to your coaches describe the correct form and watch them demonstrate it, but you do not practice the correct form yourself, you will never improve.

Math as a Musical Instrument

Learning math is like playing a musical instrument. To master a musical instrument, you need to understand music theory and learn the various hand-eye movements required to strike the right sound and tone.

This involves lots of practice. You can see someone play the piano, cello or electric guitar, watch their hands and hear the sounds, but unless you practice you will not learn how to play. Imagine how many concerts you have attended or seen on television, or how many people you have watched play the piano. Could you now go play the piano, cello or electric guitar? No. You need to practice these instruments before playing them well just like you have to practice math before you learn it.

Many of your other college courses can be learned by methods other than practicing. In social studies, for example, you can learn information by listening to your instructor, taking good notes and participating in class discussions. Many first-year college students mistakenly believe they can approach math the same way. Ask an experienced math student, and you will hear a different story. Face it, unless you are a math genius, you must practice. So, how do you practice math?

- *First,* make sure you understand the math concepts and the basics.

- *Second,* practice the homework problems over and over until the answers come to you naturally.

- *Third,* learn the vocabulary associated with problems.

- *Fourth,* try to "teach" the math to someone else.

Activity 1.2 Studying Math is like...

One of the best ways to study for math is to treat it the same way you would one of your favorite hobbies or performance-based activities. Not to say that you need to enjoy math the same way you enjoy playing basketball or singing or playing an instrument, but you certainly need to give it the same type of attention. Answer the questions below to find out how you can use your experiences participating in an activity you love to shape or reshape your approach to math.

1. Which one of the comparisons in this section is the most relatable to you? Do you play a musical instrument? Have you ever taken a foreign language class? Have you ever played a sport? Choose one of the comparisons and explain how you can use it to improve your study habits.

2. If none of the comparisons given in this section apply to you, think of one of your hobbies or activities and explain below how you can use your practice routine for this activity as an example for how to properly study math.

3. Explain, in your own words, why it is important to consistently study for math. What, for instance, makes studying for math unique?

The Types of Math Courses You Should Take

Modern math students have many options to complete the math credits required to graduate. In addition to the traditional spring, fall and summer sessions, most universities offer online courses and emporium courses. Online courses require students to learn and complete course material independently from home, while emporium courses require students to use computer programs in a specified room and at a specified time.

If you struggle with math, you need to be extremely wary of classes that require you to work independently. While these classes may ostensibly seem easier or more convenient, in truth, they have their own set of unique challenges and pitfalls. Over the course of this section, we will cover whether or not you should take online courses, late-start courses and/or summer session courses.

Before we get into the specific types of non-traditional courses available to you, however, we need to touch upon the key factors you should use to determine what traditional courses you should take: most importantly, how to choose a professor who is well-matched to your unique learning needs.

Selecting a College Professor

College and high school math instructors treat students differently. College instructors often do much less hand-holding than do high school teachers. High school math teachers frequently warn you about your grades and offer help or makeup work. College instructors expect you to keep up with how well or poorly you are doing. You must take responsibility for your own success and make an appointment to seek help from your instructor.

Students often have to choose between a full-time or part-time instructor. Sometimes, due to the increase in the number of college math courses offered in a curriculum, there are more part-time math instructors than full-time instructors. You need to think about the following questions when choosing between a full-time or part-time instructor. In fact, you need to find out the answers to these questions even when choosing between two full-time instructors.

- *What kind of reputation* do the instructors have for working with students one-on-one outside of class?

- *Do the instructors* usually keep office hours when you can visit and talk to them? If they keep them early in the morning, when you can't get to campus, then see if there is another instructor with more convenient office hours.

- *Do the instructors* help students online? More and more instructors do this.

- *Do the instructors* create a comfortable class environment in which students feel free to ask questions?

- *Do the instructors* take time to stop their lectures and answer questions?
- *Do the instructors* allow students to practice problems in class? Do they return your tests to you?

How do you find out the answers to these questions? First, most math departments keep sample syllabi, an instructor's "contract" of expectations, tests, and homework assignments. You can ask to see these. Second, counselors or advisors might know something about the different teaching styles of the instructors. Third, good math students know who the supportive instructors are. Finally, you can try to find the instructors and directly ask them these questions.

It's also worth noting that websites like RateYourProfessor.com are good guides in terms of getting a feel for a professor's teaching style—though you need to remember what you read on these sites is not always accurate. When students praise a professor, their sentiments are usually true. Negative reviews, however, don't always tell the whole story. Many great teachers are criticized simply because they expect a lot out of their students. This means that they do not cut students a break when they aren't putting in the hard work required to pass a course. Though these types of professors are tough, they often provide your best chance at truly learning material.

If a professor receives mixed reviews on these websites, it is usually due to a clash of learning styles. Some students aren't good matches with certain teachers. If you learn best a certain way, make sure to select a professor who accommodates your needs.

Online Math Courses

For those who excel at mathematics, online courses provide a convenient, compelling option for completing various math requirements. For everyone else, however, they are extremely dangerous and should only be taken after thorough contemplation.

Statistics show that students in online math classes typically achieve lower grades than those who take traditional math courses. This is usually due to two key factors:

1. *Online students* are more prone to procrastination.
2. *Online students* falsely assume that working from home will alleviate anxiety.

During my time helping students, I've run into hundreds of students who take online classes because they don't like math and figure the best way to avoid anxiety is to avoid the classroom. This way they do not have to solve problems at the board and do not have to compare themselves to other students. Unfortunately, these students almost always fail. When considering an online math course, you should use extreme caution. If you do not consider yourself a quick math-learner, you should stick to traditional courses.

Summer Sessions Vs. Fall or Spring Sessions and the Difference between Night and Day Classes

College math courses taught during summer sessions are more difficult than those taught during fall or spring. The same amount of content is presented in many fewer weeks. Students attending a six-week summer math session must learn information and master skills two-and-a-half times as fast as students attending regular, full-session math courses. There is less time between classes to study. In addition, each class is longer, making it harder to concentrate throughout the entire class.

Since math is a sequential learning experience where every building block must be understood before proceeding to the next block, you can quickly fall behind, and you may never catch up. In fact, some students become lost during the first half of a math class and never understand the rest of the lecture (this can happen during just one class session in the summer). If you must take a summer math course, take a 10- or 12-week session so that you will have more time to process the material between classes.

Night classes present similar problems, depending on how they are scheduled. Some night classes meet once a week. These classes are long, sometimes lasting four hours. An entire week goes by between classes, and it is very easy to put off studying or forget the material discussed in class. Other night classes are scheduled twice a week and there is little time after the first class to study for the next class, particularly if you work during the day. For example, if you do not understand the lecture on Monday, then you have all of Monday night to learn the material before progressing to more difficult material on Tuesday. During a night course, you have to learn and understand the material before the break; after the break, you will move immediately on to the more difficult material — that night.

Late-Start and Flex Classes

In recent years, colleges and universities have begun to develop new and innovative types of course schedules. Many institutions now offer late-start classes that begin at midterm, mostly to accommodate students who arrive at a school after a semester has already started. These late-start classes move twice as fast as normal classes, meaning many require students to be in class up to six hours a week.

Similarly, flex classes also start late — though for different reasons. Flex courses are usually intended to allow ambitious students to take multiple courses in one discipline at the same time.

Many math students like flex classes — mostly for a wrong, incredibly dangerous reason. Some students who do not care for math view flex classes as a way to put off taking a math course until late in a semester. They figure the increased amount of weekly class time is worth it if it means they will only have to take a math course for a single month. Unfortunately, many of these students fail.

This is particularly unfortunate because many developmental math course students like to take flex courses. In fact, administrators often suggest that developmental students take these classes because they offer a faster track to enrolling in credited courses. Because flex courses move about six times as fast as a one-year high school math course, many of these students struggle to keep up.

By now, you have probably figured out that late-start and flex classes fall under the high risk/high reward category. Sure you might be able to finish your math credits at a faster pace — but you also risk failing and falling even further behind.

If you are an average math student, I do not recommend taking these types of courses. The same is true if you dislike or struggle with math. Even students who excel in math should avoid late-start and flex classes during their first semester. I have seen hundreds of students fail these classes and have to repeat the same course a second or even a third time. Many of these students would have passed a regular semester course without any problem.

On the other hand, if you regularly got good grades in your high school math courses, and an uncharacteristic placement test score caused you to miss a higher level math course by just a few points, late-start and flex courses are perfectly valid options. This is especially true for those who are either taking a math study skills course or learning and using the material in this text. For everyone else, it is smarter to avoid these classes altogether.

Be Careful What You Wish For

Many students choose non-traditional courses for all the wrong reasons. What seems to be the easiest option does not always work out that way. Make sure you assess your learning strengths and weaknesses before signing up for any type of class that you have never taken before. Not only will this save you wasted energy, it might save you from failing.

How Learning Math Pays Off

Now that we have learned how math is different, how to select a college professor and why your first math test is so important, what do we want to gain from learning math?

Another way to ask this question is, "What are your reasons for attending college?" Are you going to college to better yourself? Are you going to college to obtain the career you want? Are you going to college to make more money? I ask these questions to many students who are taking math and what do you think is the most popular response? You're right! Most students say they are going to college to make more money. Students also indicate they want to like their careers and make enough money to live a better life. It does not matter if these students are going for an Associate of Science degree, an Associate of Arts degree or a Baccalaureate degree. Their goals are to graduate in the shortest amount of time and obtain a high paying career.

Students also often indicate they want their career to be secure so they will not have to keep switching employment or have to be retrained. This is especially true of men and women who are returning to college to obtain better careers to support their family. Being clear on your college goal is a way to motivate your college success. So does taking math courses mean you can obtain a higher paying career, have more career options and have a

chance at those popular careers? YES!

On the next two pages, you will see the top paying jobs for Associate of Science and Baccalaureate degrees. Associate of Science degrees are usually two-year degrees once you have been admitted to the program or once you have completed the prerequisite courses. Associate of Science degrees are used in the allied health fields, as well as electronics and computer fields. The following graph demonstrates the 15 jobs with the best pay, fastest growth and the most openings for the 21st century. It also demonstrates their national annual salary (Farr and Ludden, 2013) and what math courses are required to obtain them. The center of the graph indicates the Associate of Sciences majors.

Do you see the pattern? Four of the five highest paying jobs (dental hygienists, diagnostic medical sonographers, registered nurses, radiation therapists) require college algebra or statistics. Four of the five lowest paying jobs (veterinary technician, medical records technician, physical therapist assistant, and occupational therapist assistant) require mathematics courses below college algebra and statistics. Based on this information, if you want the most job selections and highest paying career then passing more mathematics courses is your ticket to success.

Students who are going for a Baccalaureate

degree either obtain an Associate of Arts degree at a community/junior college or are already attending a university. In most cases, these students will make more money than the Associate in Science degrees. One way to look at these majors is to plot the graph by using salaries and the increasing amounts of math courses. The following graph demonstrates the 20 top careers with the best pay, fastest growth and the most openings for the 21st century. It also shows their national annual salary per year (Farr and Ludden, Best Jobs of the 21st Century, 2013).

Again look at the pattern. Five out of the five highest paying jobs (software developer, network administrator, construction manager, engineer, computer systems analysts) require business calculus or higher. In fact, all nine careers that have salaries around $50,000 a year require business calculus or a higher math course. Four of the five lowest paying jobs (physical therapy assistant, paralegal assistant, veterinary technology assistant) require mathematics courses below college algebra and statistics. Based on this information, if you want the most job selections and highest pay then passing more mathematics courses is once again your ticket to success.

By now, using your excellent number sense, you have figured it out. The more math courses you take, the higher paying career you will get! Learning mathematics is the key to your personal and career success.

Now that you know that taking more mathematics means more career choices and better pay, how can you accomplish this goal? Effective learning strategies for successful math study skills leads to more math success. Math success helps you graduate and allows you to select majors in areas that lead to high paying jobs and more job security.

Obstacles to Success

Sometimes, self-talk and statements by others may block your motivation to be successful in your math course. Don't get in the habit of saying, "When will I ever use this math?"

Don't let obstacles get in the way of your success in math. Stay persistent and obtain the career you've always wanted.

or "Why do I have to take this math course because I will not use it in my job?" These statements may make you feel better when you are not successful in a math course. However, they also lead to poor motivation and less studying. The real questions are: "Do I need this math course to graduate?" or "Do I need this math course as a prerequisite to enter my major?" For example, if you are a business major, in most cases you will need applied calculus to be accepted to the college of business. Being successful in applied calculus is your "ticket" to your business major and making that million dollars.

In some cases you may have to take some developmental math courses in order to be ready to take the required math courses. Don't be discouraged! Thousand of students have finished their developmental math courses and have completed college algebra or calculus and are now in their careers. Remember, more math equals more money.

Best Jobs Requiring an Associate's Degree

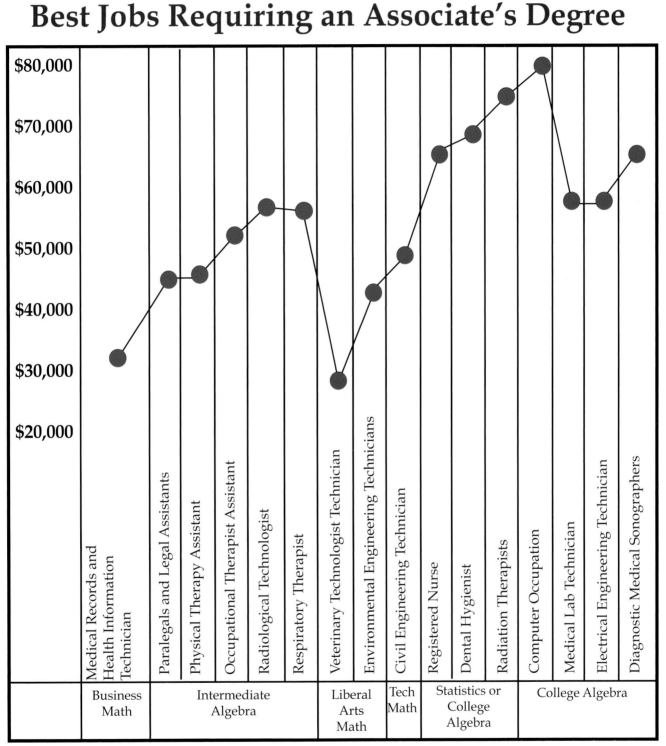

Source: *Best Jobs for the 21st Century*, Sixth Edition © JIST Works 2012
Graph: © Academic Success Press Inc. 2013

Best Jobs Requiring a Bachelor's Degree

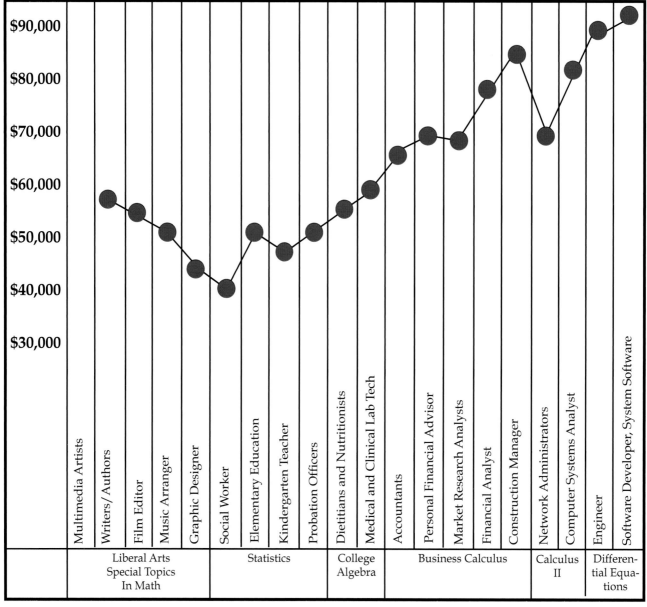

Source: *Best Jobs for the 21st Century*, Sixth Edition © JIST Works 2012
Graph: © Academic Success Press Inc. 2013

Activity 1.3 What type of career do you want?

Choosing a career is tricky. Sometimes our interests and our desire for a highly compensated career do not match up. This means that many students who do not like math will still have to take numerous math courses to obtain their degree. Fill out the form below to find out just how much math you will need to take to graduate and start your career.

1. What type of degree are you going for?

    ___ Associate's Degree

    ___Bachelor's Degree

2. What type of career do you want to have when you finish college? If undecided, then write down the general field you might want to go into (humanities, science, business, etc.)

3. How much money do you want to make in your career? Write the total in the space below.

4. Look at the charts on the previous two pages. Do you see your career? If so, see if your career goals match the amount of money you want to make. After you have done this, write down the math courses you will need to take to finish your degree.

5. If your chosen career is not on the charts, either use the Internet to look up the information you need, or visit your school's career counselor. Follow the same procedure as the question above.

Chapter 1 Summary

- The skills required for learning math differ from the skills required for learning other courses.

- Math requires sequential learning, which means one concept builds on the next concept. You must build a firm and steady foundation with each chapter. This will help you be successful.

- Thinking of learning math like learning a foreign language or a musical instrument will help you change your math study skills.

- Math isn't just numbers; it is also vocabulary.

- Keeping a positive attitude about math will help you study more efficiently.

- Passing most courses requires reading, understanding and recalling the subject material. Math students must also learn how to think like a mathematician.

- Math is the only socially acceptable course to hate and fail. However, remember you can dislike math and pass it at the same time.

- You must practice math over and over and over just like learning how to shoot a free-throw in basketball.

- When taking a math test, you not only have to understand and recall the material, you have to prove this to the instructor by correctly working the problems.

- In most other subject tests, you can just guess at the answers; you cannot guess at the answers in math tests because the answers on a math test must be precise and exact.

- Math courses are even more difficult because, in most cases, a grade of "C" or better is usually required to take the next course or, in some cases, just to pass the current course.

- There are major differences between high school and college math courses.

- The grading is exact and, in many cases, you cannot do extra credit work to improve your grade.

- Remember to study hard for your first test because it will be the easiest one and, therefore, the best opportunity to get a high grade.

- Remember, the more math you take, the more money you make!

Name: _____   Date: _____

Assignment for Chapter 1

1. Why is math considered to have a sequential learning pattern?

2. Give two examples of how math is a speed subject:

3. Give three examples of how college math is different from high school math:

4. Describe three reasons why your first math test is so important:

5. How do attitudes toward math affect learning?

6. How do summer and falls sessions differ?

7. Are flex and late-start classes good options for math students? Does it depend on the student? List your responses below:

8. How can you prepare for your first math test?

9. Describe your two personal obstacles that may prevent you from learning more math:

10. How can you overcome these obstacles:

Assessing and Using Your Math Learning Strengths

2

In Chapter 2
You will learn these concepts:

✓ How a student's knowledge and intelligence, along with quality of instruction and student characteristics, determine the level of success in a math class

✓ How to determine your best learning style

✓ How to develop "My Math Success Plan"

Ingredients for Success in Learning Math

After exploring the characteristics of math, the second step to improving your ability to study the subject is to understand your unique study skills. Just as a mechanic does a diagnostic test on a car before repairing it, you need to complete a diagnostic test to identify which of your go-to study strategies need improvement. This allows you to focus only on those learning areas that benefit you rather than wasting time on the areas in which you are already sufficiently proficient.

In order to do this, you need to develop a Math Success Plan. At the end of this chapter, you will write down your various strengths and challenges. This list will eventually become an overall attack plan for your future math courses.

Before we start exploring your learning skills, however, it helps to understand the keys to academic success. Dr. Benjamin Bloom, a famous researcher of educational learning, discovered that IQ (intelligence) and "cognitive entry skills" (knowledge about math) account for 50 percent of a student's course grade. This is highlighted in the Bloom Chart, printed on the next page. As you can see, quality of instruction represents 25 percent of a course grade, while "affective student characteristics" reflect the remaining 25 percent.

The following bullet points contain more thorough definitions of Dr. Bloom's four variables to academic achievement.

- *Intelligence,* for our purpose, is considered to be how fast a person can learn or relearn math concepts of varying difficulty.

- *Cognitive entry skills* refer to how much math people already know before entering a math course.

- *Quality of instruction* concerns the effectiveness of math instructors, lab assistants and tutors when presenting material to students in the classroom, math lab and while tutoring. This effectiveness depends on the course textbooks, curriculum, teaching style, tutoring style, teaching aids (videos, CDs, DVDs, websites, online homework) and other assistances.

- *Affective student characteristics* are characteristics people possess which affect their course grades — excluding how much math they knew before entering the math course. Some of these affective characteristics include anxiety, study skills, study attitudes, self-concepts, motivation and test-taking skills.

The first part of this chapter explores these ingredients for success in a math class — appropriate math knowledge, low level of test anxiety, effective study skills, positive attitude for studying, motivation, test-taking and personal learning style.

What You Know About Math Affects Your Grades

Going into a class with a poor knowledge of math sets you up for achieving low grades. A student placed in a math course that requires a more extensive math background than he or she possesses will probably fail that course. Without the correct math background you may fall behind and never catch up. The following information is important to know in order to make sure that you are placed in the proper math course.

Placement Tests and Previous Math Grades

The math you need to know to enroll in a particular math course can be measured by a placement test. Most colleges/universities use a standardized test such as the ACT, SAT, Compass or Accuplacer to place students into math courses. However, some colleges/universities use their own placement test to place students. Also, the grades earned in the prerequisite math courses measure your level of math knowledge. However, a few students are still incorrectly placed in math courses by these resources. So, it is important to talk to your advisor and teacher to provide any other information that might assist in properly placing you into a math course.

If the placement scores are questionable or borderline between two classes, ask the advisor if there is another diagnostic test you can take. Or, talk to one of the math instructors because they may be able to ask questions that will help determine correct placement into a math course. An inaccurate evaluation of math ability and knowledge can only lead to frustration, anxiety and

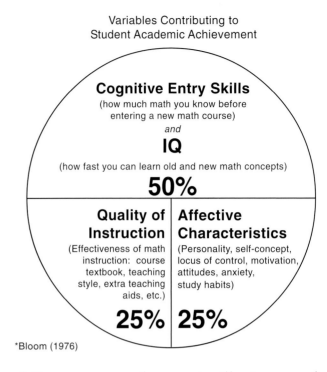

Variables Contributing to
Student Academic Achievement

Cognitive Entry Skills
(how much math you know before
entering a new math course)
and
IQ
(how fast you can learn old and new math concepts)
50%

Quality of Instruction
(Effectiveness of math instruction: course textbook, teaching style, extra teaching aids, etc.)
25%

Affective Characteristics
(Personality, self-concept, locus of control, motivation, attitudes, anxiety, study habits)
25%

*Bloom (1976)

failure; a proper placement will set you up for success!

What if you think you are not ready for the course in which you enrolled? Without the correct math background, you might fall behind and never catch up. So, if by the second class everything looks like Greek, and you do not understand what is being explained, move to a lower-level course. In the lower-level math course you will have a better chance to understand the material and to pass the course.

Most students do not want to add another math course to their lives, but taking a course that is too difficult will most likely result in problems. You will either withdraw and then re-enroll next session or, worse, fail and then take it again. So, observe what is taking place in your math class and determine what is best for you! Be honest! You want to be successful! Remember the building blocks in Chapter 1? You want to build a firm foundation. Getting into the right math course is a major factor in building that foundation.

Some students are placed in the lowest level math course offered at their college or university. If you are one of these students, check your placement test score with your instructor or counselor to see if you are in the lower quartile (bottom 25% of the test scores). If you are, then ask the instructor or math lab supervisor if they have materials that you can work on that are below the course or textbook level. You also may be able to find some of these resources on the Internet. By learning or relearning this math information, you can improve your math knowledge, which is the basis for math success. Start working on these math lessons as soon as you can, even though they may be a lower level than the first chapter of your math text.

If you have any questions about placement scores seek help immediately. If you ignore your scores and take whatever class you want, you are setting yourself up to fail a course multiple times.

Requests by Students for Higher Placement

Some students ignore their placement test scores entirely because they believe the placement scores are inaccurate. Based on this assumption, they try to encourage their advisors to move them to a higher-level math course. Even though there can be gray areas for a few students, most of the time placement scores are accurate. Also, many students try to enroll in a higher math course to avoid taking noncredit math courses, while other students do not want to repeat courses that they have previously failed. They just want to move on, thinking they can handle it. Some of these students do move on, but they may move on to further failure.

Why do students feel the need to do this? Some older students imagine their math skills are just as sharp as when they completed their last math course, which was five to ten years ago. But if they have not been practicing their math skills, they are just fooling themselves. Still other students believe they do not need the math skills obtained in a prerequisite math course to pass the next course. This is also incorrect thinking. Research indicates that students who were placed correctly in their algebra math course, and who failed it,

will not pass the next algebra math course.

I have conducted research on thousands of students who have either placed themselves or have convinced instructors to place them in higher-level math courses. The results? These students failed their math courses many times before realizing they did not possess the prerequisite math knowledge needed to pass the course. Students who without good reason talk their instructors into moving them up a course level are setting themselves up to fail.

Remember: It is better to be conservative and pass a lower-level math course with an "A" or "B" instead of making a "C" or "D" in a higher-level math course and failing the next course at a higher level.

To be successful in a math course, you must have the appropriate math knowledge. If you think you may have difficulty passing a higher-level math course, you probably do not have an adequate math background. Even if you do pass the math course with a "D" or "C," research indicates you will most likely fail the next higher math course. This is evident when many students repeat a higher-level math course up to five times before repeating the lower-level math course that was barely passed. After repeating the lower-level math course with an "A" or "B," these students can pass their higher-level math course.

The above discussions about correct placement based on the math knowledge you bring to the math course are important since 50 percent of success in a math course is attributed to intelligence and current math knowledge.

What happens when you think you are in the correct math course and you fail the first major test? This means you are in academic trouble because you may not have the background to be successful in that course. Not understanding how to solve these test problems means that you are already behind in your math course or may have been misplaced because the first test in most cases is a review of the previous math course.

My research and other math instructors' research shows that students who fail their first math tests almost never successfully complete the course. In fact some of these students keep taking the course over and over again instead of going back to a lower level course. If this is true in your case, ask the instructor whether you can have an administrative transfer to a lower level math course that he or she is teaching. If the instructor is not teaching a lower level course, ask for a recommendation of another instructor who is teaching the course and transfer to that course.

If you are attending a university that does not offer a lower level course, you may want to withdraw. (If you are on financial aid, make sure to see how withdrawing from one class affects your eligibility for financial aid.) Then next semester plan on taking a lower level math course at the community or junior college. After completing the lower level course, enroll in the university course.

If you are already at a community or junior college and failed the first test in the lowest level math course, talk to your math instructor or counselor. You may want to withdraw from the course and enroll in a math course at an adult high school or at a vocational school that matches up more with your math knowledge. Another solution is to withdraw from the class and hire a tutor and use some basic computer programs to build up your math skills, so you can be prepared to take the math course next semester. You could also stay in the course and set up a plan with the instructor to build up your math skills by having a special program in the math lab or learning assistance center. This means you will have to build up your skills that were lacking on the first test while learning the current math. This is very difficult but can be done in most cases. However, you MUST spend a lot of time on this project because if you have not caught up by the second test you will most likely not pass the course.

Your professors matter a lot more than you might think. Quality of instruction accounts for 25 percent of your grade.

Getting a good start is very important. It is not like other subjects where if you start off slow you can catch up by doing a lot of work. If you start off slow in a math course by making below a C on your first test, you may never catch up unless you follow these suggestions. Remember the goal is to complete your math courses even if it takes you longer. You will still graduate.

How Quality of Instruction Affects Your Grades

Quality of instruction accounts for another 25 percent of your grade. This instruction includes such things as classroom atmosphere, the instructor's teaching style, lab instruction, textbook content and format. All of these "quality" factors affect the ability to learn in the classroom.

Interestingly, probably the most important "quality" variable is the compatibility of an instructor's teaching style with the students'. First, you need to discover your learning style. Second, try to find an instructor who best matches your learning style. Sometimes this is difficult to find out, but a good place to start is to talk to the chair of the math department. The department chair knows the faculty. In addition, some advisors know the faculty teaching styles. Also, try to meet the instructor before the semester begins. The key is to start your inquiry early enough to get into the class you want.

If you cannot find an instructor to match your learning style, improving math study skills and using the math lab/learning resource center can compensate for most of the mismatch. You and your instructor might not be the best match, but it is still your responsibility to be successful in the course. With today's new technologies, students are able to select their best learning aids. These learning aids might be YouTube videos, computer programs and other math textbooks. Other learning resources help you learn the math outside of class when you are having difficulty understanding what is taking place in the classroom. Also, most new math books come with solutions manuals and computer programs, which make studying on your own much easier. If the textbook is still confusing, most libraries and resource centers have other math textbooks that you can use.

The quality of tutors is also a major part of the effectiveness of a math lab or learning resource center. A low student-to-tutor ratio ensures more intensive assistance. Trained tutors are essential for instruction because they know how to help students become better learners. Otherwise, tutoring sessions are just math study hall with a few helpers. The best way to work with tutors is to not only ask for assistance with math concepts but also inquire about good study strategies.

Math departments design courses so that each course covers certain math concepts. Ideally, each course curriculum prepares students for the next level of math. However,

sometimes the courses have gaps between them, or an instructor doesn't cover all the material required, leaving students unprepared for the next course. If this happens, go to your instructor immediately to explain that you did not cover the math in your previous course. Your instructor will suggest a way for you to learn it.

Even though it seems that quality of instruction is out of your control, it really isn't. Your reaction to a teaching style determines your success. If you have a positive attitude, you can find ways to create a good instructional environment.

How Affective Student Characteristics Influence Your Grades

Affective student characteristics account for about 25 percent of your grade. These affective characteristics include math study skills, test anxiety, motivation, locus of control, learning style and other variables that determine your ability to learn math.

Most students do not have this 25 percent of the grade in their favor. In fact, most students have never been taught any study skills, let alone how to study math, specifically. Students also do not know their best learning styles, which means they may study ineffectively by using those that are least effective. Until recently, little attention has been devoted to how students learn, so it is not unusual if you do not know what your learning styles are. However, later in this chapter you will have the opportunity to explore the ways you learn most effectively.

By improving your affective characteristics, you benefit from more productive learning experiences and, subsequently, higher grades. Thousands of students have improved their math study skills, lowered their anxiety, and taken control of learning by using the strategies suggested in this book. The first step in improving how you study math is to determine your best math learning style.

Activity 2.1 Test Attitude Inventory

Please provide the following information:

Name _____ Date _____

Gender (*Please circle*):   **Male   Female**   Score: T_____ W_____ E_____

Directions

A number of statements which people have used to describe themselves are given on the following page. Read each statement and then circle the appropriate number to the right of the statement to indicate how you *generally* feel:

1 = Almost Never, 2 = Sometimes, 3 = Often, 4 = Almost Always.

There are no wrong or right answers. Do not spend too much time on one statement but give the answer which seems to describe how you generally feel. Please answer every statement.

	ALMOST NEVER	SOMETIMES	OFTEN	ALMOST ALWAYS
1. I feel confident and relaxed while taking tests	1	2	3	4
2. While taking examinations I have an uneasy, upset feeling	1	2	3	4
3. Thinking about my grade in a course interferes with my work on tests .	1	2	3	4
4. I freeze up on important exams	1	2	3	4
5. During exams I find myself thinking about whether I'll ever get through school	1	2	3	4
6. The harder I work at taking a test, the more confused I get	1	2	3	4
7. Thoughts of doing poorly interfere with my concentration on tests	1	2	3	4
8. I feel very jittery when taking an important test	1	2	3	4
9. Even when I'm well prepared for a test, I feel very nervous about it . . .	1	2	3	4
10. I start feeling very uneasy just before getting a test paper back	1	2	3	4
11. During tests I feel very tense	1	2	3	4
12. I wish examinations did not bother me so much	1	2	3	4
13. During important tests I am so tense that my stomach gets upset	1	2	3	4
14. I seem to defeat myself while working on important tests	1	2	3	4
15. I feel very panicky when I take an important test	1	2	3	4
16. I worry a great deal before taking an important examination	1	2	3	4
17. During tests I find myself thinking about the consequences of failing . .	1	2	3	4
18. I feel my heart beating very fast during important tests	1	2	3	4
19. After an exam is over I try to stop worry abuot it, but I can't	1	2	3	4
20. During examinations I get so nervous that I forget facts I really know . .	1	2	3	4

Developing a
Math-Learning Profile Sheet

A more formal and more diagnostic assessment of your math learning can be conducted by assessing your test anxiety, your locus of control, and by reviewing the subtest scores of your Math Study Skills Evaluation. Complete the surveys and fill in your results in the Math Learning Profile Sheet by completing the following steps.

Step One — *Complete the Test Attitude Inventory (Activity 2.1).* The Test Attitude Inventory is a survey to assess college test attitudes and will indicate how much test anxiety you have compared to other college students. While you are taking the survey, answer the questions as if they relate to a math test. After taking the Test Anxiety Inventory, go to Appendix A and score the test. Plot your Total Score (T) above the Anxiety heading on the bottom of the graph. Use the left-hand side of the graph to put in the Total (anxiety) Score number. Make sure to plot your scores cleanly and accurately.

The anxiety score is measured in percentile norms, which compares you to other college students. For example, if you had a score of 50 percentile, then half the students tested have higher anxiety than you do and the other half have less anxiety than you. A score of 50 puts you right in the middle. High scores mean you have more test anxiety than other students and low scores mean you have less anxiety. A score from 1 to 25 means you do not have much test anxiety, a score from 26 to 50 means you have some test anxiety, and a score from 51 to 74 means you have test anxiety that may be costing you a few points on your test.

A score from 75 to 100 means you have strong test anxiety, and it likely hurts your math grades. Scores above 80 mean you have high test anxiety and need to reduce it as soon as possible by using the online How to Reduce Test Anxiety CD (found at AcademicSuccess.com). We will focus more on test anxiety in Chapter 3 (How to Reduce Math Anxiety and Math Test Anxiety).

Step Two — *Take the Locus of Control survey.* This Web-based survey is an opinion survey that estimates how much control you believe you have over life events. "Internal" students take responsibility for their lives and their grades and therefore try to improve their learning skills. "External" students believe they have little control over their lives and grades and usually blame the college or others for their poor grades. Sometimes these students do not want to change and improve.

Go to AcademicSuccess.com and click on Winning at Math Student Resources. Put in WAM as the username and Student as the password to access the site.

Click on the Locus of Control survey and take the survey. Plot the Internal Locus number above the Locus of Control heading on the bottom of Figure 2 (Math-Learning Profile Sheet).

The locus of control score is measured in percentile norms, which compare you to other individuals. For example, if you had a score of 50 percentile, then half of the other individuals tested have higher locus of control than you. A score of 50 puts you right in the middle. High scores mean you have more internal locus of control than other students, and low scores mean you have a lower locus of control. Here are a few more guidelines:

- 1 and 25 means you may have an external locus of control.
- 26 and 50 means you may have some external locus of control.
- 51 and 74 means you may have internal locus of control.
- 75 and 100 means you have a strong internal locus of control.

Many students who have difficulty in math may have an external locus of control, which could be based on their poor math attitude. Students with external locus of control can still find success in mathematics. If you do have a poor math attitude, it has already started to change after reading Chapter 1.

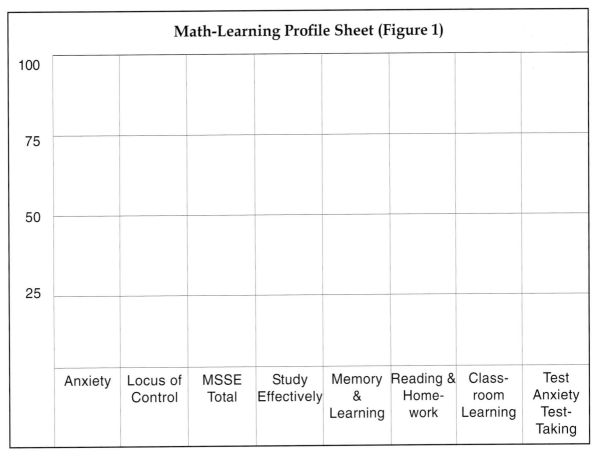

Permission is granted to copy and enlarge this figure.

To become more internal, you need to start accomplishing small goals that can lead to math success. These goals can be in the form of improving your math study skills based on the suggestions in this text. If you make a score of 20 or below, go ahead and read Chapter 9, "How to Take Control and Motivate Yourself to Learn Math." Other chapters in this book will also help you to become more internal.

Step Three — *Complete the Math Study Skills Evaluation.* This web-based survey measures your overall math skills with sub-test scores. If you have not done so already, go to www.academicsuccess.com and click on Winning at Math Student Resources. Put in "WAM" as the username and "Student" as the password to access the site. Click on Math Study Skills Evaluation (MSSE) 4th Edition and take the survey. You will get a total score and subtest scores in the following areas: Studying Efficiently, Memory and Learning, Reading and Homework, Classroom Learning, and Test Anxiety and Test-Taking.

The subtest scores for each section range from 0 to 100. These are percentage scores, not percentile scores like the Test Attitude Inventory and Locus of Control scores. The scores are divided into three ranges:

Needs Instruction (0–70),
Needs Review (71–89),
and Needs No Instruction (90–100).

Once you have completed all the surveys, plot the survey scores (if you have not done so already) on the Figure 2 (Math Learning Profile Sheet). A math-learning strengths and weaknesses profile can now be developed. Have your instructor or counselor explain the meaning of these assessment scores as they relate to how you learn math.

To better understand the Math Learning Profile Sheet, look at Figure 2, on the facing page, which features a 30-year-old married student who works part-time and has a family. According to the Math Learning Profile Sheet, she has extremely high test anxiety, internal locus of control, and poor math study skills, except in one area (Study Effectively). Despite her weaknesses, she still believes she can succeed in math and has a good attitude toward math.

Results: The student learned how to decrease her math anxiety and improve her study skills while attending my study skills class. She had failed her algebra course twice before taking my class. After taking my class, she took the algebra course again and passed with a "B"!

Figure 3, on the facing page, represents a student with a long history of failing math. His only positive scores were his low test anxiety and the Math Study Skills Evaluation subtest score in Test Anxiety and Test-Taking. He had poor study skills, poor attitude, and was external in his locus of control — all likely due to failing math so many times. This "external" student had to begin believing he could pass math through improving his study skills. He also needed support from his teachers and counselors to become more "internal" to pass math.

Results: The student improved his math study skills while attending a math study skills course, and by setting up short-term goals, he became more internal. With an increase in locus of control, he was willing to try some new learning techniques. He passed math that semester.

Figure 4, printed on page 46, represents a profile of many students that I have worked with in helping become more successful in math. This profile could be a male or female student who is returning to college having a history of math learning problems but making A's and B's in other courses. The profile's positive areas are locus of controls and math study skills (except the Test Anxiety / Test-

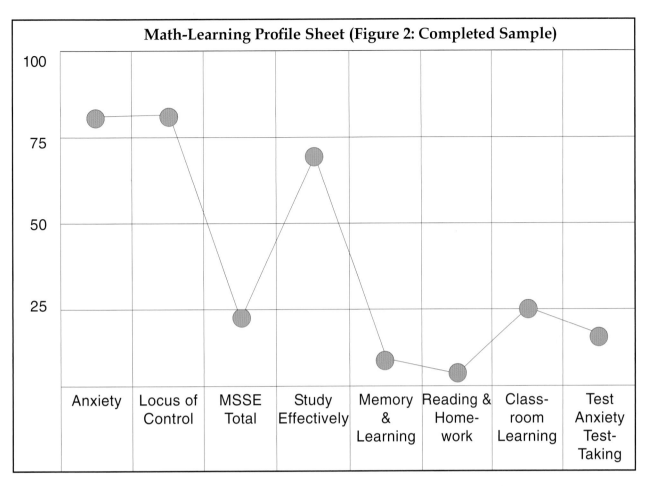

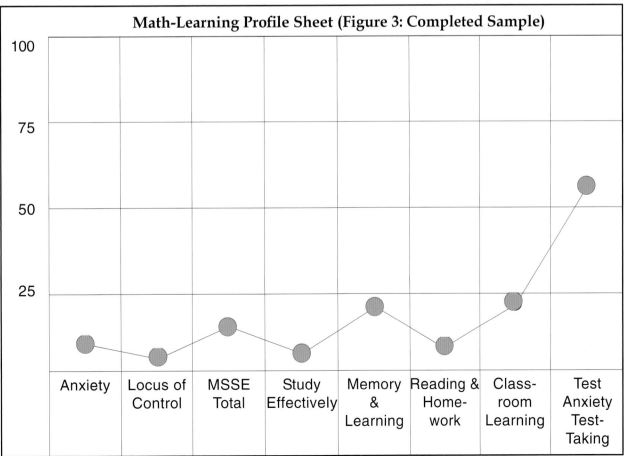

Taking subtest). The major problem areas are extremely high test anxiety and Test Anxiety/ Test-Taking along with average memory and Learning subtest scores.

These students generally have high test anxiety, poor math test-taking and test assessment skills, along with average memory and learning skills. These students need to practice the short-term and long-term relaxation techniques on the How to Reduce Test Anxiety audio file at AcademicSuccess. com, complete Chapter 3 (Managing Math Anxiety and PTSD, and How to Reduce Test Anxiety) and Chapter 8 (Improving Math Test-Taking Skills).

In general, these students are motivated to become successful in math, they just need to reduce their math anxiety and improve their math test-taking skills. Almost all of these students have become successful in their respective math courses.

From these student profiles it is evident that each student has different reasons for being unsuccessful or not being as successful as they could be in math. Their problems usually occur in the form of high anxiety and a combination of having an external locus of control and poor math study skills. These students made positive changes — and you can too — to improve your math success and grades.

Figure 5, on the facing page, represents a veteran who very much like many of the veterans that I have helped pass their math courses. These scores are from a combat veteran, but could be a representative sample of any male or female veteran returning from the wars in the Middle East. Often, these students do well in all of their classes except math. They have been out of high school for five to eight years — many of them having joined the military precisely because the G.I. Bill would pay for their higher education.

This particular student is a criminal justice major and has passed all of his classes but math. Graduation is creeping ever nearer,

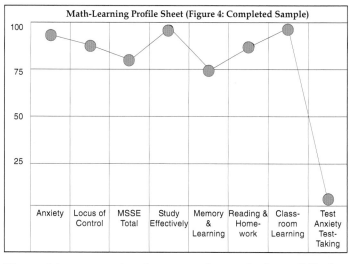

Figure 4 is a composite of many students who have difficulty learning math. These students typically make A's and B's in their other courses.

and he needs to get through his math courses to accomplish his goals.

His profile's positive areas are in the Locus of Control and Study Effectively sections. Being a combat veteran, he is very positive about taking control of his life and becoming successful. He has put in the study time required to succeed and has selected a positive study environment and keeps track of his study time. He has a average score in Classroom Learning, which means he listens in class and has some note-taking skills.

His major problems are in Anxiety, Memory and Learning and Test Anxiety. This student needs to reduce his general anxiety and may need counseling for PTSD. He can use this text to improve his memory, learning, reading, homework and test taking skills.

How well veterans fare in college is a complex issue. In general, most veterans become successful in math through effort and motivation; however, there are those who struggle. For example, veterans with a Traumatic Brain Injury (TBI) typically find it difficult to pass their algebra courses. Interestingly, these same students tend to succeed in statistics courses. Aberrations such as these require specialized help and attention. For this reason, if you are a veteran, you may want to read "My Math Success Plan" (Nolting, 2014), which is a text specifically designed to help improve math learning for wounded warriors.

Step Four — *Fill out a Math Learning Profile Sheet.* If you have not plotted your scores, go ahead and do so on the blank Math-Learning Profile Sheet at the beginning of this chapter. Based on your scores, follow the steps below to develop your plan:

1. *If your test anxiety* is over 75%, practice the relaxation techniques on the How to Reduce Test Anxiety CD (available at AcademicSuccess.com — Student Resources), and read Chapter 3.

2. *If your anxiety* is between 50% and 74%, then start practicing the relaxation techniques on track one of the How to Reduce Test Anxiety CD.

3. *If your locus of control score* is below 50%, read Chapter 9.

4. *Based on the Math Study Skills Evaluation,* read the pages that are associated with the questions that you answered with an "a" or "c," which are the areas in which you need the most help. Then read the pages that are associated with "b" as an answer.

5. *Now, based on your scores*, circle the above steps you plan to complete.

Now that you have completed these steps, you should have a solid feeling for your current ability to learn and apply math. Take note of these results as you will soon use them to fill out portions of the "My Math Success Plan" form.

By using this information as a reference, you can figure out exactly what areas you need to address with custom-built study strategies. First, however, you need to figure out your best learning style.

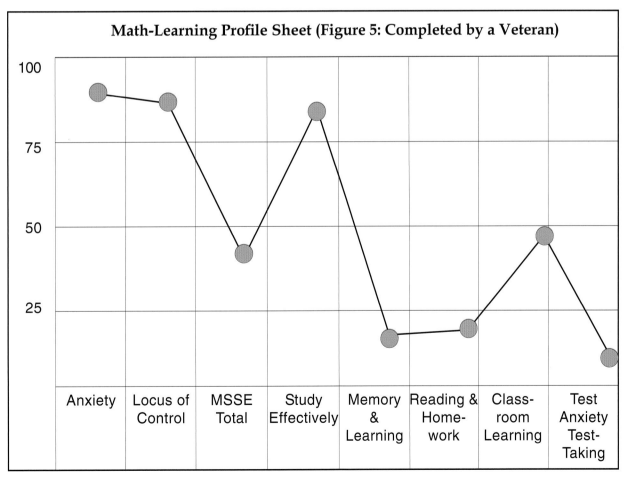

Math-Learning Profile Sheet (Figure 5: Completed by a Veteran)

Permission is granted to copy and enlarge this figure.

Determining Your Best Learning Style

A learning style is a description of the cognitive, affective, and physiological factors that shape the way a student inputs material to be learned and then demonstrates the knowledge of the material. Learning styles also pertain to the best time of day to study, environmental factors that may improve learning (silence, music, lights) and how the brain best processes the material. Research has shown that students who understand learning styles improve learning effectiveness in and outside of the classroom. Many learning style inventories are available, and students should talk to their instructors or counselors about taking one or more.

There are different types of learning styles assessments. One type focuses on learning modalities while other assessments focus on cognitive or environmental learning styles. In this chapter we will focus on modality learning styles.

Learning Modalities (Using Your Senses)

Learning modalities focus on the best way your brain receives information; that is, learning *visually* (seeing), *auditorially* (hearing) or *kinesthetically* (touching, hands-on). If one is available, take a learning style inventory that measures learning modalities. Even better, take an inventory that measures learning modalities specifically for math, such as the Learning Styles Inventory (Brown & Cooper, 1978) or the Learning Modality Inventory for Math Students (Nolting, 2008). Other learning-style inventories measure learning style, but they mainly focus on English or reading-learning modes. Sometimes students have different learning styles for math, so

an inventory that measures subject-specific learning styles is ideal. Take the Learning Modality Inventory for Math Students, found in Appendix B, to better understand your math-learning style. Based on the Learning Modality Inventory for Math Students, rank order your learning modality score by putting 1, 2 or 3 in the space below. Number one is for the learning style that is most like you. If you have a tie, pick the style you feel is most accurate.

Auditory _____

Visual _____

Kinesthetic _____

Modality learning styles are neither good nor bad. They are concerned with how you best take in information. Depending on the subject, professors teach in various ways. In the case of mathematics, most math instructors are visual learners, and they tend to teach the way they learn best. Most of these instructors will write on the board or use a PowerPoint presentation to help you learn math.

Improving Your Math Knowledge

Instructors always operate on the premise that you finished your previous math course just last week; they do not wait for you to catch up on current material. It does not matter if your previous math course was a month ago or five years ago, instructors expect you to know the previous course material — period.

Review Your Previous Math Material and Tests

There are several ways to improve your math knowledge. Review what was covered in your last math class before attending your present math course. Look closely at your final exam to determine your weak areas. Work on your weak areas as soon as possible so they can become building blocks (instead of stumbling blocks) for your current course.

If it has been some time since your last math course, visit the math lab or learning resource center to locate review material. Ask the instructor if there are any computer programs that will assess your math skills to determine your strengths and weaknesses for your course. Review math videos about the math course below your level. Also review any computer software designed for the previous math course. You can also go to Student Resources and click on "Student Math Practice and Learning Sites." These sites can help you review certain math concepts

by either working out problems or reviewing math videos. To review algebra, click on the Purple Math site and click on "How do you really do this stuff?" and review the topics from your previous math class. Review the other websites on the page to help you improve your math knowledge.

Another way to make sure you are ready for your next math class is to take all of the chapter review tests in the textbook from your last math class. If you score above 80 percent on one chapter review test, move on to the next chapter. A score below 80 percent means you need to work on that chapter before moving on to the next chapter. Get a tutor to help you with those chapters if you have trouble. Make sure you review all the chapters required in the previous course as soon as possible. If you wait more than two weeks to conclude this exercise, it may be too late to catch up (while learning new material at the same time).

Employ a Tutor

One last way to improve your cognitive entry skills is to employ a private tutor. If you have a history of not doing well in math courses, you may need to start tutorial sessions the same week class begins. This will give the tutor a better chance of helping you regain those old math skills. You still need to work hard to relearn old math skills while continuing to learn the new material. If you wait four to five weeks to employ a tutor, it will probably be too late to catch up and do well or even pass the course.

You may be able to locate a tutor by asking your instructor or the coordinator of the math lab. There also are commercial tutor centers off campus that you can pay to obtain help. However, the new fad is online tutors who help you with math. Recently one of the major networks did a national news report on how high school students were being tutored online from India. Your textbook publisher may also offer free online tutoring. Make sure to ask for references and how the tutor was trained before hiring a tutor. Also, if you are planning to use an online tutor, make sure you can learn online. Some students have difficulty with learning math online. If this is the case for you, you are better off visiting your campus' math lab to review material.

Schedule Math Courses Back-to-Back

Another way to maintain appropriate math knowledge is to take math courses every term until you complete the necessary math requirements— even if you do not like math — so that you can maintain sequential (linear) learning.

I have known students who have made "B's" or "C's" in a math class, and then waited six months to a year to take the next math course. Inevitably, many failed. These students did not complete any preparatory math work before the math course and were lost after the second chapter. This is similar to having one semester of Spanish, not speaking it for a year, then visiting Spain and not understanding what is being said.

The only exception to taking math courses "back to back" is taking a six-week "kamikaze" math course (an ultra-condensed version of a regular course), which should be avoided. These types of courses do not allow enough time for students to rehearse the math enough to maintain it in long term memory.

If you are one of the unfortunate many who are currently failing a math course, you need to ask yourself, "Am I currently learning any math or just becoming more confused?" If you are learning some math, stay in the course. If you are getting more confused, withdraw from the course. Improve your knowledge during the remaining part of the semester and re-enroll next semester.

Finding Your Best Instructor

Finding an instructor who best matches your learning style can be a difficult task. Most students are placed in their first math course by an academic advisor. Usually academic advisors know who are the most and least popular math instructors. However, advisors are reluctant to discuss teacher popularity.

To learn who the best math instructors are, ask the academic advisor which math instructor's classes fill up first. This does not place the academic advisor in the position of making a value judgment; neither does it guarantee the best instructor, but it will increase the odds in your favor. Another strategy is to ask your friends who are serious about their classes. However, if a fellow student says an instructor is excellent, make sure your learning style matches your friend's learning style. Ask your friend, "Exactly what makes the instructor so good?" Then compare the answer to how you learn best. If you have a different learning style than your friend, look for another instructor, or ask another friend whose learning style matches your own more closely. Once again, various websites also rank and collect information on college professors. While the reviews on these sites don't always tell the whole story, they nonetheless remain helpful.

If you have time, interview or observe an instructor teaching a class. This process is time consuming, but it is well worth it! Once you have found your best instructor, remain with him or her for every math class when possible. This way, you will always know that your learning style matches up with your professor's.

Activity 2.2 Use Your Learning Style to Improve Your Math Knowledge

Now that you know your preferred learning style, it is time to put it to use. Use the questionnaire printed below to figure out how to choose the resources that best fit your best way of learning.

1. Put a check mark by your preferred learning style:

   Auditory   _____
   Visual   _____
   Kinesthetic   _____

2. Based on this learning style, what type of professor should you seek out? Keep in mind how this professor may or may not teach his or her classes.

3. Think back to the last math course you completed. How did you study for this class? Did your approach follow your best learning style? Or did you adapt to the way your professor taught the course?

4. Visit one of the many online resources for ranking professors. Try to find any particular professors who seem to teach in a manner that caters to your best learning style. Write down any matches in the space below.

Creating an Individual College Success Plan for Math

In order to succeed in your college math courses, you need to develop a detailed plan for every semester. This plan must include a list of goals, and the steps and resources required to meet these goals. This book is designed to help you produce a plan that meets all of these requirements and more.

From time to time in this text, you will encounter sections titled "My Math Success Plan." The purpose of these activities is to have you use chapter information to develop a list of goals, strategies and reference materials. By the end of the book, you will have developed a comprehensive attack plan for a current or upcoming math course.

To illustrate what your finished plan might look like, we've printed a completed copy of the form on the facing page. Notice that the student who filled out this form has written her goals in a clear, concise fashion.
As you can see, to properly complete this plan, you first need to determine your best learning style. Next, you need to set your goals for your current math course(s). Finally, figure out what study strategies are best suited to your learning style, then list those strategies that address your semester goals.

After reading the first two chapters of this text, you are already able to fill out the first few sections. To do this, read the instructions printed below, then turn to "My Math Success Plan" in Chapter 9. Leave the rest blank. You will fill in these sections as you progress through the text.

Sections A and B

Section A is fairly straightforward. Simply list your name and year in college. List your current math course in Section B, and you are ready to move on!

Section C: Learning Information

Section C compiles everything you've worked on in this chapter—specifically your MSSE scores, your areas for improvement and your personal learning style preference.

Why This Success Plan Is Necessary

Creating a math success plan for every semester is important for many reasons. Here are just a few of them:

- *Plans breed confidence.* Feeling prepared for a test or a class gives you the confidence you need to succeed.

- *It lets your professors know you are serious.* By filling out a math success plan, it lets your professors know you are making their class a priority.

- *It helps you figure out what does and doesn't work.* Making a success plan allows you to take stock in what study skills actually work for you.

My Math Success Plan (Example)

Semester: Fall 2014

A: Student Information

       Name: Sally Student
       Year in College: Sophomore

B: Course: College Algebra

C: Learning Information

I am predominately a visual learner.

Based on my MSSE scores, I need to work on note-taking and homework techniques.

D: Semester Goals

1. I will obtain a 3.0 GPA.
2. I will make a "B" in elementary algebra.
3. I will improve my math study skills weaknesses by working on the suggestions from the computerized Math Study Skills Evaluation.
4. I will set up a study schedule and each week will complete a study-goals sheet.
5. I will attend tutorial sessions.
6. I will see my math instructor every two weeks and after each major test.

E: Math Study Strategies

Use math note-taking system
Color code notes
Develop a math glossary
Use online homework system
Learn relaxation techniques
Develop my own test-taking system

F: Motivation Strategies

1. I will make an appointment with my math instructor.
2. I will reward myself when completing a short-term goal.
3. I will learn the reasons for my procrastination and overcome them.
4. I will tell myself positive statements everyday.
5. I will tell myself by passing math, I will get my business degree.

Chapter 2 Summary

- Controlling math success is primarily based on improving the characteristics that affect your ability to learn math — your affective learning characteristics.

- The Math Study Skills Evaluation can help you discover how you can improve your math success.

- The major affective characteristics are study habits, anxiety and control over math.

- There are various ways to improve your math knowledge and math learning.

- Review your previous math material to have the math knowledge to start the course.

- Do not push your advisor to enroll you in a math course you aren't prepared for.

- If you are fuzzy on the math required for a particular math course, it is wise to enroll in a prerequisite course.

- Once placed in the appropriate math course, success is based on your ability to learn math.

- Students who fail their first math test are statistically more likely to fail a course than those who perform well on the exam.

- Understanding your learning modality style will improve your learning.

- Try to find an instructor who matches your learning style.

- If you are a military veteran, it is important to contact and work with your school's veteran affairs office.

- Make sure you take math every semester (except for short summer sessions) until you complete all your math courses.

- Talk to your instructor or counselor about your Math-Learning Profile Sheets and develop a learning plan.

- Students with high math anxiety need to read Chapter 3 (How to Reduce Math Anxiety and Math Test Anxiety) and listen to the "How to Reduce Test Anxiety" CD.

- Fill out sections A, B and C of your "My Math Success Plan."

Name: _____   Date: _____

Assignment for Chapter 2

1. How does math knowledge affect your math grades?

2. How long do you have to practice the study skills suggestions in this book to improve your math performance this semester? Why?

3. Based on your Math-Learning Profile Sheet, list and explain the areas in which you need to improve:

4. Why is it a bad idea to push your advisors into enrolling you in a math class you aren't ready for?

5. How does your learning style match up with your current professor's?

6. Using your Math Study Skills Evaluation, explain your strengths and weaknesses in the space below:

7. Explain your best modality learning style and five different ways you can improve your learning:

8. List and describe three ways you can improve your math knowledge.

9. What are the reasons to schedule math courses each term?

10. How can you find your best math instructor?

Managing Math Anxiety and PTSD, and How to Reduce Test Anxiety

3

In Chapter 3
You will learn these concepts:

✓ How to reduce test anxiety

✓ How to replace negative self-talk with positive self-talk

✓ Understanding math anxiety

✓ How to write a math autobiography

✓ Understanding post-traumatic stress disorder

Math Anxiety, Test Anxiety and PTSD

Math anxiety is a common problem for many high school, college and university students. It is especially difficult for students in developmental courses who normally have more anxiety than other students. There are, however, students in higher level math courses that also struggle with this problem. It is very common for students to have anxiety only about math and not in their other subjects.

Math anxiety affects students in many different ways. It affects the way they do their homework, the way they learn in the classroom and the way they choose a career. Students who have math anxiety may procrastinate with homework or put off sitting down and completing an online lesson. This behavior often leads to failure. Students also select their major based on the amount of required math, which means that those with math anxiety often settle for lower paying or dissatisfying careers.

More than anything else, math anxiety affects the way students approach and take tests. Mild test anxiety often compels students to properly prepare for a test. High test anxiety, however, causes major problems in learning and test taking, as these students avoid studying for a test when anxiety begins to afflict their thought processes. Reducing test anxiety is the key for many students to become more successful in math. These students need to learn the causes of test anxiety and figure out how to reduce its effects before their grades begin to suffer.

The same is true for students dealing with post-traumatic stress disorder. The symptoms of PTSD often flare up during high-stress situations. For many, test days bring anxiety to a fever pitch, meaning that they aren't always able to accurately portray their knowledge on an exam. If you are dealing with PTSD, you must establish a support system to get you through the most stressful days of your college career.

Several techniques have proven helpful in reducing math anxiety, test anxiety and the symptoms of PTSD. These techniques, however, are not enough to assure good grades. In order to succeed in a math class, you must couple the techniques mentioned in this chapter with effective study skills and a proper attitude.

Chapter 3 Topics Include:

- *Math anxiety* is a learned behavior based on a person's past experiences with math.

- *The definitions and causes* of math anxiety, test anxiety and PTSD.

- *The effects of test anxiety* on learning and testing.

- *PTSD symptoms,* triggers and treatments.

Understanding Math Anxiety

Math anxiety is a relatively new concept in education. During the 1970s, certain educators began using the terms "mathophobia" and "mathemaphobia" as a possible cause for a child's unwillingness to learn math. Modern psychologists define math anxiety as an extreme emotional and/or physical reaction to a negative attitude toward math.

Math anxiety affects students in many different ways. It sometimes manifests as tension, which interferes with the manipulation of numbers and the solving of math problems during tests (Richardson and Suinn, 1973). It also includes the panic, helplessness, paralysis and mental disorganization that occurs in some students when they are solving math problems. This discomfort varies in intensity and results from previous experiences in past learning situations (Tobias, 1976). There is a strong relationship between low math confidence and high math test anxiety.

Math anxiety is common among college students. In fact, counselors at a major university recently reported that one-third of students enrolled in behavior therapy programs—usually offered through counseling centers—have problems with math anxiety. It has been shown that math anxiety exists among many students who do not suffer from other tensions. It frequently occurs in students with a poor high school math background. Approximately half of students enrolled in developmental math courses suffer from some form of math anxiety—though students in high-level math courses occasionally show symptoms as well.

Today, math anxiety is accepted as one of the major problems students have in completing their math courses. It is real, but it *can* be overcome.

Math anxiety is divided into three separate anxieties: Math Test Anxiety, Numerical Anxiety and Abstraction Anxiety. Math Test Anxiety involves the anticipation, completion and feedback of math tests.

Numerical Anxiety refers to everyday situations that involve numbers and arithmetic calculations.

Numerical anxiety affects students who are trying to figure out the proper amount for a tip, thinking about mathematics, doing math homework or listening to a math lecture.

Abstraction Anxiety involves working with variables and mathematical concepts used to solve equations. Some students experience all three types of math anxiety; others deal with only one.

Most of the students I have worked with deal with Math Test Anxiety and Abstraction Anxiety. These students do not have any anxiety with numbers, but often struggle with algebra and other symbol-heavy math. Unfortunately, these symbols are extremely common in college math courses.

Causes of Math Anxiety

Since math anxiety is a learned condition, its causes are unique to each student. Nevertheless, math anxiety is almost always rooted in an individual's past experiences. Bad experiences in elementary school are one of the most common sources for students' math anxiety: coming in last in math races at the blackboard, watching a classmate finish a problem twice as fast as they do, or teachers saying, "That's okay. You just aren't good in math; you are better in English." When asked, many students with math anxiety indicate that they were made fun of when trying to solve math problems at the chalkboard. This is by far the most common story I hear when working with students. Heckled students have a hard time letting go of painful memories. Harsh words and experiences remain with these students; when they walk into a classroom or open a math book, these bad experiences often play back in their minds.

A 56 year old once indicated to me that he had a great deal of fear that his instructor might call him to the board. Even if he knew how to do a problem, he was terrified at the thought of having to display that knowledge to his peers.

Example: Over the years, math anxiety is reinforced and even increases in magnitude. In fact, many math anxious students — now 30, 40 and 50 years old — still have extreme fear about working math problems on the board. These bad memories linger well into adulthood.

Being embarrassed by family members also causes math anxiety. According to a recent study, many students claim that their parents routinely try to help them with math and this sometimes leads to serious trauma. These students say that tutoring from their guardians, mainly their fathers, often results in scolding when they are not able to complete problems. One student reported that his father hit him every time he got a multiplication problem wrong.

Brothers and sisters also tease one another about being dumb in math. This is particularly true of boys telling girls that they cannot do math. When people hear these statements enough times, they often start to believe them and associate these bad feelings with math. For some students, just hearing the word "math" triggers a response of anxiety as they consciously or unconsciously recall bad feelings or memories.

A good example of this is a student who I worked with who had completed her BS degree 15 years ago at a college that did not require much math. She was returning to college to be an elementary school teacher, which required her to take math and a placement test. As soon as I mentioned that she had to take math, she said, "I can't do math, and I will have to wait a few days to get psychologically ready to take the math placement test." She indicated her old anxiety feelings rushed through her, and she almost had an anxiety attack. This is an extreme but true example of math anxiety. In most cases math anxiety is not this bad, but remains disruptive enough to cause learning and testing problems.

Those who don't have math anxiety still have to understand it. This way they can help their classmates who need support. Also, if you do not have math anxiety now, you may develop it in the future. One way to overcome math anxiety is to find out when it first occurred and how it is still affecting you. A math autobiography is an excellent way to review previous math experiences and to learn how to overcome math anxiety. To find out more about writing a math autobiography, complete the first two activities in this chapter.

How Math Anxiety Affects Learning

Anxiety causes learning problems in several ways. Let's first start by looking at how it affects your homework. Students with high math anxiety have difficulty starting or completing assignments. Doing homework reminds some students of their learning problems in math. More specifically, it reminds them of previous math failures, which causes further anxiety. This anxiety sometimes leads to total avoidance of homework or "approach-avoidance" behavior; students start their homework, then they quit, return later, then quit again. Total homework avoidance is called procrastination. The thought of doing homework causes these students anxiety, which then causes them to put it off. Procrastination makes them feel better for a short time — until test day.

Math anxiety also affects your classroom participation and learning. Usually students with math anxiety are afraid to speak out in class and ask questions. They are also afraid of asking a question that others, including the teacher, might consider dumb. They sit in class fearful of being asked a question, looking like they understand the lecture so they will not be called on. They also take a lot of notes, even though they don't understand them, to give the illusion of comprehension. If you are one of these students, these are hard habits to break. Still, there are numerous ways to overcome them. Here are just a few:

1. *Make an appointment to talk to your math instructor.* Math instructors want to talk to you. When I do my consulting around the country, one of the major complaints I get from math instructors is that students don't come and see them. Make an appointment to see your math instructor before the first major test to discuss your math history and to ask for suggestions.

2. *Before class, ask the instructor to work one homework problem.* Write the problem on the board before the instructor arrives. This is less stressful because you are not asking the question in front of the whole class. Choose an easy question, if possible.

3. *Prepare one question from your homework and ask it within the first 15 minutes of class.* Instructors are more likely to answer questions in the first part of class when they have time instead of the end of class when time is running out.

4. *Ask a question about a problem to which you already know the answer.* That way, if the instructor asks you a question about the problem, you will know the answer. This is good practice for asking questions about things you don't understand.

5. *Use email to send questions to your instructor.* This way you can still get the answer with very little anxiety. Do not, however, overuse this option. If you send too many emails, your instructor may begin to ignore you.

6. *Set up an appointment with your disability counselor/advisor to discuss anxiety issues.* Review your test scores from your psycho-educational report, IEP or Section 504 plan. If necessary, ask for a referral to obtain help in reducing anxiety. Do not be embarrassed. Always remember to get the help you need.

7. *Set up an appointment with your veteran advisor or certifying officer.* Discuss your test anxiety and ask for helpful resources. If you have PTSD, discuss these issues. Ask for a referral to obtain assistance.

By completing these steps, you are setting up a new history of positive expriences. Not only will these tips help you become more comfortable in a math classroom, but they also allow you to change your overall attitude toward math. It is important to remember that math anxiety *can* be overcome with your effort. You don't have to live in the past with your math fears. Today is a new day and you can change how math affects you.

Activity 3.1 Revisiting Past Math Experiences

If you have math anxiety, try to remember the first time you had uneasy feelings about math. This does not include anxiety when taking a math test, which will be discussed later in this chapter. To help you remember this experience, check the appropriate response and answer the following questions:

1. Was your first negative math experience in:

    Elementary School _____

    Middle School   _____

    High School   _____

    Never   _____

2. Can you recall the incident(s)?

    Yes   _____

    No   _____

3. Was it after....

    Being called on in class and getting the answer wrong?   _____

    Getting a poor grade on a homework assignment?   _____

    A parent saying he/she cannot do math and neither can you?   _____

    Another adult telling you that cannot do math?   _____

    A fellow student telling you that you are not good at math?   _____

    A teacher telling you that you are not good at math.   _____

4. If your first negative math experience is not listed above, then write it down here:

5. If you cannot remember a specific incident, then when was the last time you told yourself that you could not learn math?

    Today   _____

    Yesterday   _____

    Last Month _____

    Last Year   _____

    Never   _____

Creating Your Math Autobiography

Now that you have finished the questionnaire, it is time to start your math autobiography. The autobiography relates to how you remember and feel about past math experiences. It also helps you explore how these past feelings and events have shaped your current life. Math autobiographies are a good healing tool that help you let go of negative experiences. To find a blank form for your math autobiography, visit AcademicSuccess.com, click Student Resources and enter the following info:

Username: Wam
Password: Student

Once you have downloaded the file, print it out and get to writing! Here are a few tips to get you started:

1. When writing your math autobiography, it is easiest to start by remembering your first negative and/or positive experiences with math. You have already written a little bit about these experiences. Use Activity 3.1 as a basis for your continued writing.

2. After you have sufficiently explained these experiences, explore how they have shaped your lifelong relationship with math. There is a good chance that your initial experiences with math continue to play a huge role in your academic career. If not, don't worry. Simply write down how you have managed to persevere through bad experiences, or have used positive experiences as fuel for continued success.

3. Finally, what are your short and long term goals in terms of redefining your relationship with math? Do you want to learn to love it? Do you want to grin and bear it long enough to pass? Whatever your goals are, it is important to stay positive. Explore these questions as you draw your math autobiography to a close.

As for what to do with your finished product, you'll need to consult your current teacher or counselor. Depending on your instructor, you may be able to hand in your completed form as your autobiography. Make sure to make a personal copy before turning it in.

Even if your instructor does not require you to hand in your autobiography, it remains important to fill one out anyway. Your math autobiography is an important tool to help you become a better math student and to help reduce your math and test anxiety.

If need be, share and discuss your math autobiography with a counselor or college psychologist. They might provide you with a few great insights into your behavior. Don't be afraid to seek out the help you need.

Understanding Post-Traumatic Stress Disorder

The number of college students who suffer from post-traumatic stress disorder continues to rise. This includes students who suffered some sort of trauma before college and those who develop PTSD during college. According to the National Institute of Mental Health (NIMH) PTSD is an anxiety disorder that some people get after seeing or living through a dangerous event. This natural fear triggers many split-second changes in the body in order to prepare it to defend against or avoid any further threats. This is called the "fight-or-flight" response and is a healthy reaction meant to protect a person from harm. In PTSD, however this reaction is changed or damaged. Even as time passes, the reactions remain activated. People who have PTSD may feel stressed or frightened even when they are no longer in danger. These students have increased anxiety. They avoid any stimuli associated with the trauma, and tend to numb emotions and emotional responses. As the number of Wounded Warriors attending college continues to increase, psychologists and counselors are focusing much more intently on PTSD.

According to the DSM-IV-TR, a PTSD (309.81) is "...the development of characteristic symptoms following exposure to an extreme traumatic stressor involving direct personal experience of an event that involves actual or threatened death or serious injury, or another threat to one's physical integrity or witnessing an event that involves death, injury or a threat to the physical integrity of another person... The person's response to the event must involve intense fear, helplessness or horror..."

Many college students have PTSD due to the following events: kidnapping, serious accident, natural disaster, car accidents; violent attacks such as, mugging, rape, torture, or being held captive; campus shootings; or simply witnessing any of these events happen to another person.

Students with traumatic brain injuries also often deal with PTSD. The most common causes of TBI among college students are vehicular accidents and sports injuries. If you have suffered either of these, seek guidance.

Here are some more facts about PTSD from the NIMH:

- PTSD can affect anyone at any age.
- Millions of Americans get PTSD every year.
- Many war veterans have had PTSD.
- Women tend to get PTSD more often than men.
- PTSD can be treated.
- Medicines are available in the most extreme cases.

Prevalence of PTSD

According to the U.S. Department of Veteran Affairs, between 7 and 8 percent of the U.S. population deals with PTSD at some point in their lives. Around 5.2 million adults have PTSD during a given year. Between 10 and 20 percent of veterans of the wars in Iraq and Afghanistan deal with PTSD, while an additional 10 percent of Desert Storm veterans also continue to manage the symptoms of the disorder.

Who is Most Likely to Develop PTSD?

Besides veterans, there are many other groups who are more likely to develop PTSD than the general public. According to the VA, the following groups are at an increased risk:

- Victims of child abuse.
- Those with other mental health problems.
- Those with family members suffering from mental health problems.
- Those who have suddenly lost a loved one.
- Alcoholics.
- People with low levels of education.
- Those prone to stress.
- People without a strong emotional support system.

Symptoms of PTSD

Post-traumatic stress disorder affects students in numerous ways. The traumatic events that lead to the disorder are usually so overwhelming and frightening that they would upset anyone. Following a traumatic event, almost everyone experiences at least some of the symptoms of PTSD, including:

- Intrusive, upsetting memories of the event.
- Flashbacks (acting or feeling like the event is happening again).
- Nightmares

- Avoiding activities, places, thoughts, or feelings that remind you of the trauma.
- Inability to remember important aspects of the trauma.
- Loss of interest in activities and life in general.
- Feeling emotionally detached
- A desire to avoid loved ones.
- Sense of a limited future (you don't expect to live a normal life span or get married).
- Have difficulty falling or staying asleep.
- Irritability or outbursts of anger.
- Hyper vigilance (on constant "red alert").

How PTSD Affects Learning

Post-traumatic stress disorder mainly affects learning by causing increased anxiety during stressful activities. Many students with PTSD are prone to panic attacks. These attacks are sometimes triggered by stress that is unrelated to the incident or events at the root of a student's disorder — particularly on test days.

The anxiety felt by students with PTSD differs from that of students with traditional test-anxiety. For students with PTSD, it isn't the test that causes the panic attack. People with PTSD learn to fear stress itself. Any discomfort at all potentially snowballs into a full blown attack. Because these students worry about having an embarrassing panic attack in public, the thought of stress is enough to create the exact symptoms they desperately want to avoid. In this way, PTSD seems to feeds on itself — making the disorder a frustrating, at times devastating ordeal.

Still, there are many ways to cope with PTSD. In the next section, you'll learn several techniques to manage the symptoms of the disorder — mostly through well-tested stress-relieving techniques. You'll also learn about the importance of seeking professional help.

Coping with PTSD

Recovering from post-traumatic stress disorder is a long, at times difficult process. Improvement is measured in small, daily victories, not overnight breakthroughs. If you are suffering from symptoms of PTSD, it is absolutely crucial that you seek professional help. The depression and fears involved with having lived through a traumatic event affect much more than your school life. When dealing with PTSD, your entire mental health is at stake. The key is to be open and honest about your situation. As painful as certain memories are, it is important that you process them before they completely take over your life.

In the meantime, there are numerous tactics you can use to cope with the symptoms of PTSD. According to the U.S. Department of Veteran affairs, the following activities help lessen the harmful effects of panic or stress attacks:

- Muscle relaxation exercises
- Breathing exercises
- Meditation
- Swimming, stretching, yoga
- Prayer
- Listening to quiet music
- Spending time in nature
- Running or jogging
- Reading

The VA also provides a few suggestions on how to put painful memories into proper perspective.

1. Remind yourself that they are just that, memories.
2. Remind yourself that it's natural to have some memories of the trauma(s).
3. Although reminders of trauma feel overwhelming, they lessen with time.

If you are dealing with PTSD, it is important to engage in positive activities. In fact, mental health professionals suggest PTSD patients use their condition as a catalyst for change. For many, this approach involves going back to school. While this is certainly a great idea, students with PTSD still need to come to college prepared to handle the stress and discomfort involved with higher education. In order to cope with the stress of tests and exams, students with PTSD should read and review the tips given in this chapter. As for the stress of daily life, here are a few more tips from the VA.

- *Write things down.* Creating "to do" lists eliminates the worry that you might forget an important date.
- *Create and focus on small attainable goals.* Doing so allows you to remain positive as you successfully check things off your list. This helps engender a feeling of forward motion.

Understanding Test Anxiety

Test anxiety has existed for as long as tests have been issued to evaluate student performance. Because it is so common, and because it has survived the test of time, test anxiety has been carefully studied over the last fifty years. Pioneering studies indicate that test anxiety generally leads to low test scores.

At the University of South Florida (Tampa), Dr. Charles Spielberger investigated the relationship between test anxiety and intellectual ability. The study results suggested that anxiety coupled with high ability can improve academic performance; but anxiety coupled with low or average ability often interferes with academic performance. That is:

Anxiety + High Ability = Improvement
Anxiety + Low or Average Ability = No Improvement

Test anxiety is a learned response brought on by environmental conditioning. A person is not born with it. It is a special kind of general stress, or a "strained exertion," which sometimes leads to physical and psychological problems. The good news? Because test anxiety is a *learned* response, it can eventually be *unlearned* through hard work and discipline. Read on through this chapter to find out more.

Definition of Test Anxiety

According to the Diagnostic and Statistics Manual of Mental Disorders, test anxiety is characterized by an "extreme fear of poor performance on tests and examinations." The DSM goes on to describe a statistical correlation between test-anxiety and various character attributes, including but not limited to low self-esteem, dependency and passivity.

One of my students once compared test anxiety to "being in a burning house with no way out." Another described it as "a sick feeling I get on test days that makes me feel like a child and makes me forget everything."

No matter how you define it, test anxiety is real, and it affects millions of students.

The Causes of Test Anxiety

The causes of test anxiety are different for each student. The initial incident could possibly have occurred in middle or high school. For many students, however, test anxiety first occurs in college when passing tests is the only way to pass a course. In most college courses, homework and extra credit do not count toward your grade. Now students must have a passing average, and, in some cases, pass an intimidating departmental final exam.

Additional pressure also exists because not passing algebra means you won't graduate, and you might not get the job you want.

PTSD is another cause of test-anxiety. As described previously, students with PTSD often fear stress itself, which in turn causes a vicious loop of self-doubt and panic. Many of these students are also dealing with Traumatic Brain Injuries, which often go hand-in-hand with memory problems. Students with TBIs are often caught in a viscious loop. First, they fear that they will forget important information on test days. Then, on test day, the stress from this fear causes them to struggle, which only reinforces their initial anxiety.

Since we have already explored your experiences with taking math tests, let's look at some of the direct causes of your math test anxiety. If you do have test anxiety, what is the main cause? If you don't know, then review the eight causes of test anxiety on the next page. Does one of these reasons fit you? If you don't have test anxiety, think of scenarios that might bring it on in the future.

If you have math test anxiety, following the suggestions in this chapter and the rest of the book can greatly reduce it. The first step was already taken by understanding how you developed test anxiety. The second step is writing the reasons.

For conveinence, here is a review of the 10 basic causes of test anxiety.

1. *Test anxiety is* a learned behavior resulting from the expectations of parents, teachers or other significant people in the student's life.

2. *Test anxiety is* sometimes caused by the association between grades and a student's personal worth.

3. *Test anxiety* develops from the fear of alienating parents, family or friends due to poor grades.

4. *Test anxiety* stems from a feeling of lack of control and an inability to change one's life situation.

5. *Test anxiety* is sometimes caused by a student being embarrassed by the teacher or other students when trying to do math problems.

6. *Test anxiety* often occurs during timed tests due to the fear of not finishing the test. This is true even when a student is capable of doing all of the problems.

7. *Test anxiety* is sometimes caused by being put in math courses that are above the student's level of competence.

8. *Students leaving* the room before the test time is up often triggers anxiety among the remaining students.

9. *PTSD* often triggers test-anxiety.

10. *TBIs* often trigger test-anxiety.

The Different Types of Test Anxiety

The two basic types of test anxiety are *emotional* ("somatic") and *worry* ("cognitive"). Students with high test anxiety have both emotional and worry anxiety.

Signs of emotional anxiety are upset stomach, nausea, sweaty palms, pain in the neck, stiff shoulders, high blood pressure, rapid shallow breathing, rapid heartbeat or general feelings of nervousness. As anxiety increases, these feelings intensify.

Even though these feelings are caused by anxiety, the physical response is real. These feelings and physical inconveniences affect your concentration and your testing speed, and sometimes cause you to "draw a blank."

Worry anxiety causes students to think about failing a test. This negative "self-talk" causes students to focus on their anxiety instead of recalling math concepts by telling themselves that they will fail the test. This talk is perhaps the worst enemy of a math student. Not only does it reinforce bad behavior, it also prohibits a student from establishing positive energy. Negative self-statements vary from student to student.

Students with worry anxiety have told me many things after not being able to solve problems:

- "What is wrong with me?"
- "I did these types of problems before."
- "I just cannot get math!"
- "Math is awful!"
- "I hate math!"
- "I don't need it for my career so why am I taking the course."
- "I am going to fail this test and this course."
- "I might as well drop this course and quit college."
- "I am dumb."

These types of statements cause more worry anxiety and divert your attention away from the test, leaving you less time to complete problems. Later on in the chapter we discuss how to get rid of these types of statements.

Students may have different levels of emotional anxiety and worry anxiety. The treatment depends on the levels of your type of test anxiety. Go to Appendix A (Scoring the Test Attitude Inventory) to measure the levels of your type of anxiety. The levels are measures in "percentile norms," which means your level of anxiety is compared to other college students.

The percentage level of my anxiety falls under (fill in percentages from your anxiety levels below).

Total worry _____

Worry anxiety _____

Emotional anxiety _____

Low levels of anxiety are between 1 and 25. Moderately low levels of anxiety are between 26 and 50. Moderately high levels of anxiety are between 51 and 75. High levels of anxiety fall between the 76th and 99th percentile.

What is your level of anxiety for each area? Students who have high test anxiety have both emotional and worry anxiety.

The Effects of Anxiety on Testing and Learning

The effects of anxiety on student learning and testing can best be explained by reviewing the Stages of Memory discussed in Chapter 5. The Stages of Memory are Sensory Input, Sensory Register, Short-term Memory, Working Memory, Abstract Reasoning, Long-term Memory and Memory Output.

When anxious students are reading a math textbook or learning mathematics in the classroom, their anxiety affects their Sensory Register and Short-term Memory. Anxiety interferes with how fast people process information and can decrease the amount of information they can hold for a short period of time. This means that less information enters Working Memory, which is where mathematics information is combined and learned.

Example: Anxiety manifests itself differently in every student. The effects of test anxiety range from a "mental block" on a test to avoidance of homework. These symptoms also range in severity.

Also, anxiety affects Working Memory by decreasing the amount of information that can be processed at the same time. This leads to poor Memory Output such as not understanding what you read or not answering a question during class.

The most recent research indicates that test anxiety strongly affects Working Memory. Authors Ashcraft and Kirk (2001) indicate that math anxiety temporarily disrupts mental processing in Working Memory that causes poorer math achievement. Math anxiety uses up Working Memory resources that make it harder to learn math. During tests, math test anxiety decreases the amount of Working Memory space, which means less information can be received and used from Long-term Memory and Abstract Reasoning. This is like using a calculator in which half of the keys are not functioning. The result is a slow down in performance and a decrease in accuracy, resulting in poorer grades.

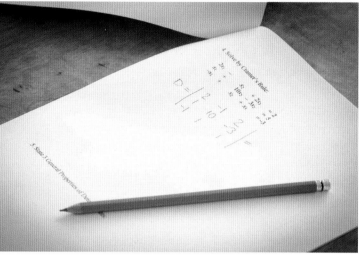

Test anxiety often makes it more difficult for math students to recall formulas and concepts on exams. This causes stress, which only strengthens anxiety.

One of the most common side effects of test anxiety is getting the test and immediately forgetting information that you know. Some students describe this event as having a "mental block," "going blank," or indicating that the test looks like Greek. After five or ten minutes into the test, some of these students can refocus and start working the problems. They have, however, lost valuable time.

For other students, anxiety persists throughout the test and they cannot recall the needed information. It is only after they walk out the door that they can remember how to work the problems. When this happens, they get mad at themselves, which increases their fears that the same thing will happen on the next test.

Sometimes students with math test anxiety do not "go blank," but it takes longer to recall formulas and concepts and to work problems. The result is frustration and loss of time, leading to more anxiety.

Since, in most cases, math tests are speed tests (those in which you have a certain amount of time to complete the test), you may not have enough time to work all the problems or to check the answers if you have mentally slowed down. The result is a lower test score because even though you knew the material, you did not complete all of the questions before the test time ran out.

Not using all of the time allotted for the test is another problem caused by test anxiety. This is particularly frustrating, because this

behavior is entirely avoidable. Most students know that they should use all of their test time to check their answers. In fact, math is one of the few subjects in which you can check test problems to find out if you have the problems correct. However, most students do not use all of their given test time, and this results in lower test scores.

Why? Students with high test anxiety do not want to stay in the classroom. This is especially true of students whose test anxiety increases as a test progresses. Test anxiety gets so bad in these situations that some students are willing to get a bad grade just to leave the classroom a little bit early.

Even more common among anxious students is the fear of what the instructor and other students will think about them for being the last one to hand in a test. These students refuse to be in the last group to finish, because they feel the instructor or other students will think they are dumb.

This is middle-school thinking, but the feelings are still real — no matter the age of the student. These students do not realize that some students who turn in their tests first fail, while many students who turn in their tests last make "A's" and "B's." Assumptions in this regard are extremely detrimental toward making good grades.

When taking a test, you need to focus on yourself and yourself only. Do not worry about what your classmates are doing. Instead, keep your eyes on your own test and imagine the relief you will feel when you hand in your test confident that you did not make any careless errors.

Another effect of test anxiety relates to completing homework assignments. Students who have high test anxiety often have difficulty starting or completing homework. The material on the homework causes them to think about previous tests or begin worrying about the next test and whether they are going to stress out in front of their classmates.

Some students begin their homework and work some problems successfully. They then get stuck on a problem that causes them anxiety, so they take a break. During their break the anxiety disappears until they start doing their homework again. Doing their homework causes more anxiety, which leads to another break. The breaks become more frequent. Finally, the student takes one long break and does not do the homework. Quitting, to them, means no more anxiety until the next homework assignment.

The effects of math test anxiety can be different for each student. Students can have several of the mentioned characteristics that can interfere with math learning and test taking.

Remember, many popular conceptions about test anxiety are entirely inaccurate. Review the 12 Myths About Test Anxiety chart, printed to the right, to see which ones you believe.

It is important to stick to the information in this book and not fall victim to advice from well-meaning but uninformed friends. Test anxiety is a very real problem and cannot be cured by simply disregarding its existence.

Now that we understand how math anxiety and math test anxiety affect learning and testing, it is time to learn how to reduce your test anxiety. The first step to doing this is to remain positve.

Tell yourself, "I can reduce my math test anxiety. It may take some time, but I *can* reduce my math test anxiety."

12 Myths About Test Anxiety

1. Students are born with test anxiety.

2. Test anxiety is a mental illness.

3. Test anxiety cannot be reduced.

4. Any level of test anxiety is bad.

5. All students who are not prepared will have test anxiety.

6. Students with test anxiety cannot learn math.

7. Students who are well prepared will not have test anxiety.

8. Very intelligent students and students taking high-level courses, such as calculus, do not have test anxiety.

9. Attending class and doing my homework should reduce all of my test anxiety.

10. Being told to relax during a test will make you relaxed.

11. Doing nothing about test anxiety will make it go away.

12. Reducing test anxiety will guarantee better grades.

Quick Section Review:

- *Test anxiety* manifests itself in many different ways.

- *There are two* types of test anxiety: emotional and worry.

- *Test Anxiety* is known to affect working memory. This diverts mental resources away from math and causes numerous mental blocks.

- *Anxious students* should make sure to use all of their alloted test time.

- *Test Anxiety* also affects homework sessions when the math on the assignment reminds them of bad test experiences.

Activity 3.2 Revisiting Past Test Experiences

If you have test anxiety, try to remember the first time you had uneasy feelings about taking a math test. To help you remember this experience, check the appropriate response and answer the questions:

Was your first negative test experience in:

     Elementary School _____

     Middle School   _____

     High School   _____

1. Can you recall the incident(s)?

     Yes   _____

     No   _____

2. Was it after....

   Your first alegbra test?   _____

   Your first math test after being out of school for a long time? _____

   After you decided to get serious about college?   _____

   When a professor told you that you needed to pass a test to pass a course? _____

   When you needed to pass a test to maintain your financial aid? _____

   After a parent asked you why you failed a previous test?   _____

   Your children asking you why you failed your last test?   _____

   If your first negative test experience is not listed above the write it down here:

   If you cannot remember a specific incident when you had test anxiety, do you expect to have any major test anxiety on your next math test? If so, write down you situation below:

How to Reduce Math and Test Anxiety, and PTSD Symptoms

To reduce math and test anxiety, you need to understand both the relaxation response and how negative self-talk undermines your abilities. These anxiety reduction techniques and positive self-statements can be used before or during your homework, class or test. These techniques need to be practiced several times before they become effective. If you have extremely high test anxiety, you need to practice long-term relaxation techniques. This mainly involves learning how to turn negative self-talk statements into positive self-talk statements.

Short-Term Relaxation Techniques

The relaxation response is any technique or procedure that helps you to become relaxed and takes the place of an anxiety response. There are both short-term and long-term relaxation response techniques, which help control emotional math test anxiety.

These techniques also help reduce worry anxiety. Among others, effective short-term

techniques include the Tensing and Differential Relaxation Method and the Palming Method. The next four subsections describe these methods in further detail. Try them all to figure out which works best for you.

Tensing/Relaxing Method

The Tensing and Relaxation Method helps you relax by tensing and relaxing your muscles all at once. Follow these procedures while sitting at your desk before taking a test:

1. *Put your* feet flat on the floor.

2. *Grab underneath* your chair with your hands.

3. *Push down* with your feet and pull up on your chair at the same time for about five seconds.

4. *Relax* for five to ten seconds.

5. *Repeat the procedure* two to three times.

6. *Relax all your muscles* except the ones that are actually used to take the test.

Deep Breathing Technique

Deep Breathing is a technique that can reduce your test anxiety. Follow these steps to Deep Breathing:

1. *Inhale slowly* and deeply through your nose by filling up the bottom of your lungs first.

2. *Stop* for a few seconds and hold your breath.

3. *Exhale slowly* through your mouth pretending like you are whistling out the air. Be sure to exhale fully and let your whole body relax. Wait a few seconds and then start to inhale as stated in number 1.

After practicing deep breathing it should become a very natural process. You may want to repeat the steps five times and then take a break. You may then want to do one more set.

If you start to get light-headed while practicing, stop for a few minutes. You were probably breathing in and out too fast. Practicing this breathing technique will make it easier to use before or during the test if needed. This technique will help some students to relax, while other students may prefer other short-term techniques.

Visualization

Have you ever daydreamed in class or during a workshop? I have asked this question to thousands of students and the answer is always yes. Then I ask them what happens when they daydream. The answer is that their minds leave the room and the body thinks it is where the mind has gone. Then I ask what would happen if you daydreamed about some relaxing place? Your mind would tell your body to relax. This process is called visualization, or using visual images in your mind to reduce test anxiety.

This technique has been used for hundreds of years. Athletes also use this technique to reduce their anxiety and to improve their game performance. You can imagine anything or anyplace in order to reduce your test anxiety. Follow these steps to practice visualization:

1. *Find* a comfortable place to sit.

2. *Close your eyes* and *think* about a relaxing place, real or imaginary.

3. *Imagine yourself* in that place, making sure to *see* it through your own eyes, not seeing yourself from afar.

4. What type of sounds do you *hear*? What do you *smell*? Are you feeling the sand between your toes or maybe the cool air? *Make the scene* as real as possible.

5. *Visualize that scene* for one to two minutes.

6. *Open your eyes* and continue to feel relaxed.

> Example: You need to develop two scenes and practice them every day until you can relax yourself in a few minutes. Then you will be ready to use them on the test.

Palming Method

The palming method is a visualization procedure used to reduce test anxiety. While you are at your desk before or during a test, follow these procedures:

1. *Close* and *cover your eyes* using the the palms of your hands.

2. *Prevent your hands* from touching your eyes by resting the lower parts of your palms on your cheeks and placing your fingers on your forehead. Do not rub or touch your eyeballs.

3. *Think* of some real or imaginary scenes that are relaxing to you.

4. *Visualize* this scene. Picture it as if you were actually there. Do this for one to two minutes.

Practice visualizing this scene several days before taking a test and the effectiveness of this relaxation procedure will improve.

Long-Term Relaxation Techniques

The Cue-Controlled Relaxation Response Technique is the best long-term relaxation technique. Cue-Controlled Relaxation works by inducing your own relaxation based on repeating certain cue words to yourself. In essence, you are taught to relax and then silently repeat cue words, such as "I am relaxed." After enough practice, you can relax during math tests. To practice these techniques, visit the Student Resources section at AcademicSuccess.com.

Managing Self-Talk

Imagine two students taking their first math test during the semester, and half way through the exam they start missing several problems. One student starts saying to himself that he is going to fail the test and might as well turn in his paper and quit. The other student says: "I might miss these problems but that is not a reason to give up and leave. I will just try as hard as I can on the other problems and I can pass."

One student feels a lot of anxiety and the other student remains calm and develops a plan. In both cases, the situation is the same, but the feelings in response to the test situation are extremely different due to their internal dialogue or self-talk. Which student are you?

Cognitive psychologists claim that what we say to ourselves in a response to an event mainly determines our mood or feeling about that event. Sometimes we say these statements to ourselves so quickly and automatically that we don't even notice. We then believe the situation is causing the feeling, when it is actually our interactions or thoughts about the event that are controlling our emotions.

This sequence is represented by the following timeline:

External Events (Math Test)

Interpretation of Events with Self-Talk

Feelings, Emotions and Reactions

Based on this psychological theory, in most cases you are responsible for what you feel. You have a choice to have positive or negative self-talk while doing your math homework or during a math test. This can determine how you feel during the test and control some of your anxiety. Some students see a math test as an opportunity to show their knowledge of the subject and are excited about that, while others see the same test as a potential failure that will lead to anger and dissatisfaction. The realization that you are responsible for your own feelings is very powerful once you fully accept it. Some points about self-talk include:

- Self-Talk is like a telegraphic message where one or two words can bring up many different thoughts and feelings.

- Self-Talk is like a scratched CD. It plays the same words over and over again.

- Self–Talk happens automatically. You don't even think about what you are saying to yourself.

- Negative self-talk during anxious situations is usually illogical, though it might seem rational at the time.

- Positive self-talk can increase appropriate behavior. Telling yourself that you can do your homework can lead to actually doing your homework.

- Negative self-talk causes avoidance and procrastination. Students who tell themselves they are not good in math don't want to do their homework and avoid it whenever possible.

Negative Self-Talk

Students who have high test anxiety usually use negative self-talk. This negative self-talk can increase the student's test anxiety and may cause them to fail. It is totally possible for students with negative self-talk to change this bad habit.

To change the negative self-talk habit, it is beneficial to understand the different types of negative self-talk. If you have negative self-talk, then review the different types to see which one matches you best. You may be one type or a combination of different types.

The Worrier —
Worriers always look for the worst-case situation. They are scared of failure. When they feel a little bit of anxiety, they blow it out of proportion and give up, believing there is nothing that can help them pass. In some extreme cases, they drop out of college believing they will never be able to pass a math course. The worrier's favorite question is, "What if . . . ?" For example, "What if I fail this test and then this class? I will not graduate and be in this dead-end job forever or all my friends will make fun of me." The Worrier can eventually give in to fear and sabotage his/herself in self-defense from disappointment.

Example: A student is taking his math test and comes to one problem that he cannot do. The student tells himself that all the rest of the problems are going to be just as hard, so he might as well start panicking now. This leads to some anxiety, which the student magnifies, causing him to give up on the test and leave.

The Victim —
"Victims" want to feel helpless and hopeless. They create anxiety by telling themselves that no matter what they do, they will not be successful in math. Victims believe there is something wrong with them that is not curable. They do not blame other factors that they can change, such as decreasing anxiety and improving their math study skills. They want to doom themselves and get into a learned helplessness mode

Negative self-talk causes students to behave in a counterproductive manner. A proper self-esteem is required for success in math classes.

that eventually stops them from even trying. They grow accustom to failure. The Victim's favorite statement is, "I can't. I will never be able to no matter how hard I try . . ."

Example: I had a student who was referred to me by a chemistry instructor after he did not complete a pre-algebra course. He indicated that he had failed or barely passed every math course he had taken since middle school. He told me he could not learn math at all and wished he could get a degree without taking math. We set up some time to work together and he received help from our tutors and study coaches. He kept telling everyone he could not do math. We assessed this student and found out that he had the exact opposite learning styles as most math instructors. I told him we could teach him by using a hands-on approach or by using manipulatives. He did not believe me. I had a meeting about this student with his professor, and I explained he believed he was a victim of math and did not want to give up that title because it meant he could and would always fail at math. To give up that label would mean he was wrong all these years and that he would have to admit he could in fact be successful in math. In our last tutoring session he was solving linear equation using Hands on Equations. In fact, after about three problems, he drew pictures on the board representing how to solve the equation. He was now doing algebra and the victim cycle was broken.

The Critic — Critics like to put themselves down. They look for internal flaws, and if they don't have any, they create some. They put themselves down when they notice other students not showing any anxiousness. They ignore their success, and instead of being proud of their accomplishments, they believe them to be a fluke. The Critic's favorite statement is, "You are too stupid to learn math!" If Critics do pass a test, they say afterward, "You could have made a better grade. Look at all those careless errors." The Critic's goal is to promote low self-esteem so that he or she will stop learning math. This behavior is disasterous come grade time. More often than not, it leads to failure.

Example: A student I worked with was repeating a math course. The student indicated that he could not do math, but nonetheless, he made a B on his first test. He was shocked by the grade and, despite starting so well, was convinced that he would fail the next exam. I asked him why and he told me that the problems he missed on this test would cause him to fail the next test. Thinking this way breeds negativity that can often lead to students setting themselves up for failure.

The Perfectionist
Perfectionists are closely related to Critics, but instead of putting themselves down for missing problems, they use the experience to push themselves toward success.

Perfectionists cannot stand mistakes or poor grades. They drive themselves to exhaustion making sure they understand every single concept. Self-worth means nothing to them because they will never be happy with anything less than perfection. This eventually leads to failure when they pass their "breaking point." Even a grade such as a 92 is not good enough. In some cases, it drives them toward causing harm to themselves.

Example: A student was making A's on her math tests until she made a C on her last test before the final. When she went to take the finial exam she had a panic attack. It caused her so much anxiety, she could not take the test. She started crying outside the math office where a faculty member spoke with her. She was soon referred to me, and we talked about her anxiety. She told me that she must make an A in the course and would not settle for a B. She was afraid to take the final because she thought a poor grade would cause her to lose her A. Her thoughts caused so much anxiety, she became physically ill and could not take the test. We started working on her test anxiety as well as her self-talk. She took the final a few days later and made a B in the course, which she was fine with.

Do any of these sound familiar?

After reading about these different types of personalities, which one can you most relate to? The person inside of you may be a combination of two different types, but there usually is one personality that dominates your perception of math. Once again, do not beat yourself up if you fall into one of these categories. In fact, just about everybody exhibits signs of at least one category. With this in mind, the next step is to learn how to cope with these problems, as well as how to begin using your personality type to become successful.

Positive Self-Talk

You can counter and control negative self-talk in several ways. Negative self-talk is easily replaced with positive self-talk. You can also develop thought-stopping techniques that reduce negative self-talk and engender positive self-talk.

Try all of the following ways to discover which one, or combination of two techniques, work best for you. The first technique is to develop positive self-talk statements. The following list of suggestions will help you develop a series of personal statements, which you should memorize as soon as possible.

1. *Use the first person tense.* **For example, "I can control my anxiety and pass this test."**

2. *Avoid using negatives in the statement.* **For example, don't say, "I will not get nervous during this test." Instead say, "I will calm myself down during the test.**

3. *Make the statements positive and realistic.* **For example, you can say, "I will be successful on this test", instead of saying, "I will make a 100 on this test."**

The Worrier, who asks, "What if I fail the test?" can counter with, "If I fail the test I will just do better on the next one."

The Victim, who believes things are hopeless says: "No way will I ever pass math." They can counter with: "I used a different way to study and take the test so I can pass the course this time."

The Critic, who puts themselves down by saying: "I cannot reduce my test anxiety and will fail." They can replace this by saying: "I know I have test anxiety but I have learned to control it."

The Perfectionist, who says, "I must make an A or I am a failure," can instead say, "I don't need an A to be successful. I just need to pass this course so I can take the next one and graduate."

These are examples of positive self-talk that can control anxiety. Additional positive self-talk statements are listed below.

- "I failed the course last semester, but I can now use my math study skills to pass this course."

- "I went blank on the last test, but I now know how to reduce my test anxiety."

- "I know that my poor math skills are due to poor study skills, not my own ability, and since I am working on my study skills, my math skills will improve."

- "I know that, with hard work, I will pass math."

- "I prepared for this test and will do the best I can. I will reduce my test anxiety and use the best test-taking procedures. I expect some problems will be difficult, but I will not get discouraged."

- "I am solving problems and feel good about myself. I am not going to worry about that difficult problem; I am going to work on the problems that I can do. I am going to use all the test time and check for careless errors. Even if I do not get the grade that I want on this test, it is not the end of the world."

Create your own positive self-talk statements in Activity 3.3, which is found at the end of this section.

Thought-Stopping Technique

Many students have difficulty controlling their negative self-talk. These students have tried to tell themselves to eliminate the negative self-talk, but no matter what they try it persists. These students need a thought-stopping technique to break this bad habit.

Thought-stopping entails focusing on unwanted negative self-talk, and then suddenly stopping those thoughts with some type of internal or external action. Actions such as yelling to yourself, "Stop that," or making a loud noise, such as slapping a desk, effectively interrupt negative self-talk.

Obviously, your location plays a role in what you should and should not do. In a homework situation, you may want to slap the desk, but obviously doing this in a crowded classroom is inappropriate.

To stop your negative thoughts in a crowded classroom, while listening to a lecture, or while during a test, silently shout to yourself, "Stop thinking about that." After your silent shout, either relax yourself or repeat one of the positive self-talk statements that you have made up. You may have to shout to yourself several times to control your negative self-talk. After every shout, use a different relaxation technique, such as positive visual scenes or positive statements that will help control your anxiety.

The way "stop-thinking" works is by interrupting the worry response before it creates the type of anxiety that gets out of control. During the interruptions, you gain control and replace negative self-talk with positive responses. Students with high worry anxiety need to practice these techniques at least one week before a test several times a day. Then, they need to keep practicing once a day until the negative self-talk completely disappears.

If needed, obtain additional help from your counselor or college psychologist to help you stop negative self-talk. Doing so prepares you to deal with inevitable adversity and sets you on the right path toward a positive math attitude.

Power of Positive Thinking

If you remain skeptical about the power of positive thinking, here is one more fact to persuade you. According to a 1985 study, conducted by psychologists Michael Scheier and Charles Carver, optimists are much more likely to succeed in life, largely because they are more capable of coping with adversity.

Negative thoughts prohibit you from improving in mathematics. Always think positive!

When they are presented with challenges, optimists manage to navigate through their negative feelings and ultimately persevere. The benefits of being an optimist don't stop there. They also live longer and sustain better overall mental and physical health than do pessimists.

Quick Section Review:

- *Students with* high-level test anxiety should focus on long-term relaxation techniques.

- *Managing self-talk* is crucial to lowering test anxiety.

- *Positive self-talk* statements must be developed in order to replace negative thoughts and thereby lower anxiety.

- *The Thought-Stopping Method* is an effective way to stop negative internal dialog before it becomes harmful.

- *Positive Thinking* is scientifically proven to breed success and confidence. Conversely, pessimists do not handle adversity nearly as well.

Activity 3.3 Creating Positive Self-Talk Statements

As you've just read, in order to succeed in a math class, you must replace negative self-talk statements with positive self-talk statements. Now that you've read the instructions in this chapter, you can go ahead and develop your positive self-talk statements in the space below. Develop four positive self-talk statements that are not in this book, making sure to use the word "I "in each statement.

Statement 1:

Statement 2:

Statement 3:

Statement 4:

Chapter 3 Summary

- General test anxiety is a learned behavior developed by having emotional and/or worry (somatic and/or cognitive) responses during previous tests.

- General test anxiety is a fear of any type of test.

- Math anxiety is usually caused by previous experiences.

- Math anxiety affects learning in class and doing your homework.

- Math test anxiety is a subclass of general test anxiety that is specific to one subject area.

- Math test anxiety, like general test anxiety, can decrease your ability to perform on tests.

- According to the U.S. Department of Veteran Affairs, between 7 and 8 percent of the U.S. population deals with PTSD at some point in their lives.

- If you are suffering from symptoms of PTSD, it is absolutely crucial that you seek professional help.

- Your ability to complete the test decreases by blocked memory and an urgency to leave the test room before checking all your answers.

- To reduce test anxiety, you must practice relaxation techniques and develop your own positive self-talk statements.

- Negative self-talk is extremely dangerous for math students. Cognitive psychologists claim that what we say to ourselves in a response to an event mainly determines our mood or feeling about that event.

- When possible, it is important for math students to replace negative internal statements with positive statements.

- According to a study conducted by Sheirer and Carver, statistically speaking, optimists are much more successful in their careers.

- Reducing your math test anxiety does not guarantee success on tests; first you have to know the appropriate material to recall during the test and have good test-taking skills.

- Increasing productive study time also builds positive experiences that can support you throughout math tests.

Name: _____   Date: _____

Assignment for Chapter 3

1. Create your personal definition of math anxiety:

2. Describe two ways math anxiety can affect learning:

    Way One:

    Way Two:

3. Describe how you know if you have math anxiety or math test anxiety:

4. List and explain the two different types of test anxiety:

    One:

    Two:

5. Describe your best short-term relaxation technique. Practice your short-term relaxation technique.

6. List and describe one of the four negative self-talk personalities that matches you the best:

7. Describe how you would use the thought-stopping techniques with positive self-statements:

8. How can you prepare for your first math test?

9. Listen to the CD How to Reduce Test Anxiety (Nolting, 1987), which can be found in the Student Resources section at AcademicSuccess.com. Practice the "Cue-Controlled Relaxation Technique" every day until it takes you two minutes or less to relax before a test. Describe the process in the space below:

10. Visit the Student Resources section at AcademicSuccess.com and complete your math autobiography.

How to Create a Positive Study Environment and Manage Your Time

4

In Chapter 4
You will learn these concepts:

✓ How to choose your best study environment

✓ The best order to study subjects

✓ How to use your school's math lab or resource center

✓ How to develop a detailed study schedule

✓ How to become a productive group worker

Setting up an Effective Study Environment

While most students understand the importance of recognizing *what* to study, many do not understand that *where* you study plays a huge role in how you do in a math course. A positive home and college study environment improves your learning experiences.

Traditional study environments include on-campus study areas, such as libraries and reading rooms, and off-campus study areas, like your house or a coffee shop. Today's students, however, have many additional options. Other study environments include math labs, Learning Resource Centers, study groups, Supplemental Instruction, collaborative learning programs and websites. These new environments require students to learn how to use resources in the math lab/LRC such as: computer programs, homework software and assessment instruments.

The learning environment in the classroom has also changed, and it now emphasizes more collaborative learning. Students now have to learn how to benefit from their collaborative classroom learning experiences and how to make the best use of the math lab or LRC. Learning outside the classroom has also changed. Students need to learn how to effectively use collaborative learning, study groups and Supplemental Instruction. To maximize learning, students need to effectively use their new study environments and learning resources.

Another way to maximize learning is to effectively manage your time. In high school, teachers and parents often manage a student's time. In college, students suddenly have more activities (work, social, study) and less time to fit them all in (and no teachers or parents handy or willing to schedule their time for them).When freshman college students are asked to give their number one reason for poor grades, they indicate that they do not have enough time to study. When students are asked how much time they study per week, most do not have any idea.

Students who do not effectively manage their study time may fail math courses. As pointed out in Chapter 1, math requires much practice (the same as mastering a sport or musical instrument) for the student to perform well on tests. Therefore, developing a good plan for studying math is key to getting good grades.

Choosing a Place to Study

Choosing a place to study is tricky business. Some study environments have too many distractions. Other study environments may be quiet, but do not have the necessary materials around to supplement your work.

For as long as students have attended college, this quandary has caused indecision and frustration. In some ways, however, modern math students have it worse than any previous generation. Thanks to laptops, tablets and smartphones, you can study anytime and anywhere, so long as you have the right attitude and a fully charged battery. This sounds like a good thing, but with an excess of options, many students become overwhelmed. As the old saying goes, the grass is always greener. With so many viable places to study, how can you be certain to choose the ideal location?

The answer to this question is deceptively simple. As long as you choose a place that suits your particular needs and establish a routine that automatically puts you in the right state of mind, you really can't go wrong.

Wherever you study, the key is to develop working familiarity with your study area. While studying in your home, choose one place, one chair, one desk or table. If you use the kitchen table, choose one chair, preferably one that you do not use during dinner. Call this chair "my study chair." If you study in the student cafeteria, use the same table each time. Do not use the table at which you play cards, video games or eat. By studying at the same place each time, you form a conditioned response. From then on, when you sit down at your study place your mind will automatically start thinking about studying. This conditioned response decreases your "warm up" time. "Warm up" time is how long it takes to actually begin studying after you sit down. Another aspect of the study environment involves the degree of silence you need for studying. In most cases, a totally quiet room is not necessary. But if you can only study with total silence, keep this in mind when selecting your study places.

Most students can study with a little noise, especially if it is constant, like music from their MP3 players or phones. In fact, some students keep on a mellow radio station or a fan to drown out other noises. However, do not turn on the television to drown out other noises while studying. That will not work! Why? Because you are likely to get distracted. Always select a study area where you can control the noise level.

All Study Areas Should Have:

1. The "tools of your trade": pencils, paper, a calculator, a computer, etc

2. A copy of your study schedule

3. Images that will reinforce your goals: pictures of people in your desired profession, images of potential rewards for your hard work, etc

4. If you need background noise, you should bring your phone or mp3 player to play ambient music or sound

5. Once you sit down, avoid getting back up, so bring light snacks and water if you think you might get hungry

Setting up Your Study Area

If you decide to study at home, signs should surround your environment that "tell" you to study. This includes a copy of your study schedule. Attach your study schedule to the inside flap of your notebook and place another copy where you study at home. It is also okay to put your schedule on your cellphone. Place your study goals and the rewards for achieving those goals where they are easily seen. Do not post pictures of your girlfriend, boyfriend or other distracting items in your study area. Instead, post pictures indicating your goals after graduation. If you want to be a nurse, doctor, or business person, post pictures that represent these goals. Your study area should always reinforce your educational goals.

When sitting down to study, have ready the "tools of your trade": pencils, paper, a notebook, a textbook, a study guide and a calculator. Everything should be well within reach. This way, when you need something, you don't have to leave your study area. The problem with getting up is not just the time it takes to get the item, but the time it takes to "warm up" again. After getting milk and cookies and sitting down, it takes another four to five minutes to "warm up" and continue studying.

The Best Way to Study Subjects

When studying, arrange your subjects in the order of difficulty. In other words, start with your most difficult subject — which is usually math — and work toward your easiest course. By studying your most difficult subject first, you are more alert and better motivated to complete the work before continuing on the easier courses, which may be more interesting to you. If you study math last, you will probably tire easily, become frustrated and quit; however, you are less likely to quit when you study a subject that interests you.

Change the Order of Study

Another approach to improving the quality of your study is to mix up the order of studying different subjects.

Example: If you have English, accounting and math to study, then study them in the following order: 1. math, 2. English, and 3. accounting. By studying the subjects in this order, one part of your brain can rest after studying math while the other part of your brain is studying English. Now your mind is "fresh" when you study accounting.

The key to this strategy is to study your easier subjects between your harder subjects. Obviously, the terms "easy" and "hard" are subjective, so you need to personalize this strategy based upon your own skills and interests. If English comes easy to you, use it as a buffer between more troublesome subjects. Not only does this strategy allow your mind rest, but it also keeps you in good spirits. The frustration that builds during difficult math study sessions is quickly forgotten after a successful bout with your favorite subject.

Deciding When to Study

Deciding when to study different types of material is also part of developing a positive study environment. Your study material can be divided into two separate types: new material and material that has already been learned. The best time to review material you've already learned is right before going to sleep. By reviewing material for the test the night before, you have less brain activity and fewer physical distractions that prevent you from recalling important material the next day.

Example: If you have an 8:00 test the next morning, you should review the material the night before. If you have a 10:00 test the next day, review the material both the night before and the day of the test. Reviewing is defined as reading the material to yourself. You also might review a few problems you have already solved to keep your mind alert, but do not try to learn any new material the night before the test.

When to Learn New Material

Learning new material should be done during the first part of the study period. Do not learn new material the night before a test. You will be setting yourself up for test anxiety. If you try to cram the procedures to solve different types of equations or new ways to factor trinomials, you will end up in a state of confusion. This is especially true if you have major problems learning how to solve new equations or factoring. The next day you will only remember not being able to solve the equation or factor the trinomials; this could distract you on the test.

Most students get tired after studying for several hours or before going to bed. If you are tired and try to study new material, it becomes more difficult to retain. It takes more effort to learn new material when you are tired than it does to review old material. When you start getting tired of studying, the best tactic is to begin reviewing previously learned material. This way, your brain stays in work mode while your body adjusts to your waning energy levels.

Find the Most Efficient Time to Study Math

The most efficient time to study is as soon as possible after the math class is over. Psychologists indicate that most forgetting occurs right after learning the material. In other words, you are going to forget most of what you have learned in the first hour after class. To prevent this mass exodus of knowledge, you need to recall some of the lecture material as soon after class as is practical.

The easiest way to recall the lecture is to rework your notes. Reviewing your notes will increase your ability to recall the information and make it easier to understand the homework assignments.

This topic is covered extensively in Chapter 6 — where you will learn how to turn a set of sloppy notes into a well-organized study tool.

Example: Mass learning — you would study three hours in a row without taking a break, then quit studying for the night. Distributive learning — you would study for about 50 minutes with a 10 minute break, study for 50 more minutes with a 10 minute break, and finish with 60 minutes of studying before stopping.

Choosing Between Mass and Distributive Learning

There are two different types of learning processes: "mass learning" and "distributive learning." Mass learning involves learning everything at one time. Distributive learning is studying the same amount of time as mass learning with the addition of several study breaks. In the past, many educators preached mass learning above all else. Now, however, most teach their students to take frequent breaks.

Benefits of Study Breaks

Psychologists have discovered that learning decreases if you do not take study breaks. Therefore, use the distributive learning procedures (described above) to study math. Study breaks keep you from becoming overly frustrated with your studies. In this way, taking regular study breaks allows you to study for longer intervals.

If you continue to force yourself to study, you will not learn the material. After taking a break, return to studying. If you still cannot study after taking a break, review your purpose for studying and your educational goals.

Think about what is required to graduate; it will probably come down to the fact that you have to pass math. Studying math today will help you pass the next test; this increases your chances of passing the course and eventually graduating. If this does not motivate you to stick with your studies, nothing will.

How to Use Math Labs, Learning Resource Centers and Emporium Learning Centers

Learning how to use your math lab or learning resource center (LRC) can improve your learning, and in turn, your grades. This is also true of those students who learn to thrive in Emporium Model learning centers, which require mandatory attendance for online learning and supplemental help.

Many students are unaware of the tutorial and learning resources offered at their college or university. Some students find out about these resources after they are failing, which in most cases is too late. You need to find the location of learning resources and how to utilize them as soon as possible after course registration.

Some colleges and universities have math labs, LRCs, Academic Enrichment Centers, computer labs, Student Support Services, Disabled Student Services or other specialized labs to help students. You should ask your instructor or counselor where to get help in math. Do not forget to ask your fellow students for recommendations to get help in math. In the meantime, here are a few of the resources available at most math labs.

Computer Programs

Locate the computer program that best goes with your text. It may be the computer software offered by the textbook publisher or commercially bought software. Ask if you can copy it and use it at another location or on your own computer.

Review the other available software programs to find the one that fits your needs. The newer computer programs are more user friendly, but some of the older programs are more effective.

Web-Based Programs

Most book companies have Web-supported materials to support student learning. These support areas could be an online tutor service, call-in tutor service, or extra homework problems and their solutions. Ask your instructor or lab supervisor about these support materials.

If your text does not have these support materials, go to the Web and find them yourself. The main difference is that you may have to pay for the services. Always check to see if a website charges.

Old Textbooks

Math is a universal language, but different textbooks describe the same topic with different English. You may understand another text better than your current text. Some textbook authors are better at explaining a topic than others. This is especially true if you are bilingual or raised in a different part of the country. If you can locate a math textbook on the same level and describing the same topic, it may be very helpful.

Example 1: If you are an auditory learner, then have the tutor orally explain to you how to solve the problem. Then repeat back what the tutor said (in your own words). Use an audio recorder to record the tutor's explanation so you can play it while doing your homework. Make sure the tutor does not just work the problem for you without explaining the reasons for each step.

Tutoring

Most students believe that tutoring is the best learning resource. However, research has shown that the sessions are useless if the tutor is untrained. Try to work with a trained tutor who has had your course. Explain to the tutor your learning style and suggest that he/she tutor you based on your learning style.

Example 2: If you are a visual learner, have the tutors write down the steps to solve the problem. Also, write down the reasons for each step or reference text pages for the reasons. If the tutor cannot write it down for you, write down the steps yourself and ask the tutor to review the steps.

Try not to schedule your tutoring sessions around lunch time since it is usually the busiest time of the day. Have your questions ready from your previous homework assignments. Focus on the concepts you do not understand, not just on how to work the problem. The more specific you are about your homework problems, the more tutorial help you will receive. Do not expect miracles! If you tell your tutor, "I have a test in twenty minutes and do not understand anything about chapter six!" — about all the tutor can do is offer to pray for you. However, past experiences have shown that those who have previously helped themselves to tutoring are most likely to be rewarded with good grades.

Practice Tests

Use practice tests to find out what you do not know before the real test. Ask if the math lab/LRC offers practice tests. Take these practice tests at least two days before the real test. This will give you at least one day to find out how to work the missed problems and another to review for the test. The more realistic practice tests you take, the better you will do on the real test. Make sure practice tests are timed and do not use any of your notes or the text.

Assessment Instruments

Assessment instruments can be used to place you into the correct course, locate your math weakness and help you understand your learning strengths and weaknesses. If you are not sure that you have been placed into the correct course, ask to take a placement test. Being placed into the correct course is a must to pass math. Ask if the lab has diagnostic math tests to locate your weaknesses. Ask about other assessment instruments, which can be used to help improve your learning.

Other helpful items include, manipulatives, models, posters, graphing calculators, YouTube videos and Google searches.

Manipulatives

If a picture is worth a thousand words, then a model is worth a million for the kinesthetic/tactile learner. If you are one of these learners, ask for what may be called "manipulatives" or "3-D models." Manipulatives and models are concrete representations of a concept that you can physically touch. A good example of a manipulative is the Hands On Equation. The Hands on Equation uses a simulated balance beam with top like objects to represent variables and dice to represent numbers. Your math lab can order the Hands On Equations by going to www.Borenson.com. Some students have made their own manipulative by using magnetic plastic numbers and letters that are put on a metal board from child games.

Students also go to sign shops and purchase the numbers and letters. The students then set up an equation by using the manipulative and moving the numbers and letters around to solve it.

Students also use the letters to represent rules such as the distributive property. You can also use these manipulatives to understand more difficult mathematical problems.

Examples: On the board put down $a(b + c) =$. Then on the other side of the equation take additional letters and place them to represent $ab + ac$. Now you have $a(b + c) = ab + bc$. Now do the steps over again until your learn it. Then put numbers in to represent the letters. Such as $2(3 + 4) = (2) (3) + (2) (4)$. Now do the multiplication on each side of the equation and you will get $14 = 14$.

The calculator is another excellent learning tool for students beginning in pre-algebra and developmental algebra. Graphing calculators match the dynamic cognitive and the kinesthetic/ tactile (hands on) learning styles.

Use the graphing calculator to see what happens when you add numbers to the equation. You can see the graph move and then understand the effects. This is an excellent way for trial-and-error learners (dynamic) to understand the equations. If you are in high-level courses, ask for

connections intended for uploading graphing calculator programs from a computer. It is important to remember, however, some colleges/universities would rather you learn developmental math without using a calculator. For this reason, you should always speak with your professors and counselors before relying on any technological help.

In general, learning math is a lot like learning to ride a bicycle. You can watch someone else do it, but you only learn by trying it yourself. You must believe in yourself and keep at it. Even if you start off wobbly, as long as you keep peddling, you are riding. But if you do not believe in yourself enough to keep peddling, you will fall. In time, you will take off the training wheels and wonder why you ever needed them. Even if you get rusty after a long absence, you will never again need training wheels.

Math is also something you learn by trying it yourself. Others can assist you with techniques, but in order to make it stick, you need to learn math on your own. As long as you keep trying, you are learning to think mathematically, and you will be able to do it. In the future, even after a long time away from math, you will remember that you were able to master math before and with a little review you still can. To find other math manipulatives online, click on the "Student Resources" section on AcademicSuccess.com. The website lists numerous helpful resources, many of which are free.

Quick Section Review

- *Math labs and learning centers* are great resources for students who struggle with math.

- *When seeking a tutor,* it is important to find somebody who shares your learning style. This way, you maximize your learning and avoid wasting time.

- *When possible, kinesthetic learners should seek out manipulatives.* Manipulatives help these students grasp key concepts and ideas.

Activity 4.1 Study Order Review

As you have already learned, when and where you study are just as important as what you study. Answer the following questions to establish a study order plan for your current or future math course.

1. Based on the information in this chapter, in what order should you study your college subjects?

2. In the space below, write down your current courses in the order you plan to study them:

   1.

   2.

   3.

   4.

   5.

3. When is the best time to study a subject the night before a test?

4. List three places kinesthetic learners can find manipulatives:

   1.

   2.

   3.

Collaborative Classroom Learning and Study Group Etiquette

Collaborative learning is a mode of learning that involves student participation in a small group to complete a desired task, assignment or project. In a math class, collaborative learning usually involves a small group of two to six students working together to solve math problems. Due to math reforms, math classes now include more collaborative learning as a mode of instruction. Here are a few examples of what you might encounter:

> Example 1: You develop a study group that is preparing for an upcoming test. Each group member makes up several sample test questions on note cards and the group discusses the answers. You are in the math classroom and the class is divided into groups of four. Each group is assigned a different word problem to solve. The student recorder listens to the group discussing the problem and writes down the solution steps. Each group shares the solution with the other groups.

The Benefits of Collaborative Learning

Collaborative learning is a mode of learning that involves student participation in a small group to complete a desired task, assignment or project. There are different types of collaborative learning exercises, which your instructor may use. Your instructor may combine traditional instruction and collaborative learning exercises. Collaborative learning has many benefits over traditional instruction. Here are just a few of them:

- Less fear of asking questions when compared to asking questions in the classroom.

- You may have a group learning style that enhances your learning.

- Sometimes an explanation of a concept or problem is more effective coming from a group member than from your instructor.

- Your instructor is free to walk around and individually help group members with difficult questions.

- The group can make up test questions and quiz each other.

Collaborative learning prepares you for the business and industry workforce. Experience with groups and team building is important to a prospective employer.

Characteristics of a Good Group Member

Being a good group member is much different than being a good individual learner. It involves unique skill sets, which may be foreign to some students. A good group member is considerate yet assertive. He or she vocalizes opinions without dominating a discussion.

Here is a short list of some of the other characteristics of a good group member:

- Complete any necessary preparation work prior to your group meeting. Little is accomplished in a group meeting if individual commitments are broken.

- Be supportive and acknowledge participation of fellow group members' ideas even if they are different from yours.

- Do not let your mind wander. Other students can usually tell when you are not paying attention.

- Encourage the group to stay on task. If discussion strays, lead the group back toward your team goal.

- Keep a good balance between being an active participant and a good listener. Speak for yourself and let others speak for themselves.

- Accept help and suggestions from other members without feeling guilty.

- Accept group members who try their hardest even if they can't solve the problems.

- Bring closure to a team session by summarizing the group's efforts. Reach consensus on any group decisions involving completion of your tasks.

Characteristics of a Good Online Group Member

As more math classes move online, modern math students are increasingly required to work with their classmates through Internet-based applications. These interactions are unique and present a series of new challenges. Good online group members share similar characteristics with traditional group members. Still, there a few more things to consider:

- Make sure you sign in to the group meeting at the correct time. Don't be late; in fact, aim to be early.

- Focus on the group work instead of being on Facebook or tweeting someone at the same time. Even if you're an adept multitasker, it is nonetheless rude to split your attention between your group and social media.

- Take notes on your computer while listing how to do the problems.

- After the chat group, summarize what you have learned and what you will do next to learn the material.

Supplemental Instruction

Supplemental Instruction (SI) is an academic support program in which a student who has already passed a course helps tutor the course with the same instructor the next semester. The SI leader models effective classroom learning and facilitates study groups for current students. In these study groups, students learn how to study while learning the course work. The SI leader is trained in effective learning strategies and also knows what it takes to get a good grade in a course with a particular instructor.

Colleges and universities, in many countries, use Supplemental Instruction. If you have SI in your class, the leader will introduce himself or herself on the first day of class. If you do not have SI in your class, find a tutor who will work with a group from your class in a similar way.

How to Develop a Study Schedule

Before starting to develop a study schedule, let's look at studying and learning effectiveness based on educational psychology. Educational psychologists have conducted research on studying and memory and found out the best time to study is right after class. Research shows that most students lose up to 50% of the information learned in class by the next day. This means that the closer you can schedule doing homework, reviewing your notes or reading your textbook after class, the more likely you'll retain the information.

If possible, when working out your schedule, reserve a one or two hour space right after class for studying. If you have back-to-back classes, then schedule study time for as soon as possible after your last class. Even if your schedule has very few breaks, spend at least a few minutes reviewing your notes the same day. Remember, studying right after class is the best way to learn.

Educational psychologists have also conducted research to see what students remember most clearly the next day after studying several subjects. The research indicates that the subject you studied last is what you remember best the next day. This means that you may want to review your most challenging subject before going to bed each night. This is especially true the night before a test.

Biological Clock

Research also shows that your biological clock has a significant impact on your ability to develop study habits. Most of us learn best at different times of the day.

Try to schedule your study times to match your daily biological clock. If you are a morning person, then don't schedule your study time for late at night. If you are a

late-night person, then don't schedule your study time for early in the morning. It will take about two weeks to develop this new schedule into a habit. Once you have, your body and your mind should sync up, giving you the best chance to retain information.

Schedule Weekly Study Time

Now let's look at how you can develop a study schedule while keeping these important points in mind. There are two basic reasons for developing a study schedule: To schedule your study time and to become more efficient at studying.

In order to become a more efficient studier, you need to set aside a certain amount of study time each week. Rather than setting up a number of daily study hours, you should focus on the number of hours, per week, you plan to devote to studying.

How many hours do you study per week? Ten hours, 15 hours, 20 hours, 30 hours?

Without knowing the amount of your study hours per week, you will not know if you are studying at a productive rate. Many students believe they are studying enough to make their desired grade, when in truth, they are coming up drastically short.

Example: If your goal is to make a B average, and with studying 15 hours per week you make all B's on your tests, then the goal has been met. However, if you study 15 hours per week and make all D's, then you need to increase your study time and/or change your study methods. By monitoring your grades and the number of hours you study per week, you can adjust your study schedule to get the grades you want.

By monitoring your grades and the number of hours you study per week, you can adjust your study schedule accordingly.

Example: You are at the mall on a Sunday afternoon, shopping for clothes, when you start feeling guilty. You have not started studying for that math test on Monday. If you had created a study schedule, you could have arranged to study for the math test on Saturday and still have been able to enjoy the mall on Sunday.

The second reason for developing a study schedule is to use time more efficiently. Efficient study means knowing when you are supposed to study and when you do not have to study. This approach will help keep you from thinking about other things you should be doing when you sit down to study. The reverse is also true. When doing other, more enjoyable things, you will not feel guilty about not studying.

A study schedule should be set up for two reasons: To determine the amount of study time you need, per week, to get the grades you want and to set up peak efficient study times.

How to Prioritize Your Time

To develop a study schedule, review the Planning Use of Daily Time chart printed on page 100. Use the chart to map out planned study times—feel free to make enlarged copies if you wish.

The best way to begin to develop your study schedule is to fill in all the times you cannot study. Do this by following the steps printed on the next few pages. Some of these steps may not apply to you. If so, replace the step with something unique to your schedule.

1. *Fill in all your classes by putting code C.* For example, if you have an 8:00-9:30 class, draw a line through the center of the 9:00 a.m. box on the study schedule.

2. *Fill in the time you work with code W (W = work).* This may be difficult, since some students' work schedules may change during the week. The best way to predict work time is to base it on the time you worked the previous week, unless you are on a rotating shift. Indicate your approximate work times on the study schedule. As your work hours change, revise the study schedule. Remember: Your study schedule should be structured around the number of hours a week you plan to study. Realize that while your work times might change every week, your total weekly work hours usually remain the same.

3. *Decide the amount of time it takes to eat (E = eat) breakfast, lunch and dinner*; this time slot should include both food preparation and clean up. Keep in mind that the amount of time it takes to eat may fluctuate. Eating time also includes time spent in the student cafeteria. If you have an 11:00-12:00 or 1:00-2:00 lunch break, you

might not eat during the entire time; you could be there both socializing and eating. Still put code E in the study schedule, since the main use of your time is for eating.

4. *Include your grooming time (G = grooming).* Some grooming activities include taking a bath, washing your hair or other activities that you do to get ready for school, dates or work. Grooming varies from minutes to hours per day for college students. Mark your study schedule with code G for the usual amount of time spent on grooming. Remember that more time might be spent on grooming during weekends.

5. *Include your tutor time (T = tutor).* This is not considered study time. Tutor time is strictly that which you spend in a tutoring session. If you have a tutor scheduled or meet weekly with your instructor, mark these times with code T in the study schedule.

6. *Reserve time for family responsibilities on the study schedule (F = family responsibilities).* Some family responsibilities include taking your child on errands, mowing the lawn, grocery shopping and taking out the garbage. Also, if you have arranged to take your children some place every Saturday morning, then put it on the study schedule using code F.

7. *Figure out how much time is spent on cleaning each week (CN = cleaning).* This time can include cleaning your dorm room, house, car, and clothes. Cleaning time usually takes several hours a week. Indicate with code CN that you have cleaning time on the study schedule, and make sure it is adequate for the entire week.

8. *Review your sleep patterns for the week (SL = sleep).* Your sleep time will probably be the same from Monday through Friday. On the weekend, you might sleep later during the day and stay up later at night. Be realistic when scheduling your sleep time. If you have been sleeping on Saturday mornings until 10:00 a.m. for the last two or three years, do not plan time at 8:00 a.m. to study.

9. *Figure the amount of weekly social time (SC = social time).* Social time includes being with other people, watching TV or going to church. It can be doing nothing at all or going out and having a good time. You need to have some social time during the week or you will burn out, and you will probably drop out of school. You may last only one semester. If you study and work too hard without some relaxation, you will not last the entire school year. Some daily social time is needed, but do not overdo it.

10. *Figure the amount of travel time to and from work (TR= travel time).* Travel time could be driving to and from college or riding the subway. If possible, use travel to listen to recordings of your class or to review notes. Travel time may vary during different times of the year.

11. *Recall other time obligations that have not been previously mentioned (O = other).* Other time obligations may be aspects of your life, which you do not want to share with other people. Review the study schedule for any other time obligations and mark them.

Once you have finished all of the steps, count up all the blank spaces. Each blank space represents one hour. You might have several half-blank spaces, which each represent one-half hour. Add together the number of blank spaces left and write the total in the oval, which is located on the lower right-hand corner of the study schedule.

Next, figure how many hours you have to study during the week. The rule of thumb is to study approximately two hours per week for each class hour. If you have 12 real class hours (not counting physical education) per week, you should be studying 20-24 hours per week to make A's and B's. Write the amount of time you want to study per week in the square, located in the lower left-hand corner of your study schedule. This is a study "contract" you are making with yourself.

If the number of contracted (square) study hours is less than the number in the oval, then fill in the times you want to study (S = study). First, fill in the best times to study. If there are unmarked spaces, use them as backup study time. Now you have a schedule of the best times to study. On the other hand, if you want to study 15 hours a week and have only 10 hours of space, you have to make a decision. Go back over your study-schedule codes and locate where you can change some times.

If you have a problem locating additional study time, make a priority time list. Take the hours away from the items with the least priority. Complete the study schedule by putting in your best study times. Also, feel free to use one of the many computer-based, phone-based and tablet-based software applications that send you notifications about important events or due dates. These programs, which usually come pre-installed, send you text messages or emails to make sure you don't miss important points on your schedule.

How to Choose the Grade You Want

Determine what grade you want to make in the math course and write the grade on the study schedule. The grade should be an A, a B or a C. Do not write an N, W, X or F because these grades mean you will not successfully complete the course. Do not write D because you may not get credit for the course or be allowed to take the next course. In fact, it is not wise to write C, either, because most students who make a C usually fail the next math course. Your selected grade is now your goal.

Currently, you have a study schedule representing the number of hours of study per week. You also have a course grade goal. After you have been in the course for several weeks and get back the results of your first tests, you will know if you are accomplishing your goal. Should you not meet your goal, improve the quality and quantity of your studying or lower your course grade goal.

How to Create a Weekly Study Plan

By using the information from your completed copy of the Planning Use of Daily Time chart, you will know which time slots are available for study. You can use this information to both develop an effective study plan for the next week and establish weekly study goals.

Each Sunday, use an enlarged copy of your Weekly Study Goal Sheet to plan the best use for your study time during the next week. The first priority, when completing the chart, is to establish the best time to study math. Math should be studied as soon as possible after each class session. Therefore you should choose study times that are as close to class time as possible. Be sure to indicate where you will study. Are you going to go to the math lab? Or are you going to study in a group at someone's home or workplace?

Once you have indicated in the Weekly Study Goal Sheet your math study times and locations, fill in your study goals for other subjects. If your math class is the last class of the day, schedule your math study time in the first study-time slot. Therefore, you would choose to begin studying your daily math at 3:00 on Monday, Tuesday, Wednesday and Thursday. You will mark the box on the math line for Monday, Tuesday, Wednesday and Thursday with: 3 p.m., daily work, home.

Planning Use of Daily Time

	Monday	Tuesday	Wednesday	Thursday	Friday	Saturday	Sunday
6:00							
7:00							
8:00							
9:00							
10:00							
11:00							
12:00							
1:00							
2:00							
3:00							
4:00							
5:00							
6:00							
7:00							
8:00							
9:00							
10:00							
11:00							
12:00							

Grade goal: _____

CODES: C=Class, **W**=Work, **E**=Eating, **G**=Grooming, **T**=Tutor, **F**=Family, **CN**=Cleaning, **SL**=Sleep, **SC**=Social Time, **TR**=Travel, **O**=Other, **S**=Study

Permission is granted to copy and enlarge Figure 11.

Weekly Study Goal Sheet

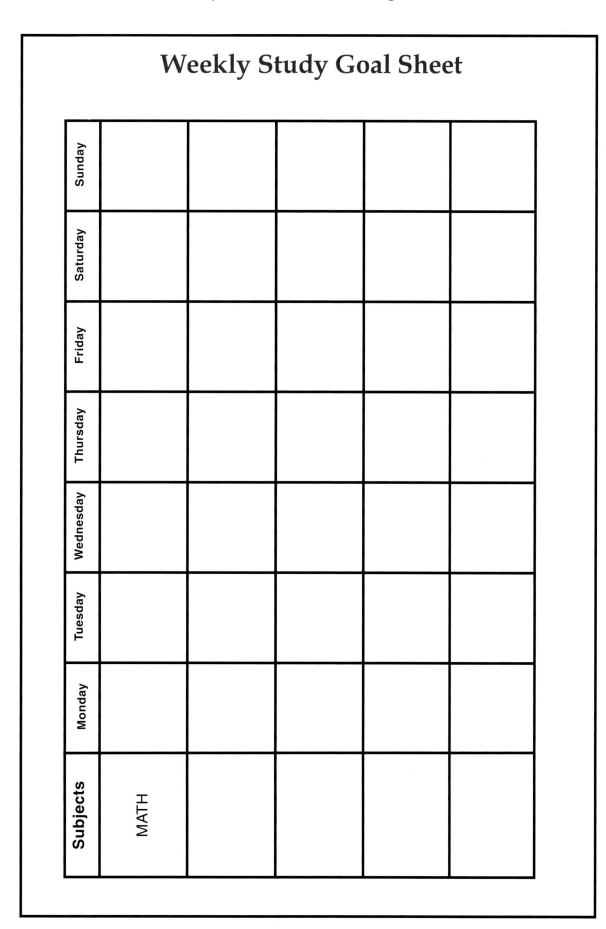

Subjects	Monday	Tuesday	Wednesday	Thursday	Friday	Saturday	Sunday
MATH							

How to Manage Work and Study Schedules

Most college students work and attend college at the same time. Some college students even try to be full-time students and employees. This can be dangerous because many full-time college students who attempt to work full time wind up dropping out. Students who work and attend college at the same time must manage their time very carefully and balance their work and study schedules.

Students can be successful in college while working; however, it takes effective time management along with excellent reading and study techniques. Make sure you are not setting yourself up to be successful at work while failing college. If necessary, drop to part-time work while in college and work overtime to obtain enough money to attend college. Also, it is better to "stop out" of college for a term and work instead of juggling both. This is especially true if your work is causing you to fail classes. However, you should only "stop out" for one semester because many students who stay out of college more than one semester don't come back. The suggestions below can help you best manage work and study:

- Try to find a job that allows you some opportunity to study.
- Try to arrange to work right after class. Do not go home first. Take work clothes with you to school if needed. Study during lunch or during breaks.
- Try to review your notes during work if the job allows.
- Record class lectures and play them during your travel to and from work.
- Take only 12 semester hours,which will qualify you as full-time for financial aid but will not over-burden your time.
- Take one easy course each semester.
- Do not wait until the weekend to do your homework.

If you are short on time and still need to work, you may want to ask about working at your college through the College Work Study program. This program is federally funded and is based on financial need. The college does not pay you. The money comes from the federal government.

If you do not qualify for College Work Study, you may still be able to work on campus through department funds. For example, you may be able to work in the library or at a food services location. These funds come directly from the college or department based on their budget. The downside is that colleges tend to pay lower wages than outside employers. However, colleges work with your schedule and there is no driving time or gas money involved. I have had many students work for me as tutors or study coaches up to 25 hours a week, and they thought it was a good opportunity. See if working at you college is a good option for you.

Activity 4.2 Setting a Semester G.P.A. Goal

As promised, it is now time to revisit the "My Math Success Plan" chart you began in Chapter 2. Later on in this text, you will come up with numerous semester goals. This activity focuses on the first of these goals: setting a semester G.P.A. marker.

In the space below, write out your semester schedule. To the right, fill in an ambitious (but realistic) grade objective. While doing this, consider the overall G.P.A you desire. Do you want a 4.0 average, (all A's), a 3.0 average (all B's), a 2.5 average (B's and C's), or a 2.00 average (all C's)? Do not choose any average below 2.00; you will not graduate with a lower average. Be realistic when deciding upon an overall grade point average.

Course	Credit Hours	Grade Objective
1.		
2.		
3.		
4.		
5.		
6.		

Total Hours:

Final Semester Grade Point Average:

Are the goals you set realistic? If so, explain why or why not in the space below:

Chapter 4 Summary

- A positive study environment can improve your math grades.

- Establishing several appropriate study places can increase your learning potential.

- Using distributive learning and studying new and old material at the appropriate times can improve your learning skills.

- Studying at the most efficient time, which is right after math class, can improve your learning.

- Being an effective collaborative learner will not only help you in math, it will help you in your future career.

- Learning how to use the math lab/LRC resources, which match your learning modality, enhances learning. Therefore, make sure you try each resource at least once to see how it helps you.

- Study skills and math lab/LRC resources can compensate for a mismatch of teaching and learning styles through tutoring.

- The main reason freshman students give for making poor grades is lack of study time.

- You have now completed a study schedule and a Weekly Study-Goal Sheet indicating both the times to study and the number of study hours per week.

- The number of study hours you contracted with yourself can change based on the grades you want.

- If you do not receive the grade you want in math, or your desired overall average during the semester, then increase the quality and quantity of study time.

- If you are working, have a family and are attending college full time, your time management is extremely important.

- Full time parents who are also students need to be creative in developing a workable study time.

Name: _____   Date: _____

Assignment for Chapter 4

1. List three ways to improve your study environment:

    Way One:

    Way Two:

    Way Three:

2. What should you do when you cannot study?

3. What are your best math lab/LRC resources?

4. What are two reasons for developing a study schedule?

    Reason One:

    Reason Two:

5. List five creative ways to study.

    One:

    Two:

Three:

Four:

Five:

6. What is the main reason freshman college students give for their poor grades?

7. Complete the Planning Use of Daily Time (page 98), select your math course grade, select your overall GPA for the semester, then complete your Weekly Study-Goal Sheet (page 101).

8. When should you learn new material?

9. In what order do you need to study your courses?

10. What should you do when you cannot study?

Understanding and Improving the Memory Process

5

In Chapter 5
You will learn these concepts:

✓ Understanding the memory process

✓ How each stage of the memory process affects your learning

✓ How to use your best learning style to improve memory

✓ How to use number sense

✓ General memory techniques

Understanding the Stages of Memory

To understand the learning process, you must understand how memory works. You learn by conditioning and thinking, but memorization is different from learning. For memorization, the brain must perform several tasks including receiving, storing and recalling the information. By understanding how memory works, you learn at which point your memory is failing you.

Most students usually experience memory trouble between the time the brain receives information and the time the information is stored. There are many techniques for learning information that can help you receive and store information without losing it in the process. Some of these techniques will be more successful than others, based on your skills and how you best learn.

How You Learn

Educators tell us that learning is the process of "achieving competency." More simply put, it is how you become good at something. The three ways of learning are by conditioning, thinking and a combination of conditioning and thinking. *Conditioning* is learning things with a maximum of physical and emotional reaction and a minimum of thinking. *Thinking* is defined as learning with a maximum of thought and a minimum of emotional and physical reaction.

Conditioning Example: Repeating the word "pi" to yourself and practicing where the symbol is found on a calculator are two forms of conditioned learning. This type of learning involves the use of your voice and hand-eye coordination, both of which require very little thinking.

Thinking Example: Learning about "pi" by thinking is different than learning about it by conditioning. To learn "pi" by thinking, you would have to do the calculations necessary to result in the numeric value, which the word "pi" represents. You are learning, using your mind (thought activities), and you are using very little emotional or physical energy to learn "pi" in this way.

Years of research indicates that the best way to learn math is to combine conditioning with thinking. The most successful way to do this is to learn by thinking first and conditioning second.

Learning by thinking means you learn by:

- Observing,

- Processing and

- Understanding the information.

The Stages of Memory

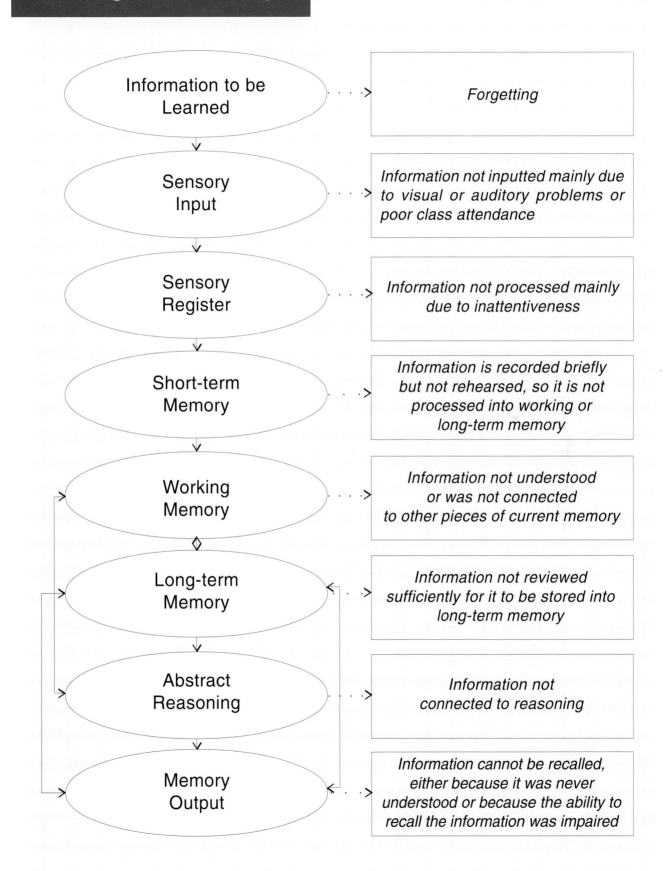

Understanding the Stages of Memory

Memory is different from learning; it requires the reception, storage and retrieval of information. This memory process is still being explored, but the presented model best represents how students learn mathematics. The memory process starts with the sensory input, proceeds through the sensory register into short-term memory, and then into working memory, where it goes directly into long-term memory, abstract reasoning or memory output (see the Stages of Memory chart).

Information also goes through long-term memory and/or abstract reasoning and then into memory output. The double arrows in the Stages of Memory Chart demonstrate how working memory goes both ways. The reception of information is through the sensory input. The storage is through the sensory register, short-term memory, working memory, long-term memory and abstract reasoning. The retrieval of this information is usually through doing homework and taking tests. It is important to understand that information can be lost through each stage.

As we discuss each stage of memory, locate your memory strengths and where your memory is breaking down. Understanding how the stages of memory affect learning helps improve your grades.

Sensory Input and Sensory Register

You receive information through your five senses (known as the sensory input): what you see, feel, hear, smell and taste. This process behaves differently in every course.

The sensory register briefly holds an exact image or sound of each sensory experience until it can be processed. If the information is not processed immediately, it is forgotten. The sensory register helps us go from one situation to the next without cluttering up our minds with trivial information. Processing the information involves placing it into short-term memory. Students who don't attend class do not ever reach this stage of memory and lose valuable information.

If students have visual or auditory impairments, information must be processed differently or through another sense. For example, deaf students may need interpreters or real time captioning while visually impaired students may need large print, audiobooks, recorded lectures or Braille texts.

Example: In math classes, you use your sense of vision to watch the instructor demonstrate problems and to read printed materials. You use your sense of hearing to listen to the instructor and other students discuss problems. Your sense of touch is used to operate your calculator and to appreciate geometric shapes. In chemistry and other classes, however, you may additionally use your senses of smell and taste to identify substances.

How Short-Term Memory Affects What You Remember

Information that passes through the sensory register is stored in short-term memory. Short-term memory involves visual information or auditory information. Remembering something for a short time is not hard for most students. By conscious effort, you remember the math laws, facts and formulas received by your five senses. You recognize and register them in your mind as something to remember for a short time.

Example: When you are studying math, you can tell yourself the distributive property is illustrated by $a(b+c)=ab+ac$. By deliberately telling yourself to remember that fact (by using conditioning — repeating or writing it again and again), you can remember it, at least for a while, because you have put it in short-term memory.

Psychologists have found that short-term memory cannot hold an unlimited amount of information. You may be able to use short-term memory to remember one phone number or a few formulas but not five phone numbers or ten formulas. Items placed into short-term memory usually fade fast, as the name suggests.

Example: Looking up a telephone number in the directory, remembering it long enough to dial, then forgetting it immediately. Learning the name of a person at a large party or in a class but forgetting it completely within a few seconds. Cramming for a test and forgetting most of it before taking the test.

In many college classes, information is processed so quickly that no time is allowed for practicing and understanding the math. Instructors are required to cover an immense amount of information and students are lucky if they capture all of it and understand it for a brief moment. The memory process, for the most part, stops at short term in the classroom. That's why students need to have good note-taking skills to record the information, so it can be reviewed later on for better understanding.

How Working Memory Affects What You Remember

Working memory (or long-term retrieval) is that process in the brain that works on problems for a longer period of time than short-term memory. Working memory, then, offers an increase in the amount of time information is held in memory. (An increase in the volume of information that can be held requires long-term memory.)

Working memory is like the amount of RAM in a computer. Working memory uses the information (such as multiplication tables) recalled from long-term memory, along with new information to learn new concepts. It is the ability to think about and use many pieces

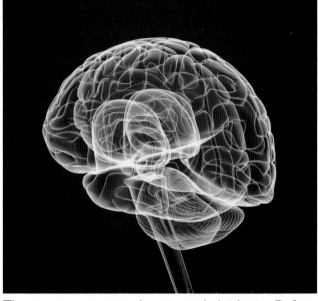

The memory process is extremely intricate. Before you can fix memory problems, you must understand how the process works.

of information at the same time. For instance, when you solve a linear equation in a math class you must use all the math that you learned in elementary school like addition, subtraction, and multiplication. You then have to add this to the new rules for linear equations.

Working memory can be compared to a mental workspace or an internal chalkboard. Just like a chalkboard, working memory has limited space, which can cause a "bottleneck" in learning. It involves the ability to recall information after learning has been consistently interrupted over a period of several minutes. Students with working memory problems may listen to a lecture and understand the information as it is explained. When the instructor goes back to something discussed earlier, however, the student has difficulty explaining or remembering things they thought they knew just a few minutes earlier. These students have difficulty remembering series of steps long enough to understand the concept.

Over-learning information by storing them in long-term memory can free up working memory to solve problems. Studying every night helps put information into long term memory which makes it easier when it is time to use working memory to learn new information.

Working memory goes both ways in the memory process. First, it leads into long-term memory and abstract reasoning. Second, working memory brings information out from long-term memory and abstract memory to use in learning new concepts. How information is remembered largely depends upon the subject. When learning a mathematical concept, working memory goes into abstract memory. When learning historical dates or definitions of words, information goes directly into long-term memory. Students use working memory to do their homework and when answering test questions. The amount of space in working memory is critical to answering test questions just like the amount of RAM is critical to running computer programs.

Example: In calculating 26 x 32, you would put the intermediate products 52 (from 2 x 26) and 780 (from 30 x 26 — remember 3 is in the 10's place, so make it 30) into working memory and add them together. The more automatic the multiplication, the less working memory you use. If you cannot remember your multiplication, you use up working memory trying to solve the multiplication problem.

Recent research indicates that working memory is affected by test anxiety. Many students who have test anxiety indicate that during tests they recognize problems but cannot remember how to work them. This happens because anxiety takes up working memory space, leaving less working memory to solve the problems. When anxiety levels go down, such as right after the test is over, some students remember how to solve problems because their working memory is freed up. This accounts for the "I knew I knew it" syndrome.

How Long-Term Memory Affects What You Remember

Long-term memory is a storehouse of material that is retained for long periods of time. Working memory places information in long-term memory and long-term memory is recalled into working memory to solve problems. It is not a matter of trying harder and harder to remember more and more unrelated facts or ideas; it is a matter of organizing your short-term memories and working memories into meaningful information.

In most cases long-term memory is immeasurable. There is so much room in long-term memory, no one has measured its total capacity. Long-term memory also relates more to language skills than abstract skills. Students with good long-term memory and poor abstract skills can sometimes do well in every subject except math and the physical sciences. These students can use their long-term memory language skills by learning the vocabulary. By understanding the language of mathematics they can put into words how to solve math problems and recall these words during the test instead of depending mainly on their abstract memory. This information must be reviewed many times for it to get into longterm memory. This concept will be explored more in later chapters.

How Reasoning Affects What You Remember

Reasoning (abstract memory) is thinking about memories, comprehending their meanings and understanding their concepts. Abstract reasoning involves learning how the rules and laws apply to solving math problems. Without understanding a concept, you cannot transfer information into abstract reasoning.

The main problem most students face is converting information from working memory to long-term and abstract reasoning. To place information into long-term memory, students must understand math vocabulary and practice problems.

To place information into abstract reasoning, students must understand a concept and remember it. Most students use long-term memory and abstract reasoning to solve problems. Depending on their skills in these areas, they may choose one or the other.

Role of Memory Output in Testing

Memory output is what educators call a "retrieving process." It is necessary for verbal or written examinations. The retrieving process is used when answering questions, doing homework or taking tests. It is the method by which you recall information stored into long-term memory and through abstract reasoning are able to verbalize it or put it on paper.

This retrieval process comes directly from long-term memory. For example, "What are whole numbers?" This is a fact question that comes from long-term memory. The retrieval process also comes from abstract reasoning. However, most math problems are solved through working memory by using information from both long-term memory and abstract reasoning. For example, "solve: $3y - 10 = 9y + 21$". For this problem you are pulling in number facts from long-term memory and the rules for solving equations from abstract reasoning.

Three things block memory output: insufficient processing of information into long-term memory or reasoning, test anxiety, and poor test-taking skills. If you do not place all of the information you learned into long-term memory and abstract reasoning, you may not be able to answer test questions.

Test anxiety decreases your ability to recall important information or totally blocks out information. During exams test anxiety affects working memory by decreasing how much information it processes at one time. Students who work on test-taking skills often improve their memory output.

Assessing Your Memory Strengths and Weaknesses

Understanding the stages of memory helps answer this common question about learning math: "Why do I understand the procedures to solve a math problem one day and forget

how to solve a similar problem days later?"

There are three good answers to this question. First, after initially learning how to solve the problem, you did not rehearse the solving process enough for it to enter your long-term memory. Second, you did get the information into long-term memory, but the information was not reviewed frequently enough and was forgotten. Third, you memorized how to work the problem but did not understand the concept.

There are also other areas where the memory process breaks down. The following are some common problems students have in learning, preceded by what stages of memory each problem affects:

Sensory Input
- Visual or hearing impairment.
- Dyslexia.

Sensory Register
- Trouble understanding information in a noisy classroom.
- Not knowing what information is important.

Short-Term Memory
- Being a poor note-taker .
- Not being able to write down the steps of problems.

Working Memory
- Having a poor homework system.
- Not reading the text.

Long-Term Memory
- Not reviewing your homework problems.
- Not reviewing your notes.
- Not knowing the meaning of vocabulary.

Abstract Reasoning
- Not understanding properties, rules and key concepts.
- Not applying the properties, rules and concepts.

Memory Output
- Breakdown in one or more stages of memory.
- Inadequate test-taking skills.
- Test anxiety.

Activity 5.1 Discovering Your Memory Strengths

Now that you have a better understanding of the stages of memory, it is time to do a self-assessment to discover your memory strengths and those areas in which you need to improve. Look at the Stages of Memory Chart and put an "S" by those memory stages in which you are strong. Label those stages your average memory stages with an "A." Put a (W) by those areas you consider yourself weak. Once you have done this, answer the questions printed below.

1. What weak area(s) did you have in the Stages of Memory and how can you improve them?

2. In what area(s) are you average, according to the Stages of Memory, and how can you improve them?

3. What were your strong areas in the Stages of Memory about which you can be proud?

Using Your Learning Style to Improve Memory

There are many different techniques that can help you store information in your long-term memory and reasoning. Using your learning sense or learning style and decreasing distraction while studying are very efficient ways to learn. Using your best learning sense (what educators call your "predominate learning modality") improves how well you learn and enhances the transfer of knowledge into long-term memory/reasoning.

As you'll remember, the learning senses are vision, hearing, touching, etc. Ask yourself if you learn best by watching (vision), listening (hearing), or touching (feeling).

Another helpful tool is the Learning Styles Modality Inventory for Math Students, available in Appendix B. It is the only learning style inventory that has specific modality math learning style information. This means by taking the inventory, you learn the specific ways you prefer to learn math. Based on your preferred learning style, practice those learning suggestions first. Remember, learning styles are neither good nor bad. They are based on genetics and environment, not ability or intelligence.

The next few sections in the textbook cover the five major types of learners and provide specific tips on how each type can streamline the memory process. Find the section that best suits your particular needs and progress accordingly.

In the meantime, here is a quick refresher on the five major types of learners:

- *Visual Numeric Learners* prefer to learn by reading and writing.
- *Auditory Numeric Learners* prefer to learn through lectures and other verbal communication.
- *Tactile Concrete Learners* prefer to learn through hands-on learning.
- *Social Individual Learners* prefer to learn either by themselves or by one-on-one tutoring.
- *Social Group Learners* prefer to take part in group learning.

Multiple Senses

If you have difficulty learning material from one sense, try learning material through two or three senses. Involving two or more senses improves your learning and remembering. Review the figures in this section on using your learning styles. Whenever possible, combine learning styles. If your primary sense is visual, and your secondary sense is auditory, write down equations while saying them out loud. Writing and reciting the material at the same time combines visual, auditory, and some tactile/concrete styles of learning. Likewise, studying with a pen or highlighter is a visual as well as a tactile/concrete way to improve your concentration. Placing the pen or highlighter in your hand forces you to concentrate on what you are reading. After you write and recite the material back to yourself, do it five or ten more times to over-learn it.

Improving Memory for Visual and Auditory Learners

Most college students are either visual or auditory learners. While it is easier to find math teachers and tutors to accommodate these learning styles than it is for other methods, students who learn this way should still learn to maximize their chances of success. With that in mind, read the section on this page that is specific to the way you prefer to learn and then take a look at the adjoining chart (printed on the facing page). These charts present easy-to-implement strategies that are custom designed to help specific types of learners improve their success in math.

Visual (Watching) Learner

Visual learners—also known as Visual Numerical Learners—study best by repeatedly reading and writing down material. These learners get more out of reading a textbook and watching their professors write on the board than they do listening to lectures.

A visual way to decrease distractions is by using the "my mind is full" concept. Imagine that your mind is completely filled with thoughts of learning math, and other distracting thoughts cannot enter. Your mind

has one-way input and output, which only responds to thinking about math when you are doing homework or studying.

Auditory (Hearing) Learner

If you are an auditory learner—one who learns best by hearing the information—then learning formulas is best accomplished by repeating them back to yourself, or recording and listening to them. In-class and Web-based lectures are perfectly suited to your learning style, which gives you plenty of study options.

Reading out loud is one of the best auditory ways to get important information into long-term memory. Stating facts and ideas out loud improves your ability to think and remember. If you cannot recite out loud, recite the material to yourself, emphasizing the key words.

An auditory way to improve your concentration is by becoming aware of your distractions and telling yourself to concentrate. If you are in a location where talking out loud will cause a disturbance, mouth the words "start concentrating" as you say them in your mind. This usually increases the length of time you are able to concentrate.

Visual Numeric Learner

These students learn math best by seeing it written. If you are a visual numerical learner, you may learn best by following these suggestions:

1. Use worksheets, workbooks, handouts, additional math texts and any other additional written materials.

2. Play games with, and get involved in activities with, visual printed materials such as multiplication or algebra flash cards.

3. Use visually orientated computer programs, DVDs, homework programs and math websites like those mentioned in this text.

4. Watch YouTube videos on learning math.

5. Rework your notes using the suggestions in this text.

6. Make "3 X 5" note or flash cards putting the variables and numbers in different colors.

7. Use Study Stacks to develop your own virtual flash cards or use the virtual flash cards already developed (www.academicsuccess.com — Student Resources — Student Math Practice and Learning Sites.)

8. Use video websites from your text or AcademicSuccess.com — Student Resources — Student Math Practice and Learning Sites.

9. Use different colors of ink to emphasize different parts of each math formula.

10. Visualize numbers and formulas in detail.

11. Ask your tutor to show you how to do the problems instead of telling you how to do the problems.

12. Take pictures of the board with your cellphone, or use your phone to record a lecture.

Auditory Numeric Learner

If you are an auditory numerical learner, you may learn best by following these suggestions:

1. Say the numbers to yourself or move your lips as you read the problems.

2. Record your class and play it back while reading your notes.

3. Read aloud any written explanations.

4. Make sure all important facts are spoken aloud with auditory repetition.

5. Read math problems aloud and try solutions verbally as you talk yourself through .

6. Record directions to difficult math problems and refer to them when solving those specific types of problems.

7. Record math laws and rules in your own words, by chapters, and listen to them every other day (auditory highlighting).

8. Use your smartphone or tablet to record a lecture.

9. Explain to the tutor how to work the math problems.

10. Explain to group members how to solve math problems.

11. During the test, sub-vocally talk yourself through the problems.

12. Take the test in a private room and talk to yourself out loud to solve the problem.

Improving Memory for Tactile/ Concrete Learners

A tactile/concrete learner needs to feel and touch material to learn it. Tactile concrete learners, who are also called "kinesthetic" learners, tend to learn best when they concretely manipulate information. Unfortunately, most math instructors do not use this learning sense. As a result, students who depend heavily upon feeling and touching for learning will usually have the most difficulty developing effective math learning techniques. This learning style creates a problem with math learning because math is more abstract than concrete. Also, most math instructors are visual abstract learners and have difficulty teaching math tactilely. Ask for the math instructors and tutors who give the most practical examples and who may even "act out" the math problems.

As mentioned before, a tactile concrete learner will probably learn most efficiently by hands-on learning. Also, learning is most effective when physical involvement with manipulation is combined with sight and sound. For example, as you trace the face you also say the words out loud.

Based on the Learning Styles Inventory for Math Students, tactile concrete learners best learn math by manipulating the information that is to be taught. If you are a tactile concrete learner, you may learn best by following the suggestions in the figure printed on the next page. Try as many of these suggestions as possible and select and practice the best suggestions that help. If you do not have these manipulatives or don't know how to use them, ask the math lab supervisor or instructor if they have any manipulative materials or models. If your math lab does not have any manipulative materials, ask for help to develop your own.

Tactile/concrete learners can also use graphing calculators to improve their learning. Entering keystrokes makes it is easier to remember how to solve the problems. This is also an excellent way to remember how to solve a problem when using a calculator during a test. Another way tactile/concrete learners can learn is to trace the graph with their fingers when it appears on the calculator. They should say and trace every equation to "feel" how the graph changes when using different equations.

A tactile/concrete way to improve your study concentration is by counting the number of distractions for each study session. Place a sheet of paper by your book when doing homework. When you catch yourself not concentrating put the letter "C" on the sheet of paper. This will remind you to concentrate and get back to work. After each study period, count up the number of "C's" and watch the number decrease.

Tactile/Concrete Learner

These students learn math best by hands on learning. If you are a tactile concrete learner, you may learn best by following these suggestions:

1. Cut up a paper plate to represent a fraction of a whole.

2. Fold up a piece of paper several times and cut along the fold marks to represent a fraction of a whole.

3. In order to understand math concepts, ask to be shown how to use Cuesinaire or algebra titles as manipulatives.

4. Try to use your hands and body to "act out" a solution. For example, you may "become" the car in a rate-and-distance word problem.

5. Obtain diagrams, objects or manipulatives and incorporate activities such as drawing and writing into your study time. You may also enhance your learning by doing some type of physical activity such as walking.

6. Find a way to physically interact with common mathematics techniques. For an example, follow the directions below.

F (a) (c)

O (a) (d)

I (b) (c)

L (b) (d)

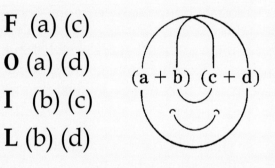

$(a + b)$ $(c + d)$

FOIL is used to remember the procedure to multiply two binomials. To use FOIL, multiply the following:

- the First terms ((a) (c))
- the Outside Terms ((a) (d))
- the Inside Terms ((b) (c))
- the Last terms ((b) (d)).

To learn FOIL, trace your finger along the FOIL route.

7. Ask to use the Hands-On-Equations Learning System using manipulatives to learn basic algebra. You can go to their website (www.borenson.com) to learn more about this system and other systems to help you learn math.

8. Go to one of the "learning stores," usually in your local mall, to see if they sell manipulatives. You can also try a K-12 learning resource center to see if they have manipulatives, such as magnetic boards, that you can put letters and numbers on and move around. Also, talk to the coordinator of students with disabilities to see if they use manipulatives when tutoring their students with learning disabilities.

9. Tear up a piece of paper into several pieces and put an x on some of the pieces. Mark the other pieces with numbers 0 to 9. The pieces with the x can represent the variable and the other pieces can represent the numbers. You can now use the pieces of paper to set up and solve equations.

10. Use the virtual manipulative websites at www.academicsuccess.com — Student Resource website or Google "college math manipulative."

Improving Memory for Social Learners

If you are a social individual learner, learning math may best be done individually. You may learn best by yourself, working with computer programs and being individually tutored. In some cases, social individuals may have to meet in groups to develop practice tests but leave socializing to a minimum.

If you think you are a social individual learner and visual learner, computers are one of the best learning tools available. If you are a social individual learner, based on past experiences, you may learn best by following the 10 suggestions in the Social Individual Learner figure on the next page. Try as many of these suggestions as possible, then select those that are most helpful.

A problem that a social individual learner may encounter is working too long on a problem for which they could have received help. Social individual learners must understand that getting help is okay, especially if it saves study time and makes them more study efficient.

Social Group Learner

If you are a social group learner (one who best learns in a group), then learning math may best be done in study groups and in math classes that have collaborative learning (group learning). Social group learners may learn best by discussing information. They can usually develop their own study groups and discuss how to solve problems over the phone. If you are a social group learner and an auditory learner, then you definitely learn best by talking to people. If you are a social group learner, you may learn best by following the 10 suggestions in the Social Group Learner Figure. Try as many of these suggestions as possible and select and practice those that are most helpful.

A learning problem that a social group learner may have is talking too much about other subjects when in a study group. This is called being off task. You may want to have a student serve as a discussion monitor to let others know when they need to get back on task. Also, social group learners need to know that they still must study math individually to be successful. During this individual study session, prepare questions for the group. This will maximize the value of your time.

Remember: When working in a group, complete any necessary preparation work prior to your group meeting. Little is accomplished in a group meeting if individual commitments are broken. Also, encourage the group to stay on task. If discussion strays, lead the group back toward your team goal. Bring closure to a team session by summarizing the group's efforts. Reach consensus on any group decisions involving completion of your tasks.

Social Individual Learners

These students learn math best individually. If you are a social individual learner, you may learn best by following these suggestions:

1. Study math, English or other subjects alone.

2. Utilize videos or audio files to learn by yourself (on or offline).

3. Prepare individual questions for your tutor or instructor.

4. Obtain individual help from the math lab or hire your own tutor.

5. Set up a schedule and study area so other people will not bother you.

6. Study in the library or in some other private, quiet place.

7. Use group study times only as a way to ask questions, obtain information and take pretests on your subject material.

8. Use math learning websites such as the ones at www.academicsuccess.com—Student Resources—Student Math Practice and Learning Websites.

9. Use the math homework sites listed in your text.

10. Set up virtual tutoring as needed.

Social Group Learners

These students learn math best in groups. If you are a social group learner, you may learn best by following these suggestions:

1. Study math, English or other subjects in a study group.

2. Sign up for math course sections that use cooperative learning (learning in small groups).

3. Review your notes with someone in a group.

4. Obtain help in the math lab or other labs where you can work in groups.

5. Watch math videos with a group and discuss the subject matter.

6. Listen to audio lectures (online or offline) and discuss them with a group.

7. Post pictures of your homework on Facebook and discuss it with your friends in the comment section below.

8. Form a study group. Each member should bring ten test questions with explanations on the back of the page. The group should complete all the test questions and share the answer.

9. Arrange a meeting with your instructor and several other students to go over math problems.

10. Develop an online chat group to help each other solve problems.

General Memory Techniques

Now that you know how to use your best learning style to improve your memory, it is time to learn a few techniques that help you remember specific information. These techniques are especially helpful when studying for tests.

A Good Study/Math Attitude

Having a positive attitude about studying will help you concentrate and improve your retention. This means you need to have at least a neutral math attitude (you neither like nor dislike it), and you should reserve the right to actually learn to like math. View studying as an opportunity to learn rather than as an unpleasant task. Tell yourself that you can learn the material and that learning it will help you pass the course and graduate.

Be a Selective Learner

Being selective in your math learning will improve your memory. Prioritize the materials you are studying. Decide which facts you need to know and which ones you can ignore. Narrow down information into laws and principles that can be generalized. Learn the laws and principles 100 percent.

Also, you must learn the math vocabulary in each chapter to continue to understand the instructor and math material.

Example: If you have been given a list of math principles and laws to learn for a test, put each one on an index card. As you go through them, create two piles: an "I already know this" pile and an "I don't know this" pile. Then, study only the "I don't know this" pile until it is completely memorized and understood.

Become an Organizer

Organizing math material into idea/fact clusters helps you learn and memorize it. Grouping similar material in a problem or calculator log are examples of categorizing information. Do not learn isolated facts; always connect them to other similar material.

Use Visual Imagery

Using mental pictures or diagrams is especially helpful for visual learners and those who are right-hemisphere dominant. Mental pictures and diagrams involve 100 percent of your brainpower. Picture the steps to solve difficult math problems in your mind.

Example: Use the Foil Method to visually learn how to multiply binomials. Memorize the face until you can sketch it from memory. During a test, you can then sketch the face onto your scratch paper and refer to it.

Make Associations

Association learning can help you remember better. Find a link between new facts and some well-established old facts and study them together. The recalling of old facts will help you remember the new ones and strengthen a mental connection between the two. Make up your own associations to remember math properties and laws.

> Example: When learning the commutative property, remember that the word "commutative" sounds like the word "community." A community is made up of different types of people who could be labeled as an "a" group and a "b" group. However, in a community of "a" people and "b" people, it does not matter if we count the "a" people first or the "b" people first; we still have the same total number of people in the community. Thus, a+b=b+a. When learning the distributive law of multiplication over addition, such as a(b+c), remember that "distributive" sounds like "distributor," which is associated with giving out a product. The distributor "a" is giving its products to "b" and "c.

Use Mnemonic Devices

The use of mnemonic devices is another way to help you remember. Mnemonic devices are easily remembered words, phrases or rhymes associated with difficult-to-remember principles or facts. Chances are you've used these devices since elementary school.

> Example: A mnemonic device to remember the Order of Operations is "Please Excuse My Dear Aunt Sally." The first letter in each of the words represents the math function to be completed from the first to the last. Thus, the Order of Operations is Parentheses (Please), Exponents (Excuse), Multiplication (My), Division (Dear), Addition (Aunt), and Subtraction (Sally).

Using mnemonic devices can improve a student's mathematics learning. Students making up their own mnemonic devices can remember them better than the ones given to them. Try to make up your own mnemonic device, but if you have difficulty, use the mathematic mnemonic devices on the Winning at Math Student Resource website.

> Example: FOIL is a common math acronym. FOIL is used to remember the procedure to multiply two binomials. Each letter in the word FOIL represents a math operation. FOIL stands for First, Outside, Inside and Last, as it applies to multiplying two binomials such as (2x+3)(x+7). The First product is 2x (in the first expression) and x (in the second expression). The Outside product is 2x (in the first expression) and 7 (in the second expression). The Inside product is 3 (in the first expression) and x (in the second expression). The Last product is 3 (in the first expression) and 7 (in the second expression). This results in F $((2x)(x))$ + O $((2x)(7))$ + I $((3)(x))$ + L $((3)(7))$. Do the multiplication to get $2x^2$+ 14x + 3x + 21, which adds up to $2x^2 + 17x + 21$.

Use Acronyms

Acronyms are another memory device to help you learn math. Acronyms are word forms created from the first letters of a series of words. Using acronyms improves a student's mathematics learning. Making up your own acronym devices is the best way to remember them. If you are having difficulty making up acronyms then use the Winning at Math Student Resource website.

How to Develop Practice Tests

Developing a practice test is one of the best ways to evaluate your memory and math skills before taking the real test. You want to find out what you do not know before the real test instead of during the test. Practice tests should be as real as possible and should include the use of time constraints.

You can create a practice test by reworking all the problems that you have recorded in your problem log. Another practice test can be developed using every other problem in the textbook chapter tests. You can also use the solutions manual to generate other problems with which to test yourself. Check to see if the math lab/LRC has tests on file from previous semesters, or ask your instructor for other tests. For some students, the group method is a better way to prepare for a test.

If group work improves your learning, you may want to hold a study group session at least once a week. Make sure the individual or group test is completed at least three days before the real test.

Completing practice math tests will help you increase testing skills. It will also reveal your test problem weaknesses in enough time for you to learn how to solve the problem before the real test. If you have difficulty with any of the problems during class or after taking the practice test, be sure to see your tutor or instructor.

After taking the practice test(s), you should know what parts you do not understand (and need to study) and what is likely to be on the test. Put this valuable information on one sheet of paper. This information needs to be understood and memorized. It may include formulas, rules or steps to solving a problem.

Use the learning strategies discussed in this chapter to remember this information. A good example of how this information should look is what students might call a mental "cheat sheet." Obviously, you cannot use the written form of this sheet during the real test. If you cannot take a practice test, put down on your mental cheat sheet the valuable information you will need for the test. Work to understand and memorize your mental cheat sheet. Chapter 8 (Improving Math Test-Taking Skills) will discuss how to use the information on the mental cheat sheet — without cheating.

How to Use Number Sense

Number sense is a lot like common sense. It is the ability to see if your answer makes sense without using algorithms. (Algorithms are the sequential math steps used to solve problems.) These following two examples demonstrate solving two math problems (from a national math test given to high school students) using algorithms and number sense.

Example One: Solve 3.04 x 5.3. Students use algorithms to calculate this problem by multiplying the number 3.04 by 5.3, in sequence. 72 percent of the students answered the problem correctly using algorithms.

Example Two: Estimate the product of 3.04 x 5.3. Answer given the choices below:

   A) 1.6   B) 16   C) 160   D) 1600

Only 15 percent of the students chose "B," which is the correct answer. Twenty-eight percent of the students chose "A." Using estimating to solve the answer, a whopping 85 percent of the students got the problem wrong.

These students were incorrectly using their "mental black board" instead of using number sense. In using number sense to answer, you would multiply the numbers to the left of the decimal in each number to get an estimate of the answer.

To estimate the answer you would multiply 3 (the number to the left of the decimal in 3.04) by 5 (the number to the left of the decimal in 5.3) and expect the answer to be a little larger than 15.

It appears that the students' procedural processing (the use of algorithms) was good, but when asked to solve a non-routine problem using estimating (which is easier than using algorithms), the results were disappointing.

Example: Solve 48 + 48 by rounding off. Rounding off means mentally changing the number (up or down) to make it more manageable to you, without using algorithms. By rounding off, 48 becomes 50 (easier to work with). 50 + 50 = 100. If the choices for answers were 104, 100, 98 and 96, you would then subtract four from the 100 (since each number was rounded up by 2) and you get 96.

Another example of using number sense or estimating is in "rounding off." Taking the time to estimate the answer to a math problem is a good way to check your answer.

Another way to use number sense is to check your answer to see if it is reasonable. Many students forget this important step and get the answer wrong. This is especially true of word or story problems.

Examples: When solving a rate-and-distance problem, use your common sense to realize that one car cannot go 500 miles per hour to catch the other car. However, the car could go 50 miles per hour.

The same common-sense rule applies to age-word problems where the age of a person cannot be 150 years but could be 15.

Further, in solving equations, x is usually a number that is less than 20. When you solve a problem for x and get 50, then this isn't reasonable, and you should re-check your calculations.

Also remember, when dealing with an equation, to make sure that you put the answer back into the equation to see if one side of the equation equals the other. If the two sides are not equal, you have the wrong answer. If you have extra time left over after you have completed a test, you should check answers using this method.

Metacognition — Putting It All Together

Metacognition is a new concept in mathematics that looks at what students are thinking when solving math problems. Using your memory process to learn how to solve math problems is the first step, but you must also be able to apply concepts to solve homework or test problems. The key to your success is the self-monitoring of problem solving, not memorizing how to do the problems. Memorization of steps instead of understanding the rules and principles leads to passive learning and unsuccessful problem solving. It is important that you develop a reliable method. Joy (1991) in her article, "Ideas in Practice: Metacognition and Mathematical Problem Solving," suggests a math solving model based on metacognition. This model of plan, monitor and evaluate is a framework for solving math problems also supported by other researchers.

Planning consists of understanding what the problem wants, the strategies to solve the problem and potential obstacles. It also includes understanding what information is required, doing the calculations and predicting the outcome.

Monitoring is putting the steps in order, keeping one's place, identifying and finding errors, understanding when additional information is needed, knowing when to use another strategy and knowing when you have part of the answer.

Evaluating includes knowing if the answer seems right (number sense), putting the answer back into the equation, doing the opposite of the function to see if the answer is correct, and measuring the efficiency of the plan and monitoring.

Using metacognition to solve math problems increases your homework and test-taking success. We will cover this method in much more detail in ("Chapter 7: How to Improve Your Reading and Homework Techniques") and (Chapter 8: "Improving Your Math Test-Taking Skills").

Chapter 5 Summary

- Remembering what you learn begins with understanding the relationship between receiving (sensing), storing (processing) and retrieving (recalling) information.

- Having enough working memory to recall information from long-term memory to solve a problem is important.

- Transforming working memory into long-term memory is the major memory problem for most students.

- While studying, many students do not complete this memory-shifting process.

- Understanding the stages of memory and using memory techniques can help you store information in long-term memory.

- Understanding your best learning style and how to use it will dramatically improve your grades.

- Common memory techniques include maintaining a good math/study attitude, becoming a selective learner, becoming an organizer, using visual imagery, making associations, using mnemonic devices and using acronyms.

- Developing practice tests can also help you learn where your memory is failing you, and creating practice tests helps you increase your test-taking skills.

- Memory output skills (or recalling long-term memory or reasoning into working memory) can be improved.

- Use your imagination to adapt these learning techniques to the math material you need to understand and learn.

- One way to improve these skills is to become more automatic with your mental processing of numbers and using number sense.

- Using a calculator can free up more working memory to help you solve the problem.

- Using the metacognition model of planning, monitoring and evaluating will improve your math success.

Name: _____   Date: _____

Assignment for Chapter 5

Directions: Read each of the scenarios and identify the learning process stages in which the math student messes up. Also list other issues that might be interfering with the student's learning process. Then identify what the student could do to improve his or her math learning process.

1. The night before the test, David got out his elementary algebra book, class notes, and the few homework problems he did. To his dismay, as he reviewed his notes, which were detailed and organized, he realized that although he kind of understood everything, he didn't know it as well as he should and definitely did not know how to do the word problems without looking at his notes. All of a sudden, David panicked. Then he remembered that there would be five more tests and he would just go ahead and wing this one because he was sure he would be more prepared for the other tests. After all, he had learned his lesson.

   A: List the stages in the learning process that David did not complete:

   B: Identify other issues that interfered in his success:

   C: List suggestions for improvement:

   D: Describe environmental factors affecting the learning experience:

2. While sitting in her math class on Monday morning, Mary kept thinking about how many hours of work she was asked to put in for the week. The math that the professor was teaching looked familiar from high school, so she didn't worry about taking careful notes. She had to figure a way to get out of working Thursday night so she could study for her history test. Tuesday night rolled around, and Mary sat down with her math textbook to do a few problems so she wouldn't be totally lost in class the next day. She was tired from work and never had figured out how to read the math book. She tried a few problems first and then read the book when she couldn't remember how to do them. She couldn't find the explanation in the book when she flipped through the chapter. So, Mary decided she would just wait and get caught up on her math on the weekend and went to bed.

   A: List the stages in the learning process that Mary did not complete:

B. Identify other issues that interfered in her success:

C. List suggestions for improvement:

D. Describe environmental factors affecting the learning experience:

3. Tom earned a "D" on his first math test. That was enough to wake him up to taking class seriously. He listened in class, took notes, and did the homework. He even saw a tutor a couple of times to get help on some word problems he didn't understand. As the test got closer, though, Tom started worrying. He had a hard time concentrating while reviewing for the test, but he still seemed to understand everything better than he did for the first test. He reviewed his notes, practice problems, and the textbook. On test day, Tom took a look at the test and panicked. His face turned blotchy red. He knew he knew the material but just couldn't get it out on the paper. He left a third of his test blank and left fifteen minutes early.

    A: List the stages of the learning process that Tom did not complete:

    B: Identify other issues that interfered with Tom's success:

    C: List suggestions for improvement:

    D: Describe environmental factors affecting the learning experience:

HOW TO IMPROVE LISTENING AND NOTE-TAKING SKILLS

6

IN CHAPTER 6
YOU WILL LEARN THESE CONCEPTS:

✓ How to listen effectively and identify the important information in an instructor's lecture

✓ How to develop listening and recording habits that improve the content of your notes

✓ How to design a system of note-taking, like the "Seven Steps to Math Note-Taking"

How to Become an Effective Listener

Listening and note-taking skills in a math class are very important, since most students do not read the math text or have difficulty understanding it. In most of your other classes, if you do not understand the lecture you can read the book and get almost all the information. In the math class, however, the instructor can usually explain the textbook better than the students can read and understand it. Students who do not have good listening skills or note-taking skills are at a disadvantage in learning math. Most math understanding takes place in the classroom. Students must learn how to take advantage of learning in the classroom by becoming effective listeners, calculator users and note-takers.

You can become an effective listener using a set of skills, which you can learn and practice. To become an effective listener, you must prepare both physically and mentally.

It is also important to point out, students are now receiving their lectures online. For example, you may be in an Emporium model classroom with computers or taking an online course. Both of these systems feature math lectures online, so you cannot ask questions. This type of delivery system requires a different type of note-taking in order to learn the material.

Sitting in the Golden Triangle of Success

The physical preparation for becoming an effective listener involves where you sit in the classroom. Sit in the best area to obtain high grades, "The Golden Triangle of Success." This area is illustrated on the picture located below. Students seated in this area (especially on the front row) directly face the teacher and will most likely pay attention to the lecture. This is a great seating location for visual learners. There are also fewer tendencies for distraction by activities outside the classroom or by students making noise or movement in the classroom.

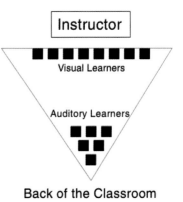

Back of the Classroom

The middle seat in the back row is another point in "The Golden Triangle" for students to sit, especially those who are auditory (hearing) learners. You can hear the instructor better because the instructor's voice is projected to that point. This means that there is less chance of misunderstanding the instructor, and you can hear well enough to ask appropriate questions.

Sitting in "The Golden Triangle of Success" forces you to pay more attention during class and be less distracted by other students. This is very important for math students because math instructors usually go over a point once. If you miss that point in the lesson, then you could be lost for the remainder of the class.

Warming Up for Math Class

The first step of mental preparation for note-taking involves "warming up" before class begins. Just as an athlete must "warm up" before a game begins, you must "warm up" before taking notes. "Warm up" by reviewing the previous day's notes, reviewing the reading material, reviewing the homework, preparing questions, and working one or two unassigned homework problems. This mental "warm up" before the lecture refreshes your memory, making it easier to learn the new material. Students who "warm up" are "ready to go" as soon as the instructor starts lecturing, and they keep up with what is discussed in class.

How to Become an Active Listener and Learner

In many ways, math class is like a race. Every session follows the same pattern:

1. *On your mark* — sit in your desk.
2. *Get set* — get focused and be ready to take notes when the instructor begins.
3. *Go* — keep a steady pace with note-taking.
4. *Last lap* — stay focused, even if you are tired.
5. *Finish line* — class is over. You have good notes. Time to practice for your next race.

In order to complete this process, you must become an active listener. Active listening means integrating the thinking and learning process with listening and recording information.

First, it involves learning the instructor's lecture style, how he or she indicates when information is important. What information do they tend to leave out? Is it best to keep the book open during lecture? How parallel is the lecture with the book? The pace of the instructor's lecture is important. If it is too slow, you must think of ways to remain focused like finding sample problems in the book. If it is too fast, you must find a way to make short cuts in recording information while still getting the details.

Second, you must be a participant in the class, asking questions, listening to other students' questions. Be willing to ask questions for clarification when confused because if you are confused, so is someone else. Questions are another way to force an instructor to repeat information or provide more details. Sometimes it is easy to fall into the frame of mind where you just go to class, get the notes down, planning to learn it later. That is passive listening. No more sitting in the back, slouched in the desk, waiting to write whatever the instructor puts on the board.

What do you think about while in the math class?

First, listen for the instructor to discuss what you learned when you previewed the chapter as a "warm up." Sometimes it helps to have the book open to the chapter the instructor is talking about. You can compare the information from the lecture with the book.

Second, if the instructor is speeding on, ask a question to help you understand what is being discussed. This also gives a mental break for everyone. Just don't ask too many questions that are irrelevant. Classmates do not appreciate those questions.

Third, as the instructor is explaining how to do something, listen for the explanation of why particular steps are completed. If you do not hear the "why," be brave and ask the instructor. Usually the answer will include the rules, properties or laws that explain why certain steps are taken. This will help you and many of your classmates understand what is going on. Make sure you record this information in your notes.

There will be times when the instructor has to present so much information at a fast pace, all that you can do is make sure you get it down. One trick is to sit next to someone who is trying to listen as intently as you. Then, when one of you spaces out, the other one will still be focused in and getting the notes down. At the end of class you can compare notes and fill in each other's gaps. If you can, sit close enough to each other to be able to look at each other's notes in order to fill in the gaps. This is particularly helpful in a class that meets for a long time. The catch is that in these situations, you must review the notes as soon as possible because you didn't have as much time to think about the information in class.

So how do you go about reviewing your notes as soon as possible? I have asked this question to many students and have never accepted the answer that they did not have enough time. If you try hard enough, you can always find enough time to review your notes. Try to find time between your classes or during lunch. Even better, get to you next class early and use the quiet time before class to go over everything you just wrote. Even three to five minutes of review improves learning. This is time incredibly well spent. Not only are you embedding fresh information into your memory, you are actively and continuously studying for future exams.

Remember, class time should be considered a valuable study period where you can listen, take notes and learn at the same time. Some students think listening to the instructor and taking notes is a waste of valuable time. Too often, students sit in class and use only a fraction of their learning ability. One way to learn more in class is to memorize important facts when the instructor is talking about material you already know. Another technique is to repeat back to yourself the important concepts right after the instructor says them in class. Using class time to learn math is an efficient learning system.

Speaking with a Professor About Your Notes

Some students have difficulty asking questions in class or they run out of time to record the notes before class is dismissed. When this happens, write down as much as you can and leave a blank area between the steps that you don't know how to do or could not record. However, you still need to know the information you left blank to understand how to solve the problem.

So what is your next step? Go see your instructor or tutor to help you solve the problem.

When you approach your instructor or tutor do not say, "I don't know how to work this problem." Instead say something like, "I recorded several steps, but could not understand (or record) the third step." Instructors and tutors like this approach because it shows them that you were trying in class, and they now know exactly where you got stuck. Ask the instructor or tutor, "Is this problem similar to some of the other problems I have in my notes, and what is the difference?" Then complete the steps in the problem by writing them in your notes.

Next, ask your instructor to give you a similar problem to see if you can work it. This is how you can move the math concept from short-term memory to long-term memory or abstract reasoning. If you get stuck on the similar problem, get immediate help. Tell the instructor or tutor what you are thinking so they can figure out what concepts you are missing.

When you solve the problem, show yourself and the tutor or instructor that you understand that concept. Now you are actively listening because both you and the instructor and tutor are working together.

Activity 6.1 Assessing Your Listening Strengths

Now that you have become an effective listener, it is time to assess what strategies you have been using and which strategies you can use to improve these skills. In the section below, answer the questions and then compare your answers to a classmate's.

1. What 'warm up strategies' have you been using in your math class?

2. With this new information, what new strategies can you use to "warm up" for your math class?

3. What active learning strategies have you been using in your math class?

4. What new active learning strategies can you use in your math class?

5. The progression of a math class is very similar to a race. After each race stage below, put a personal statement starting with "I will" on how you will complete that stage.

   a. On your mark—

   b. Get set—

   c. Go—

   d. Last lap—

   e. Finish line—

How to Become an Effective Classroom Note-Taker

Becoming a good note-taker requires two basic strategies. One strategy is to be specific in detail. In other words, copy the problems down, step by step. The second strategy is to listen for the general principles, general concepts and general ideas and record them in your notes.

Copying from the Board

While taking math notes, you need to copy each and every step of each problem on the board, even though you may already know them. While in the classroom, you might understand each step, but a week later you might not remember unless all the steps were written down. In addition, as you write down each step, you are memorizing it. The major reason for recording every step of a problem is to understand how to do the problems while the instructor is explaining them instead of trying to remember unwritten steps when you are studying on your own. It may seem time consuming; however, it pays off during homework and test time.

There will be times when you will get lost while listening to the lecture. Nevertheless, you should keep taking notes even though you do not understand the problem. This will provide you with a reference point for further study.

Put a question mark (?) by those steps you do not understand. As you take notes on confusing problem steps, skip lines; then go back and fill in information that clarifies your misunderstanding of the steps in question at some later point. Ask your tutor or instructor for help with the uncompleted problem steps and write down the reasons for each step in the space provided.

Also, ask your professor for permission to use your smartphone to take a picture of the board. Because many phones allow panoramic photographs, it is possible to create a single image of the entire board. This method does not, however, take the place of taking proper notes. Only view the images you create as a backup or use them to ensure you copied everything down correctly.

Remember, the goal is to get all the details without writing an essay. A procedure to save time while taking notes from the board is to stop writing complete sentences. Write your main thoughts in phrases. Phrases are easier to jot down and easier to memorize. Another strategy to streamline taking notes off the board is to develop an abbreviation system.

An abbreviation system is your way to reduce long words to shorter versions, which you still can understand. By writing less, you can listen more and have a better understanding of the material. For good examples of proper abbreviations , see the chart printed below.

The Goals of Note-Taking

The goal of note-taking is to take the least amount of notes and get the greatest amount of information on your paper. This could be the opposite of what most instructors have told you. Some instructors tell you to take down everything. This is not necessarily a good note-taking system, since it is very difficult to take precise, specific notes while at the same time understanding the instructor. On the other hand, some instructors ask you to stop taking notes during a lecture and just listen. These instructors know that when explaining a major point you need to listen and not write. If you are doing both, you may not understand the important concept. Let these instructors explain the major point and then record your notes. If you didn't have enough time to take the notes, see the instructor during his/her office hours or get the notes from a friend. Getting notes from another student instead of doing your own notes is not a good idea. Notes from other students are thoughts that pertain to their math knowledge to remind them how to do problems that they don't know how to solve. You might not have the same knowledge as they do, so the notes may not help you.

Abbreviations

E.G.	(for example)
CF.	(compare, remember in context)
N.B.	(note well, this is important)
∴	(therefore)
∵	(because)
⊃	(implies, it follows from this)
>	(greater than)
<	(less than)
=	(equals, is the same)
≠	(does not equal, is not the same)
( )	(parentheses in the margin, around a sentence or group of sentences indicates an important idea)
?	(used to indicate you do not understand the material)
O	(a circle around a word may indicate that you are not familiar with it; look it up)
TQ	(marks important materials likely to be used in an exam)

1, 2, 3, 4	(to indicate a series of facts)
D	(shows disagreement with statement or passage)
REF	(reference)
et al	(and others)
bk	(book)
p	(page)
etc.	(and so forth)
V	(see)
VS	(see above)
SC	(namely)
SQ	(the following)
Comm.	(Commutative)
Dis.	(Distributive)
A.P.A.	(Associative Property of Addition)
A.I.	(Additive Inverse)
I.P.M.	(Identity Property of Multiplication)

It is best to take your own notes and then compare them to a classmate's notes to gain additional information.

What you need to develop is a note-taking system in which you write the least amount possible and get the most information down while still understanding what the instructor is saying. The first step to this system is to know when to take notes.

When to Take Classroom Notes

To become a better note-taker you must know when to take notes. The instructor will give cues that indicate what material is important. Some cues include:

- Presenting usual facts or ideas

- Writing on the board

- Summarizing

- Pausing

- Repeating statements

- Enumerating, such as, "1, 2, 3" or "A, B, C"

- Working several examples of the same type of problem on the blackboard

- Saying, "This is a tricky problem. Most students will miss it."

- Saying, "This is the most difficult step in the problem."

- Saying these types of problems will be on the test, such as coin or age word problems

- Explaining bold-print words

- Saying, "This will be on the test."

- The instructor makes a special point of a particular PowerPoint slide, or the instructor brings up one of many Web-based resources

You must learn the cues your instructor gives indicating important material. If you are in doubt about the importance of the class material, do not hesitate to ask the instructor about its importance. If you are not sure if something is important in the lecture, write it down just in case.

While taking notes you may become confused about math material. At that point, take as many notes as possible, and do not give up on note-taking.

When important cues indicate that this information may be on the test, make sure to put TQ in the margin of your notes. These TQs could be the instructor indicating that this information will be on the test. If an instructor does the same type of problem several times and tells you that you must know how to work these types of problems, it is TQ. These TQs need to be reviewed and learned before each test. List these TQs on a separate page in the back of your notebook to review for the test and final exam.

When to Take Online and Emporium Class Notes

If you are taking an Emporium or online math course, taking notes may become confusing because there may not be formal lectures. The note-taking rules have changed for these courses; however, you still need to take notes. Remember the purpose of note-taking is to provide a resource for working homework problems and preparing for tests. I have worked with hundreds of students in these types of course who did not take notes and failed. Many had successfully completed their homework but did not have any notes or very few notes to review for the major tests. Some cues to take online/Emporium notes include:

1. If the instructor conducts a mini-lecture

2. If the instructor conducts a "pull out" section of students

3. When you ask for help from the class tutor or instructor

4. When you email the instructor or tutor for help on a problem

5. When it takes you three tries to get the homework problem correct

6. When you view the video lecture and don't understand the concept

Activity 6.2 Assessing Your Note-Taking Skills

Now that you have a better understanding of how to become a good note-taker, it is time to do a self-assessment to discover your strengths and those areas in which you need to improve.

1. Show your math notes to a classmate and see if he or she can read and understand the notes. Write down what they said about your notes.

2. List the type of math abbreviations you use in your notes:

3. Make up some math abbreviations you can use for your notes, and write them below:

4. What cues do you need to listen for when you take notes?

5. Based on reading this section, list five additional cues you can use to take notes:

The Seven Steps to Taking Notes in Math Class

Since most students are not court reporters, the key to effective note-taking is to record the fewest words while retaining the greatest amount of information. As you know, it is very difficult to record notes and, at the same time, fully understand your instructor. The "Seven Steps to Math Note-taking" system was developed to decrease the amount of words you write down and to maximize your math learning.

The system consists of three major components. Steps One through Three focus on recording your notes. Steps Four through Six focus on checking yourself to see how much information is retained. This is done by recalling key words and concepts and putting a check mark by misunderstood information. Recalling information is one of the best learning techniques. Step Seven, the third component, is a math glossary.

Before we get into the specifics of these steps, however, let's first explore how to set up your notes page. Great notebooks are organized and legible; they follow and stick to a singular design.

One of the best math note-taking methods is demonstrated in the figure on the next page. The "Modified Three Column Note-Taking Method" allows you to record everything you need to know to solve math problems in an easy-to-follow guide.

To set up this system, do the following on regular notebook paper:

1. *Label the top space* between the notebook ring and the red line, "Key Words."

2. *Label the other side* of the red line, "Examples."

3. *Next, label "Explanations/ Rules"* about four inches from the red line.

4. *Draw a vertical line* between the "Examples" and "Explanations/Rules" sections.

5. *Record the same information* on the next 10 pages. After using this system for 10 pages, you may not need to label each page.

Modified Three Column Note-Taking Method

Key Words/Rules	Examples	Explanations
Solve a linear equation	$5(x + 4) + 3(x - 4) = 2(x - 2)$	Have to get x on one side of the = and numbers on the other side of the =.
Distributive Property	$5x + 20 + 3x - 12 = 2x-4$	Multiply numbers to the left of the ( ) by each variable and number in the ( ).
Commutative Property	$5x + 3x + 20 - 12 = 2x-4$	Regroup numbers and variables.
Combine like terms	$8x + 8 = 2x - 4$	Add x's together and numbers together .
Additive Inverse Property	$8x - 2x + 8 = 2x - 2x -4$ $6x + 8 = -4$	Subtract 2x from both sides to get variables all on the left side of the =.
Additive Inverse Property	$6x + 8 - 8 = -4 - 8$ $6x = -12$	Subtract 8 from both sides to get numbers all on the right side of the =.
Multiplicative Inverse Property	$\dfrac{6x}{6} = \dfrac{-12}{6}$	Divide both sides by 6 to get x by itself on the left side of the =.
Simplify	$x = -2$	Solution. Now, check your answer.
	Insert new problem	

Once you have set up your page, follow the seven steps listed below.

Step One — Record each problem step in the "Examples" section.

Step Two — Record the reasons for each step in the "Explanation/Rules" section by using abbreviations; short phrases, not sentences; keywords, properties, principles or formulas.

Step Three — Record key words/concepts in the left two-inch margin either during or immediately after your lecture by reworking your notes.

Step Four — Cover up the "Example and Explanation" sections and recite out loud the meaning of the key words or concepts.

Step Five — Place a check mark by the key words/concepts that you did not know.

Step Six — Review the information that you checked until it is understood.

Step Seven — Develop a math glossary for difficult-to-remember key words and concepts.

After practicing this note-taking system, you may want to modify it to meet your personal note-taking needs. Some students wait and convert their notes into a three column system after class. They also put information from the math book into the three columns. Other students use graph paper and turn it landscape in order to make the columns wider.

In some cases, auditory abstract learners do not take extensive notes. I have seen these students take down only a few notes and spend most of their working memory understanding abstract concepts. For the most part, this is fine. If you are this type of student, however, you should at least take a few notes in order to remind yourself of key concepts. You should also still develop a math glossary. It is very important for you to remember the vocabulary that connects to abstract learning. Knowing these words frees up working memory to solve difficult equations on important tests.

Creating a Math Glossary

The third component in the Seven Steps to Math Note-Taking is devoted to developing a math glossary. Since math is sometimes considered a foreign language, understanding math vocabulary becomes a key to learning math. A math glossary for each chapter dramatically improves learning and allows you to better remember key concepts. Your glossary can be a combination of lecture notes, text readings or text notes (the latter two are discussed in the next chapter).

A good glossary is a key to success for students who have good language skills but have difficulty learning math. Even though math is an abstract subject, it is still learned through using language to recall how to work problems. In fact, some students talk their way through solving equations by using their math vocabulary.

For this reason, a math glossary should be created for each chapter to define math vocabulary words and concepts. Label a section in the back of your notebook "Math Vocabulary for Chapter One." Your glossary should include all words printed in bold print in your text, words emphasized by your instructor and any other words you do not understand. If you are not sure whether or not a word is important, add it anyway just in case.

The glossary should be divided into three areas, which include the book definition, your definition in your own words, and, if appropriate, an example. When you are finished, your glossary will look similar to the note-taking system you learned about in the last section. If you cannot explain the math vocabulary in your own words, ask your instructor or tutor for help. If your instructor or tutor cannot help you, then go to www.academicsuccess.com and click on "Student Resources." From there, click on "Math Practice and Learning." Go to "Other Support Sites" and click on the sites that mention a math glossary or math vocabulary. Look up the definitions of the words and then try to put the definitions in your own words. Review your math glossary every week.

Some students record vocabulary words with a digital recorder. If you use a recorder, leave a few seconds between a word and its definition. The definition should be in your own words. These vocabulary words are usually the words that you could not remember from your glossary. To practice your vocabulary words, play the recording when you have a few minutes between classes by using a recorder and headphones. This process keeps the words active in your mind until they finally pass into your long-term memory.

Once you listen to the vocabulary word, pause the recording and repeat the definition back to yourself. Replay the recording and listen to the definition. If you did not repeat it back correctly, then continue repeating it until you get it right. Keep practicing until you can correctly repeat back all the definitions. This is an excellent way for auditory math learners to memorize and learn vocabulary. Other types of learners can also use this learning system, because the repetition drills these words into your long-term memory.

Students who are visual or kinesthetic (hands on) learners may be able to learn math vocabulary more effectively by developing a virtual web-based math glossary. StudyStack.com is a free website that is designed to help people memorize and learn information.

Using the StudyStack website, you can use your computer to develop and display a stack of "virtual cards" of information that you want to learn. Just like flashcards, you can review the cards at any time, at your own pace, and you can discard the cards that you already know. The site is set up to find information on any subject, to develop your own flashcards, to play games such as

| Vocabulary Card Examples | |
Front	Back
Multiplicative Identity Additive Identity	Identity property a times 1 = a Additive identity a + 0= a
Order of polynomials	Place the terms in descending order of exponents. Highest on the left to lowest on the right. x cubed, next x squared, x to the first, constant (number).
Decimals — rational numbers and irrational numbers	Rational numbers have terminating or repeating decimal equivalents. e.g. ¾ = .75, 5/7 =.714285714285… Continuing but non-repeating or nonterminating decimals are called irrational numbers (e.g. the square root of 2 and pi).

hangman and matching, and also to help you study anytime/anywhere, 24/7. You can also print out the cards and export them to your cellphone, tablet or computer.

Visual math learners can also learn vocabulary the old fashion way — by putting a vocabulary word on one side of a flashcard and the definition on the other side. Auditory math learners can also develop flash cards, making sure to say the information out loud while learning the information. It is also helpful to write vocabulary words next to the homework problems they are associated with. The examples above are 3x5 cards that show only words. These memory devices can be even more effective if you include pictures or other diagrams.

How to Rework Your Notes

A good note-taking system does not stop when you leave the classroom. As soon as possible after class, rework your notes to decrease the chances you will forget something important. This is an excellent procedure to transfer math information from short-term to long-term memory and abstract reasoning.

Remember: Most forgetting occurs right after learning material. You need to rework your notes as soon as possible. The longer you wait, the more you forget and have to relearn.

1. *Rewrite the material you cannot read or will not be able to understand a few weeks later.* If you do not rework your notes, you will become frustrated when you come across illegible writing while studying for a test. Another benefit of rewriting your notes is that you immediately learn new material. Waiting means it will take more time to learn material.

2. *Fill in the gaps.* Most of the time, when you are listening to a lecture, you cannot write down everything. Locate the portions of your notes, which are incomplete. Fill in the concepts that were left out. In the future, skip two or three lines in your notebook page for anticipated lecture gaps.

3. *Add additional key words and ideas in the left-hand column.* These key words or ideas were the ones not recorded during the lecture. Example: You did not know you should add the opposite of 18 to solve a particular problem, and you incorrectly added 18. Put additional important key words and ideas (such as "opposite"and "negative of") in the notes; these are the words that will improve your understanding of math.

4. *Add to your problem log the problems which the teacher worked in class.* The problem log is a separate section of your notebook that contains a listing of problems (without explanations — just problems) your teacher worked in class. If your teacher chose those problems to work in class, you can bet that they are considered important. The problems in this log can be used as a practice test for the next exam. Your regular class notes will not only contain the solutions but also all the steps involved in arriving at those solutions. These notes can be used as a reference when you take your practice test. This process prepares you for exams by giving you a basic feel for potential test questions.

5. *Add calculator keystroke sequences to your calculator handbook.* The calculator handbook can be a spiral-bound set of notecards or a separate section of your notebook that holds only calculator-related information. Your handbook should also include an explanation of when that particular set of keystrokes is to be used.

6. *Reflection and synthesis.* Once you have finished going over your notes, review the major points in your mind. Combine your new notes with your previous knowledge to have a better understanding of what you have learned today.

How to Use an Audio Recorder While Taking Notes

If you have problems recording all the information in your math class, ask your instructor about using an audio recorder. To ensure success, the recorder or phone application must have a counter and must be voice activated. This way, you can start and stop during lectures while also keeping track of when a particular piece of information was mentioned.

Most recording applications display a sliding time bar, which allows you to know exactly where you are in a lecture. When you find you are in an area of confusing information while you are recording the lecture, write down the beginning and ending times in the left margin of your notes. When reviewing your notes, the counter number will be a reference point for obtaining information to work the problem. You can also reduce the time it takes to listen to the recording by using the pause button to stop the recording while your professor is covering unnecessary material during a lecture.

Most smartphone applications also contain valuable organization and time-saving tools. Remember, however, that you must always ask permission before using your smartphone in class.

Don't Be Afraid to Ask Questions

To get the most out of a lecture, you must ask questions in class. By asking questions, you improve your understanding of material and decrease your homework time. By not asking questions, you create unnecessary confusion during the remainder of a class period.

Also, it is much easier to ask questions in class about potential homework problems than it is to spend hours trying to figure out the problems on your own.

If you are shy about asking questions in class, write down any questions you may have and read them to your instructor. If the instructor seems confused about the questions, tell him or her that you will discuss the problem after class. Most professors are more than willing to help you during the moments immediately following a lecture.

Another trick is to prepare a question before class. This question can be something you are confused about, or something you already know. By forcing yourself to ask a question—any question—at the onset of a lecture, you can alleviate any nervousness you may have about asking questions in the future.

To encourage yourself to ask questions, remember:

- You have paid for your instructor's help.

- Other students probably have the same or similar questions.

- The instructor needs feedback on his or her teaching to help the class learn material.

- Not asking a question can stop your learning.

- There is no such thing as a "stupid" question.

- Asking questions during class lets a professor know you are interested in his or her lecture. Engaging a teacher during class makes it much more likely they will help you when you get confused.

The Advanced Color-Coded Note-Taking Method

Some students are starting to use an advanced note-taking system that involves color-coding specific types of information. Nate—a colleague of mine—developed this color-based note-taking system from the Modified Three Column Note-Taking system described in previous sections.

The color code system can greatly improve your notes. It is especially effective with visual learners who can practice visualizing the notes in color and later recall these visualizations during tests. The overall key to this note-taking system is organization and consistency. Make sure to use a pen with four different colors. If you are working on a computer, simply rework your notes with different colors of text.

Also, it is important to use the following guidelines:

1. *New sections* need to be labeled and started on a new page.

2. *The colors* you use should be consistent throughout the semester.

3. *Organize notes* in a three-column format.

To prepare for this advanced note-taking system, follow the steps below on regular notebook paper:

1. *Label the top space* between the note-book ring and the red line, "Topic" or Objective."

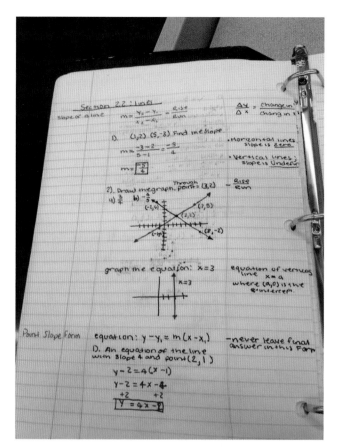

2. *Label the other side* of the red line, "Problem Main Steps" and under that "Intermediate Steps."

3. *Next, label* "Personal Notes" about four inches from the red line.

4. *Label* "Example" below the Topic and Objective.

5. *Record the same* information on the next 10 pages. After using the system for a while, you may not need to label the top of every page.

Once you have set up your pages, follow the 10 steps printed below. If you get confused, consult the graphic printed on the facing page.

Step One — Write down your example problem in the "Problem Steps" column in your "Example" section.

Step Two — Write down the topic or objective of your example problem in the left column. If you don't know the topic or objective, ask your instructor.

Step Three — Write down the problem steps. Make sure to color code these steps using black for main steps and red for intermediate steps.

Step Four — Explain each step in your "Personal Notes" column. If you don't know the reasons for the steps, ask your instructor, look up the reasons after class, or ask your tutor.

Step Five — Check your answer by putting the solution back into the equation or doing the opposite of the function to get the original problem.

Step Six — Cover up the "Personal Notes" section and say out loud the reasons for each step. This is an excellent rehearsal for preparing for a test.

Step Seven — Place a mark by any information in your "Personal Notes" section that you do not know or remember.

Step Eight — Review the information you do not know until you think you have a grasp on it. Visualize the information by closing your eyes and seeing the notes in color.

Step Nine — Develop a math glossary for the information in your "Personal Notes" section that was hard to remember.

Step Ten — Review your math glossary until you understand key vocabulary and concepts.

This system is more advanced than the Modified Three Column Note-Taking method. For visual learners, this system improves the transfer of information from short-term memory to long-term memory. Auditory and kinesthetic learners can also use the system by rewriting their notes and saying the steps out loud. Compare your own notes with other student's notes. If you find a student's notes that are better than yours, ask him or her if you can take a picture with your smartphone. Use this picture to fill in your notes later.

Topic or Objective	Problem Main Steps Intermediate Steps	Personal Notes

Example: Solve the equation $x^2 - 3 = -2x$.

Topic or Objective	Problem Main Steps / Intermediate Steps	Personal Notes
Solving a Quadratic Equation by Factoring	$x^2 - 3 = -2x$ $+ 2x \quad\quad +2x$ $x^2 + 2x -3 = 0$ $\underline{\;3\;} \times \underline{\;-1\;} = -3$ $\underline{\;3\;} + \underline{\;-1\;} = 2$ $(x + 3)(x - 1) = 0$ $x + 3 = 0 \quad\quad x - 1 = 0$ $-3 \quad\quad -3 \quad\quad +1 \quad\quad +1$ $x = -3 \quad\quad\quad x = 1$ $(-3)^2 - 3 = -2(-3) \quad (1)^2 - 3 = -2(1)$ $9 - 3 = 6 \quad\quad\quad\quad 1 - 3 = -2$ $6 = 6 \quad\quad\quad\quad\quad -2 = -2$	—set the equation equal to zero — find two numbers that multiply to be the constant and add up to be the middle coefficient —write the equation in factored form using these numbers —set each factor equal to zero and solve — make sure to check your answer by plugging it back into the original equation.

How to Take Notes for Online and Emporium Model Courses

Modern math students have more course options than any generation in the history of higher education. Two of the newest options, online courses and emporium model courses, differ greatly from classes held in traditional math classrooms.

Online distance courses allow students to use course software to complete a class outside of the classroom. Students are required to finish a pre-set curriculum by a certain date, though they are mostly left to complete the work where and when the want.

Emporium Model courses, on the other hand, are taken in specified classrooms on specified dates. These courses, often held in computer labs, do not typically include lectures, nor do they require students to work at a specific pace. These courses often use similar software to that used in online distance courses, though students typically benefit from having a professor or a group of tutors in the room to answer their questions.

Because there are no planned lectures, most emporium students dive immediately into their homework without taking any notes—this despite the fact that most math software programs allow students to easily

find specific passages from the required textbook and even provide extremely detailed, video-based walkthroughs. Having observed many emporium classes, however, I've noticed most students prefer to rely on built in support buttons, which answer their questions as they progress through their assignments. This practice—also common among online distance learners—is extremely dangerous. While these support buttons are often helpful, they are intended to provide reminders, not to take the place of proper lectures.

Just because you are allowed to move at your own pace does not mean that you should skip lectures and move directly to assignments. If you want to succeed in your online or emporium course, you must treat it exactly the same way you would a traditional course. This means that you must read the text and take copious, detailed notes.

With this in mind, online and Emporium courses require their own, unique note-taking system. Traditional classroom notes are mainly taken to help you complete your homework assignments. Online and Emporium notes are taken to help you review for online quizzes and tests. This means that it is more important than ever to remember every step to every type of problem.

Note-Taking Memory Cues and Steps

The first thing you should notice about this note-taking system is that it looks similar to the "Seven Steps to Math Note-Taking" system given in the previous unit. Any similarities between the two systems are all cosmetic. The memory cues and problems steps are much different in the Emporium system.

Using this system enhances your math learning as you complete new units in your software. It also provides you with a set of comprehensive study guides for quizzes and tests. Students can use this note-taking system in two different formats. Some students will use it while doing their homework. Other students will use their regular note-taking system and then transfer their notes into this system after class. I prefer that you use the first way because it will save you time in the long run; however, if you do not have access to the Internet at home, you may have to use the second system and rework your notes when you get back from class. If this is the case for you, you may want to print out or write down the problem steps you find through the "Help" and "Example" buttons in your software. This way you won't be at a disadvantage come test day.

When taking notes in an online or emporium model course, you should focus on any problem that you had to attempt two or three times. Also, focus on any problems on which you required help from your professor, lab assistant or online tutoring program.

Setting up Your Notebook Page

Before you take any notes, you first need to label the top of your notebook page with the homework section and problem numbers the notes refer to. Also, include the date on which

you are working on these problems. Once you've done this, complete the following steps:

1. *Label the top* space between the notebook ring and the red line, "Key Words."

2. *Label the other* side of the red line, "Examples."

3. *In the spot* to the right of "Examples," label a third section "Explanations/Rules."

4. *Draw vertical lines* on each side of the "Examples" section. By doing so, you are setting up three different columns.

5. *Record the same* information on the next 10 pages of your notebook. After using this system for 10 pages, you may not need to label each page.

Seven Steps to Taking Online or Emporium Notes

Once you have set up your page, follow the seven steps listed below:

Step One — Record a problem and each of its steps in the "Examples" section.

Step Two — Record the reasons for each step in the "Explanation/Rules" section by using abbreviations; short phrases, not sentences; keywords, properties, principles or formulas. If you do not know the explanations for a particular step, click on your "Help Me Solve This" or "Example" button. Condense this information in sentence(s) above and/or below the problem. If you do not understand the phrases you find in the help sections, click on the "Textbook Help" button and locate the definitions of any words you don't know. If you still have difficulty, click on the "Video" button or ask your instructor or tutor for help.

Step Three — Record key words and rules in the left two-inch margin either during or immediately after an online lecture by reworking your notes. If you are in the middle of an assignment, find these words at the right of each step in the "Help Me Solve" and "Examples" sections.

Step Four — Cover up the "Example and Explanation" sections and recite out loud the meaning of the key words or concepts.

Step Five — Place a check mark by the key words/concepts that you did not know.

Step Six — Review the information that you checked until it is understood.

Step Seven — Develop a math glossary for difficult-to-remember key words and concepts.

When you finish, your notes should look like the notecard printed on the next page. After practicing this system, you may want to modify it to write down only the explanations that you do not understand or feel you might forget. As mentioned earlier, some students wait to convert their notes into a three column system until after class. This is perfectly fine. The key is to organize the details in your notes into a system that connects problem steps with the reasons the steps are necessary.

The Importance of Emailing Your Professors

Students taking online courses especially need to develop and use this note-taking system. Online students do not have the luxury of taking notes while asking a tutor or instructor to help them solve the problems. Online students must depend more on "Help" and "Example" buttons. If these buttons don't help you understand how to solve a problem, you need to take notes from the support videos and textbook.

Taking all these notes may be time consuming; however, you need to put the information in your own words in order to better understand the concept.

The next logical question is, "What do I do if after taking the notes from various resources, I still don't understand how to solve the problem?"

The answer is very obvious but according to many online instructors most students don't do it. *Email your instructor and ask about how to solve difficult problems.* That is not to say that the instructors don't get emails from their students. The emails they do get are usually technical questions about accessing or operating online homework. Many math instructors wish the questions were about solving homework problems.

Emailing math instructors to help you solve homework problems is similar to using the listening skills we discussed earlier in this chapter. Don't email the instructor the problem just to indicate that you cannot do the problem; send the problem along with your attempted problem steps, and indicate where you got stuck. After the instructor helps you solve the problems, take notes on the steps.

Next, ask the instructor to guide you to online resources for solving similar problems. Check those resources to see if you did review them or if they are new resources.

If you email your instructor a question about a problem, you will probably make his or her day. Conversely, the Instructional Technology team at your college loves to answer technological problems. Direct to them any and all such inquires.

If you are in the Emporium model, don't be afraid to ask your instructor or tutor to help you with notes. Most students have difficulty filling in "Explanation" sections. Have the tutor or instructor explain the reasons for a problem's steps. Don't, however, write down their explanation. Rephrase the explanation into your own words, and ask them if this is what they meant. Then write down your explanation because you remember your own words better while taking tests. This translation helps transfer math concepts into long-term memory and abstract reasoning.

Emporium/Online Three Column Note-Taking Method

Key Words and Rules	Examples	Explanations
Words from the right side of problem	The problem	Sentences that describe the next step or sentences at the end of the problem
Solve a linear equation.	$5(x + 4) + 3(x - 4) = 2(x - 2)$	Get x on one side of the = sign and a number on the on the other side
Distributive Property	$5x + 20 + 3x - 12 = 2x - 4$	Use the distributive property: multiply number outside () by the variable and number
Add like terms	$8x + 8 = 2x - 4$	Add numbers and like variables
Additive Inverse	$8x - 2x + 8 = 2x - 2x - 4$	Get numbers on one side
Subtract like terms	$6x + 8 = - 4$	Get the variable on one side.
Additive Inverse	$6x + 8 - 8 = - 4 - 8$	Get the x on one side and the number on the other
Simplify	$6x = - 12$	Simplify the equation.
Multiplicative Inverse	$\dfrac{6x}{6} = \dfrac{- 12}{6}$	Divide by 6 to get x
Simplify	$x = -2$	Solution. Does it make sense?

Chapter 6 Summary

- Effective listening is the first step to excellent note-taking.

- The effective listener knows where to sit in the classroom (The Golden Triangle of Success) and practices good listening techniques.

- The goal of note-taking is to write the least amount possible to record the most information.

- This allows you to enhance your ability to listen to the lecture and increase your learning potential in the classroom.

- The Modified Three-Column Note-Taking Example is an excellent example to use for both taking notes and testing yourself on the information. Make sure you practice covering up the left side of the note page and recalling the information. Do not waste your time studying information you already know.

- Making a math glossary can especially help students with good language skills understand mathematics.

- Use the StudyStack website to develop your own virtual flash cards and review them any time you want by using your computer, cell phone, PDA or iPod.

- Rework your notes as soon as possible after class. When reworking your notes, make sure you complete your problem log; it will become very important when preparing for tests.

- If you wait too long to review your notes, you might not understand them and it will be more difficult to learn them.

- Reworking your notes will improve not only your understanding of math but also your grades in the course.

- Online and Emporium students need to use a special note-taking system that differs in many ways from traditional note-taking systems.

- When using an online and Emporium note-taking system, write down information from the "Help" and "Explanation" windows in your software.

- Don't be afraid to email your instructor for help sovling problems.

- When beginning an online or Emporium course, figure out exactly who you need to contact should you have any technical problems.

Name: _____   Date: _____

Assignment for Chapter 6

1. Review and use the Modified Three-Column Note-Taking figure as a model for your notes. List and define the key words that were discussed while using this system:

2. In the space below, describe the listening and questioning skills you need to communicate with your instructor when visiting his or her office:

3. Why do you need to copy down each step of the math homework?

4. List and define three ways a math glossary can improve math learning:

    Reason One:

    Reason Two:

    Reason Three:

5. What are three reasons to rework your notes?

    Reason One:

    Reason Two:

    Reason Three:

6. How can you encourage yourself to ask questions in classroom and online courses?

7. How does asking questions in math class decrease the time you will spend on homework?

8. Who is the classmate with whom you can compare math notes?

9. In the space below, describe the steps to emailing your instructor about the problem you are having difficulty with:

10. List and explain the Seven Steps to Math Note Taking. If you are taking an online or Emporium model class, list the Seven Steps to Taking Online Math Notes instead.

    1.

    2.

    3.

    4.

    5.

    6.

    7.

How to Improve Your Reading and Homework Techniques

7

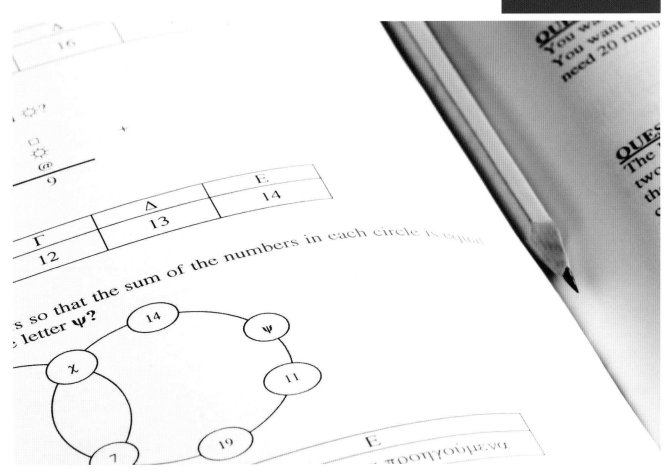

In Chapter 7
You will learn these concepts:

- ✓ How to effectively read your math texbook
- ✓ How to effectively complete math homework
- ✓ How to read an online math text
- ✓ How to complete online homework
- ✓ Ways to recall what you have learned
- ✓ How to study with other classmates

Math Textbooks and Homework

Knowing how to read a math textbook and complete homework is absolutely vital to succeeding in mathematics. Understanding and retaining material from your text makes it much more likely that you will follow lectures and succeed on tests. While this is true in all college courses, having the skill set to read and digest information from a text is more important in math than perhaps any other subject.

Unfortunately, many students struggle with math textbooks, which are far more technical and harder to follow than those used in other courses. Worse, because math instructors know how to read and learn from these books, they often assume that students are capable of figuring out how to solve math problems through assigned readings. The truth is, most students are never taught how to read a math text. This disconnect is at the heart of many students' struggles with the subject.

It is not enough to merely dive into a math textbook—you must develop a system. The same is also true of homework. Most math students do not have a homework system. They begin their homework by going directly to the problems and trying to work them. When they get stuck, they usually quit. This is not a good homework system. A good system improves success in homework. It also helps your overall understanding of math. Two key components to a good math study system deal with using the textbook as a resource of information and completing homework to learn math well enough to perform well during a timed test. This chapter helps you design such a system, which allows you to learn from your homework and to use the math textbook as an invaluable resource for information.

It's also worth noting that more and more math classes are either being taught online or through the Emporium model. These courses require students to read online textbooks and complete online homework problems. Reading online texts requires a new set of reading skills that most students don't have. In most cases, students don't read the online text or section of the text that is paired with the homework problems. They see no value in reading this material. Also most students start doing homework without a homework plan. After several tries, they may get a few problems correct, but they soon forget how exactly they got there.

In order to succeed in these course, you need to learn how to read online textbooks and complete online homework.

When to Read Your Textbook

Most students don't read math textbooks because in the past many math textbooks were poorly written. These books were difficult to understand, composed mostly of example problems, and written for instructors instead of students. Now, math textbooks are more student friendly and feature more support materials. When we discuss reading a math textbook, we are also focusing on the additional products that come with the textbook. This includes solution manuals, online texts, problem hints, support websites and tutor sites.

Math instructors and students often debate over the best time to read a math textbook. Some instructors prefer that students read the textbook before coming to class. Other instructors prefer students read the textbook after class. If students read their textbook before going to class, they become familiar with key vocabulary words and concepts. You don't need to understand every bit of material when you read your book before class. Yet, understanding even just a third of the material will free up your mind to understand more material during a lecture. For this reason, I recommend reading ahead two or three sections and putting question marks by material you don't understand. Make a list of the vocabulary words that will most likely appear in a lecture. When your instructor starts discussing the material, have your questions ready and take good notes. When they start discussing a topic you marked, pay special attention. If you do not understand your instructor's explanation, you MUST ask questions. If there is not enough time for questions, make an appointment with your instructor to go over the material. Reading the text before a lecture helps you better understand it and know when to ask questions.

Reading the textbook after a lecture also has its benefits. This method reinforces the material learned in class and further explains misunderstood information. Instructors who believe in this format think they can explain mathematical concepts better than the textbook or don't want you to get confused by its explanations. Reading the textbook after a lecture helps students to remember notes taken during class. The textbook also explains mathematical concepts in different, more understandable ways. In addition, the textbook might cover material that was not discussed in the lecture that will help clarify a concept.

Reading a mathematics textbook before or after the lecture may depend on how well the book is written. It also depends on your cognitive learning style. Try both ways and see which one works best.

How to Read the Syllabus

As you probably already know, a course's syllabus tells you what to expect from a class and when you should complete assignments. You need to read and study the syllabus. The syllabus often contains a course title, course number, the instructor's name, reading assignments, dates to complete chapter sections, which homework problems to complete, absence policy, drop dates, withdraw dates, test dates, a test make-up policy, a grading scale and how the course is graded. Students need to use this valuable information to their advantage.

Some students know how to use the syllabus to their advantage, checking it before and after every class period. I have worked with hundreds of students who after adding two or three classes figured out they were in the wrong math course after examining the syllabus. The course level was too high for them and, based on the syllabus, they dropped down to the next math level during the first week without penalty.

Other students come to me while failing a course, knowing the date they can still get a W (withdraw) without getting an F. They usually take the W, and we start to prepare to take the course again the next semester. Some students who know the test dates, make sure they are off from work the day before the test to allow for more study time. In addition, many students, knowing the grading system for their particular course, figure out what their overall grade is in the class after each test. They use this information to adjust their schedule for reading the text and doing their homework. Knowing, understanding and using the syllabus to your advantage can help in your learning and also improve your math grades.

I have some students that come to me who do not understand the syllabus and figure it out too late to use it to their advantage. For example, a student came to me during the last two weeks of a semester wanting to withdraw from a math course. I asked her if she was failing the course and she said no. The student said that she was in the wrong course because she took this course two years ago and made a B. She learned about being in the wrong course when being "blocked" from registering for the next course. I asked her if she reviewed her course syllabus to make sure she was in the correct course. She indicated that she never read the syllabus.

Another student came to me in the last part of a semester indicating he was failing the course and wanted to withdraw. Receiving an F in the course would eliminate his financial aid next semester. I asked him if he read the syllabus to see when that last day to drop the course with a W (instead of an F) was. He said no. He did not have his syllabus, and I informed him that it was the previous week.

A third student indicated that his instructor was not fair to him because she would not let him make up a missed test. He indicated that he made up one missed test before. I asked the student about the instructor's test make up policy on the syllabus. The student indicated that he did not know what it was and had lost his syllabus. We found out that the instructor had a "one make-up test" policy and then there were no more make-ups. The student then admitted that he volunteered to work overtime instead of taking the test, and that if he had known about the policy he wouldn't have come to that decision. Make sure you understand the syllabus to avoid these problems.

The Importance of Distance Learning Syllabi

Students taking distance learning courses MUST know and understand the syllabus. If you are in a distance learning course, the syllabus is your BOSS.

The syllabus for distance learning courses is very important and will tell you what to do and when it should be done. You MUST read and study the syllabus. It should be a week-by-week description of the course. The syllabus should be lengthy and in great detail. If possible, read the syllabus before you sign up for the course. Ask the department secretary or instructor if the syllabus is online or if they can fax or email it to you. Looking at the syllabus will give you an idea on how the course is designed and if the instructor is experienced in teaching distance-learning courses. Read it thoroughly because the instructor is not there to tell you the important parts, and you do not want any surprises. Highlight the important dates of assignments, tests, and projects. If the course does not have a syllabus, or if it is a very short syllabus, then consider not taking the course. It is a warning sign that the instructor might be relatively new to the learning environment or not detailed in presentation of material.

The first section on the syllabus to look at is the computer and software requirements: minimum computer speed, RAM, email, software and internet connection. Even if you meet the minimum requirements, it may take a long time to download the files and send them. If you don't meet the minimum requirement, obtain another computer or don't take the course. I know several students who learned this lesson the hard way. They signed up for their distance-learning class, and when downloading the files, their computers crashed. Look at the course requirement and the grading system. You must completely understand what you are expected to learn and how you will be graded. You need to know how the text will be used. In some cases your grades will come from tests, papers and outside projects. You need to know what percent each one will count and when they are due. Write down these dates and put them where you can easily refer to them. Just like in regular classes, instructors expect papers to be emailed on time and tests taken at the correct time.

Remember: The importance of a course syllabus cannot be overstated. If you keep the document handy, nothing—not a test, nor an assignment—will surprise you. Make sure to store your syllabus in a safe, easy-to-remember place. Always refer to it before approaching your professor with questions about the course's schedule or due dates. Many professors make their syllabi as detailed as possible so that they don't have to answer the same quesitons over and over again.

How Math Textbooks are Different

As mentioned in previous chapters, reading a math textbook is more difficult than reading other textbooks. They are written differently than English or social science textbooks. Math textbooks contain condensed material, which takes longer to read. Mathematicians can reduce a page of writing to one paragraph, using math formulas and symbols. To make sure you understand that same information, an English instructor might take that original page of writing and expand it into two pages. Mathematicians pride themselves on how little they can write and still cover a concept. This is one reason why it may take two to three times as long to read a math book as it might any other book.

The way you read a math textbook is different from the traditional way you are taught to read textbooks in high school or college. Students are taught to read quickly or skim the material.

If you do not understand a word, you are supposed to keep on reading. Instructors of other courses want students to continue to read so they can pick up the unknown words and their meanings from context. This reading technique may work with your other classes, but using it in your math course often causes confusion. By skipping major concept words or bold-print words, you will not understand what you are reading and therefore will not be able to do your homework. Reading a math textbook takes more time and concentration than reading your other textbooks.

If you have a reading problem, it is wise to take a developmental reading course before taking math. This is especially true with math reform delivery, where reading and writing are more emphasized. Reform math classes deal more with word problems than do traditional math courses.

If you cannot take a developmental reading course before taking math, then take it during the same semester as your math course.

Now that you know the importance of reading the math text or online text, the next step is to review the method you currently use to read your textbook. To start the evaluation, complete activity 7.1.

Activity 7.1 How do you approach your math text?

This short self-assessment will help you understand how you approach reading the math text. Most students don't read the text because they believe it doesn't help them. Even some students who read the text don't do it effectively. By completing this questionnaire and comparing your answers to the methods given in upcoming sections, you will know exactly what you are doing right and exactly what you are doing wrong.

1. Check the appropriate area that best describes your usual textbook reading tactics.

    When reading my textbook:

    _____ I read the entire selection.

    _____ I skim the contents and move right on to the problems.

    _____ I only read the part that pertains to my homework.

    _____ I don't bother reading the text at all.

    Does reading the math text help improve your math learning?

    _____ Yes

    _____ A little

    _____ Not at all

    _____ This question doesn't apply to me. I don't read my textbooks.

2. If reading the textbook does not help you, then explain why in the empty space below:

3. In the space below, explain how you typically approach reading your textbook:

10 Steps to Better Understand What You Read

Before practicing the Ten Steps to Understanding Reading Materials, you need to get to know your textbook. Each textbook has its own organizational pattern for presenting information. It is important to understand how the book works.

- Are there learning objectives at the beginning of the chapter that can be used as a checklist to make sure you are learning everything important?

- How are the vocabulary words highlighted? Are they just bold print? Are they in highlighted boxes?

- How are the mathematical rules highlighted?

- Does each section of the chapter have learning objectives?

- Are the homework problems at the end of the chapter arranged according to the chapter sections?

If you can't figure out how your textbook is organized, go to your instructor or a learning center to receive assistance in "figuring the book out." Once you understand how to use your book, then take the following steps and adapt them in a way that they work for you.

There are several appropriate steps in reading a math textbook:

Step One — *Skim the assigned reading material in order to get a general idea of what the chapter is about.* Skimming is an excellent skill to develop. First, it is an excellent way to get familiar with what will be covered in the next class. Second, as you sit down to study your math after the lecture, it helps you to see how all the "pieces of the puzzle" fit together. Third, after you have learned the material, it is a good strategy to use as a quick ten-minute review so that you do not forget what you learned.

Here are the steps I suggest:

- Read the chapter introduction and/ or learning objectives and each section summary and/or learning objectives. As you read, try to see the connections between each section. Remember, when you skim, do not try to learn the material; you simply want to get an overview of the assignment.

- As you skim, think about similar math topics that you already know. What do you already know about the chapter objectives?

- As you skim the chapter, circle (using pencil) new words that you do not understand. You can also skim after learning the material, pretending you are a tutor explaining how each objective connects with one another. You can even explain in your own words what each vocabulary word means as if you were tutoring. This skimming also helps you remember what you have spent so much time learning.

Step Two — *While reading the textbook, highlight the material that is important to you.* However, do not highlight more than 50 percent of a page because the material is not being narrowed down enough for future study. If you are reading the textbook after the lecture, highlight the material that was discussed in the class. Material discussed both in the textbook and lecture usually appears on the test. The purpose for highlighting is to emphasize the important material for future study.

Step Three — *When you get to the examples, go through each step.* If the example skips any steps, make sure you write down each one of those skipped steps in the textbook for better understanding. Later on, when you go back and review, the steps are already filled in. You will understand how each step was completed. Also, by filling in the extra steps, you are starting to over-learn the material for better recall on future tests.

Step Four — *Revise your marks and highlights.* Maybe you marked them the first time while skimming. If you understand them now, erase the marks. If you do not understand the words or concepts, then reread the page or look them up in the glossary. Try not to read any further until you understand all the words and concepts.

Step Five — *Take notes from your math textbook on principles, properties and rules.* Taking meaningful notes after reading a math textbook helps students remember what they have read. These notes also serve as a review sheet for preparing for a test. This note-taking system is different from taking notes in the classroom. These notes become a quicker resource for information while completing homework and are beneficial in learning math vocabulary. The steps are as follows:

- Before reading the math book, label the top of your notebook page with the chapter and section numbers. For example, at the top of the note page put Chapter 2.3 to 2.6.

- Divide the page into three columns. Label the left one "Terms," the middle one "Examples" and the third one "Definitions and Explanations."

- As you read about principles, properties or rules, write down their names, define them, give one or two examples and explain the process.

Terms	Example	Definitions/Explanation
Multiplication principle	$1/3x = -15$ $3(1/3x) = 3(-15)$ $x = -45$	Def. = for real numbers a, b, c, with c not = to 0, if a=b then ca=cb Multiply each side of the equation by 3 (this isolates the x). Multiply the other side by 3.

Step Five — *Learn math vocabulary words.* If you do not clearly understand some words, add these words to the note-taking glossary in the back of your notebook. Your glossary will contain the bold print words that you do not understand. You should have the book definition and the definition in your own words. If you have difficulty understanding the bold-print words, ask the instructor for a better explanation. You should know all the words and concepts in your notebook glossary before taking the test.

Step Seven — *If you do not understand the material, follow these eight points, one after the other, until you are comfortable with the information.*

1. Go back to the previous page and reread the information to maintain a train of thought. Make sure you have learned the previous information correctly.

2. Read ahead to the next page to discover

if any additional information better explains the misunderstood material.

3. Locate and review any diagrams, examples or rules that explain the misunderstood material.

4. Read the misunderstood paragraph(s) several times aloud to better understand its meaning.

5. Refer to your math notes for a better explanation of the misunderstood material.

6. Refer to another math textbook, computer software program or DVD that expands the explanation of the misunderstood material.

7. Define exactly what you do not understand and call your study buddy for help.

8. Contact your math tutor or math instructor for help in understanding the material.

Step Eight — *Reflect on what you have read.* Combine what you already know with the new information that you just read. Think about how this new information enhances your math knowledge. Prepare questions for your instructor on the confusing information. Ask those questions at the next class meeting.

Step Nine — *Review your math textbook notes and math glossary several times a week.* Anytime you have a spare five to ten minutes, review your notes or vocabulary words. These short periods of time allow you to study in little chunks and become confident in your understanding of the material. Try reviewing before the math lecture starts, between classes, or at lunch. Over a period of several weeks you will be amazed at how much you can learn. This process can ensure that you know the information before taking a test.

Step Ten — *Write anticipated test questions.* Research has noted that students have about 80 percent accuracy in predicting test questions. Think about what is the most important concept you just read and what

problems the instructor could give you that would test the knowledge of that concept. Make up four or five problems and add them to your problem log (this was part of your note-taking system). Indicate that these questions are from reading the textbook. Review the questions and answers before taking the next test. By using this reading technique, you have:

- Narrowed down the important material to be learned,

- Skimmed the textbook to get an overview of the assignment

- Carefully read the material and highlighted the important parts,

- Recorded important information into a three column note-taking system, and,

- Added to your note-taking glossary unknown words or concepts.

Now that you understand the benefits of reading your textbook, you need to decide when to schedule time to read the text and how not to procrastinate. As mentioned earlier, it is best to read the text before doing your homework. Look at your study schedule and see when you have scheduled your homework time. Do you have time to read the textbook before that time, or do you want to include reading your textbook as part of your homework time?

When I ask students for the reasons they do not read the text, many tell me that they simply had other things to do. In almost every case, these other things were not that important. When we discuss this issue, students usually admit they do not like reading the text, and they use distractions as an excuse to get out of it. In most cases, these students claim that they have read their math texts in the past, and it did not help them learn how to complete problems. What these students don't realize, is that the only reason they experience ineffective study sessions is that they've never been taught how to correctly read a math text.

If you want to pass your math course, this is an absolutely vital skill.

How to Read an Online Textbook

Reading an online textbook differs a great deal from reading a traditional textbook. The objectives are the same—you still want to have a better understanding of math and eventually transfer information into your long-term memory—but because online texts come in many different formats, these books require much more preparation before reading.

Before reading an online text, you need to become familiar with how the e-book is formatted. Each online text or e-book has its own organizational pattern for presenting information and resources. It is important to understand how the book works. Before reading, you must ask yourself a series of questions.

- Are there learning objectives at the beginning of the chapter or chapter sections that can be used as a checklist?

- How are the vocabulary words highlighted? Are they bold print?

- Are they in highlighted boxes?

- Can you electronically highlight the text?

- Can you mark a page and come back to it?

- How are the mathematical rules highlighted?

- Does the chapter have a vocabulary check that can become your glossary?

- Does the chapter have highlights or review sections with definitions and concepts?

- Are there additional resources to support chapter readings?

If you have difficulty understanding how to use an online textbook, then go to your instructor, learning center or math lab to receive assistance. Understanding how to use the text improves your ability to learn math.

Some students do not read their textbook until they have difficulty solving homework problems. Even though this is not a good strategy, I realize that this is a reality for many students. For this reason, after going through the steps for reading an online text, I will present a strategy for how to read a section of the text that pertains only to a particular homework problem you are trying to solve.

With that out of the way, it is time to get on to the specific steps you need to follow to read on online text. Note that many of these steps are similar to those given in the previous section for traditional textbooks. These steps, however, take into account the technological aspects that make reading an e-book unique.

The following 10 steps are designed to help you read and digest information from textbooks presented on computer screens, tablets, or other mobile devices.

Step One — *Click or swipe through the assigned reading material or section(s) pertaining to the homework.* This is a good idea for many reasons. First, doing so gives you a general idea of the material covered in a given section and thereby gives you a leg up on your homework. Second, this gives you a good idea where to turn when you get stuck on a particular homework problem. Third, it makes it easier to review information before taking quizzes or tests.

To skim effectively, stick to the following pattern:

1. Read the chapter introduction or first page of the section.

2. In the chapter introduction, review the learning objectives. As you read, try to see the connections between each section. Remember, when you skim, do not try to learn the material; you simply want to get an overview of the assignment. If you are reviewing a section just read the first page.

3. As you skim the section(s), highlight new words you do not understand. If you are reading on a tablet, many applications allow you to drag your finger over a particular word or line. Doing so brings up a menu, which usually gives you the option to highlight. The e-book keeps track of these highlights — usually in a folder or submenu — and allows you to return to them at any time. If you are on a computer, look for similar options, or write down the vocabulary words in your notebook. This is also a good time to go to the end of the chapter and review vocabulary words and chapter highlights. To skim the section(s) click through the pages to see what will be presented and the type of problems at the end of the section.

Step Two — *Read with concentration.* Now it is time to highlight specific material within a text — not just vocabulary words, but key concepts and formulas. Remember, the purpose for highlighting is to emphasize the important material for future study and review. Click through the pages and use the electronic highlighting method mentioned before to mark important material. Do not, however, highlight more than 50 percent of a page. This does not allow you to narrow information down enough for future study.

If you are reading a section after watching a video, highlight the material discussed on the video. Material discussed both in the textbook and during a video usually appears on tests.

Step Three — *Take notes from your math chapter section.* For every example, review each step even if you know the steps. If the example skips any steps, mentally tell yourself the step. If you don't know the step ask for help. You will now understand how each step was completed. By mentally going through these steps you are preparing for your homework and are starting to over learn the material for better recall on tests.

Step Four — *Revise your marks and highlights.* Maybe you already marked them while skimming. If you understand them now, remove the highlight. If you do not understand the words or concepts, then reread the page or see if they are in the vocabulary check or chapter highlight. If the vocabulary or words are not there, go to www.mathwords.com or knot.org/glossary/atop.shtml, which are math vocabulary websites. Try not to read any further until you understand all the words and concepts.

Step Five — *Take notes from the text.* The notes should only be on the principles, properties, rules and concepts. Taking meaningful notes, either during or after reading the math textbook, helps students remember what they have read. These notes also serve as a review sheet while preparing for a test. This note-taking system is different from taking notes in the classroom. These notes are a quick resource for information while completing homework and are beneficial in learning math vocabulary.

The steps are as follows:

- Before reading your online math book, label the top of your notebook page with the chapter and section numbers. For example, at the top of the page write "Chapter 1.1 – 1.3."

- Divide the page into three columns. Label the left one "Terms," the middle one "Examples" and the third one "Definitions/Explanations."

- As you read, or after you read, write down the principles, properties rules or concepts that you do not know, writing the term, example and definition/ explanation. If your text has a vocabulary check or chapter highlights section, use that information to fill in the columns. Refer to Chapter 6 for more information.

Step Six — *Develop a Math Glossary.*
Math is a foreign language, and you need to understand its vocabulary. Review the math vocabulary from your notes, and if you do not clearly understand some words, add these words to the note-taking glossary in the back of your notebook. The back of your notebook should be labeled by chapter and section with a list of these vocabulary words. Your glossary can contain the bold print words that you do not understand. You should have the book definition and the definition in your own words.

If you have difficulty understanding the bold-print words, ask your instructor or tutor for a better explanation. You need to know all the words and concepts in your notebook glossary before taking a test. These vocabulary words should be reviewed every week until the final exam.

Step Seven — *Develop a strategy for understanding difficult material.* If you did not understand the material follow these suggestions to improve learning:

1. Click or swipe back to the previous page and reread the information to maintain a train of thought. Make sure you have learned the previous information correctly.

2. Click or swip ahead to the next page to discover if any additional information better explains the misunderstood material.

3. Locate and review any diagrams, examples or rules that explain the misunderstood material.

4. Read the misunderstood paragraph(s) several times aloud to better understand its meaning.

5. Replay any math videos pertaining to a confusing section.

6. Refer to another math textbook, computer software program or DVD that expands the explanation of the misunderstood material. This includes YouTube videos or other online resources.

7. Define exactly what you do not understand and either call, e-mail or write a Facebook message to your study buddy for help.

8. Contact your math tutor or math instructor for help in understanding the material.

Step Eight — *Reflect on what you have just read.* Combine what you already know with the new information that you just read. Thinking about how this new information enhances your math knowledge.

Prepare questions to email your instructor about the confusing information. If your class is an Emporium Model course ask those questions at the next class meeting. It is important that you understand what you've read before moving on.

Step Nine — *Review your math notes and math glossary.* This review should occur every week. When you have a spare five to 10 minutes, review your notes or vocabulary words. These short reviews allow you to study in little chunks and become confident in your math understanding. Try reviewing before you start your math homework. Over a period of several weeks you will learn a lot. This process ensures that you know more math material before taking the test.

Step Ten — *Write anticipated test questions.* Research has noted that students have about 80 percent accuracy in predicting test questions. Think about what is the most important concept you just read and how those concepts could be turned into test questions.

Make up four or five problems and add them to your problem log (this was part of your note-taking system). Indicate that these questions are from reading the textbook. Review the questions and answers before taking the next test.

How to Read a Single Online Chapter Section

Reading a section of an online text involves a condensed version of the steps listed above. In most cases you are reading this section of the chapter because you are having difficulty answering specific homework problems. With this in mind, the purpose of reading this section is mainly to answer the homework problems and prepare for quizzes or tests.

Below are the steps for reading a section of an online textbook or e-book. Adapt these steps that will work best for you.

Step One — *Concentrate on important information as you read the section.* Click or swipe through the pages and use the electronic highlighter to mark the information relating to the probllem. If you understand very little information, you should review the video and then reread the section.

Step Two — *Go through examples similar to your problem.* For those examples, review each step and compare those steps that are related to your problem. Write the problem steps next to your problem steps for comparison. Going through example problem steps helps you solve your problem.

If you do not understand words or concepts in your problem, review your book's vocabulary or chapter highlight sections. If the vocabulary or words are not there, go to www.mathwords.com or knot.org/glossary/atop.shtml, which are math vocabulary websites.

Step Three — *Take notes from your math chapter section.* The notes should be related to the principles, properties, rules and concepts of the problem you don't understand. Take the notes the same way as mentioned in the previous section and expand the "Terms" section to include vocabualry words. These notes can be used to help you solve this problem or similar problems or review for quizzes or tests. Now you have math notes and a glossary system.

Step Four — *Find additional resources.* If you did not understand the material, seek out YouTube videos or other math-based websites that contain information specific to your problems.

Step Five — *Review your math notes.* This review should occur every week. Review your math notes before reading the next section or homework. This process will help you to become more successful in reading the sections and problem solving.

By using this technique you can:

- Better understand the math textbook sections,

- Answer homework problems,

- Prepare for quizzes and tests,

- and recall information on your quiz or test day.

Activity 7.2   Establishing Study Period Goals

Before beginning your homework, it is important to establish goals for the study period. Do not just grab a coke and chips, sit down and turn to the homework problems. Ask yourself this question, "What am I going to do tonight to become more successful in math?" By setting up short-term homework goals and reaching them, you will feel more confident about math. This also improves your self-esteem and helps you become a more internally motivated student.

Study-period goals are set up either on a time-line basis or an item-line basis. Studying on a time-line basis is studying math for a certain amount of time. Studying by item-line basis means you will study your math until you have completed a certain number of homework problems.

No matter what homework system you use, remember this important rule: Always finish a homework session by understanding a concept or doing a homework problem correctly. Do not end a homework session with a problem you cannot complete. You will lose confidence since all you will think about is the last problem you could not solve instead of the 50 problems you correctly solved. If you did quit on a problem you could not solve, return and rework problems you have done correctly.

In the space below, set up a few example homework tasks. Be sure to set goals that you can complete. Be realistic.

Goal 1:

Goal 2:

Goal 3:

Goal 4:

$$x^2 - 7x + 10 = 0$$
$$(x - 2)(x - 5) = 0$$
$$x - 2 = 0 \quad \lor \quad x - 5 = 0$$
$$x = 2 \quad \lor \quad x = 5$$

Math Homework Techniques

Why do math instructors assign homework? That is a good question. I have asked this question to students, math instructors and math department chairs. Some of them knew the answer, but I was surprised when some of them, including the instructors, did not know the answer. Again, let me ask you the question, "Why do instructors assign math homework?"

Yes, you are correct. Homework is given not just to waste time but to have you practice the math problems often enough to understand the mathematical concept that can be put into your abstract reasoning or long-term memory. In other words, you do math homework to remember how to do the problems during the test. However, just memorizing how to do the problems will create difficulty recalling how to do them on the test.

Doing your homework is an excellent time to practice doing problems as if on a test and to understand the mathematical concepts. Completing homework needs to be a learning experience.

Now that you know the reasons to do your homework, I have another question. "Has anyone taught you the best way to do your homework?" Probably not. The next section will answer that question.

Doing your homework can be frustrating or rewarding. Most students jump right into their homework, become frustrated and stop studying. These students usually go directly to the math problems and start working them without any preparation. When they get stuck on one problem, they flip to the back of the textbook for the answer. Then, they either try to work the problem backwards to understand the problem steps, or they just copy down the answer.

Other students go to the solution guide and just copy the steps. After getting stuck several times, these students will inevitably quit doing their homework assignment. Their homework becomes a frustrating experience, and they may even quit doing their math homework altogether.

Now that you know how some students do their homework, the next step is reviewing how you do your own homework.

To start the evaluation, complete Activity 7.3 (located on the facing page).

Activity 7.3 Math Homework Assessment

This short self-assessment will help you understand how you approach your homework. Many students don't do all their homework because they believe doing every problem doesn't help them. Even students who do all the homework sometimes don't do it effectively.

1. Check the appropriate area that best describes your usual homework tactics.

    When doing homework:

    _____   I complete the entire assignment.

    _____   I finish some of the assignment.

    _____   Honestly, I don't really do my math homework.

    Does reading the math text help improve your math learning?

    _____   Yes

    _____   A little

    _____   Not at all

    _____   This question doesn't apply to me. I don't do my math homework.

2. If doing your math homework does not help you learn math, then explain why in the empty space below.

3. In the space below, explain how you typically approach doing your math homework:

10 Steps to Doing Your Math Homework

The following 10 steps are designed to help you complete traditional homework assignments from printed textbooks. If you are in an online class, go ahead and turn to the next section, "10 Steps to Doing Your Online or Emporium Math Homework."

Step One — *Review the textbook material that relates to the homework.* You can also use your glossary and textbook notes in your notebook. A proper review will increase the chances of successfully completing your homework. If you get stuck on a problem, you will have a better chance of remembering the location of similar problems. If you do not review prior to doing your homework, you could get stuck and not know where to find help in the textbook.

Step Two — *Review your lecture notes that relate to your homework.* If you could not understand the explanation in the textbook on how to complete the homework assignment, then review your class notes.

Step Three — *Do your homework as neatly as possible.* Doing your homework — organized and neatly — has several benefits. When approaching your instructor about problems with your homework, he or she will

be able to understand your previous attempts to solve the problem. The instructor will easily locate the mistakes and show you how to correct the steps without having to decipher your handwriting. Another benefit is that, when you review for midterm or final exams, you can quickly relearn the homework material without having to decipher your own writing.

Example: Problem: 2 (a + 5) = 0. What property allows you to write the equation as 2a + 10 = 0? Answer: The distributive property.

Step Four — *Write down every step of every problem.* Even if you can do the step in your head, write it down anyway. This will increase the amount of homework time, but you are over-learning how to solve problems, which improves your memory. Doing every step is an easy way to memorize and understand the material. Another advantage is that when you rework the problems you did wrong, it is easy to review each step to find the mistake.

Step Five — *Understand the reasons for each step and check your answers.* Do not get into the bad habit of memorizing how to do problems without knowing the reasons for each step. Many students are smart enough to memorize procedures required to complete a set of homework problems. However, when slightly different problems are presented on a test, they cannot solve the problems. To avoid this dilemma, keep reminding yourself about the rules, laws, or properties used to solve problems. A good idea is to write each name of the rule, law or property by several of the homework problems. Then, the homework becomes a test review.

Example: Solve this equation:
6x + 5 = 4x + 1.

The answer is x = -2.

Now put this back into the equation:
 6 (-2) + 5 = 4 (-2) + 1

Reduces to -12 + 5 = -7, which is -7 = -7.

If one side of the equation equals the other, you have the correct answer. If not rework the problem.

Once you know the correct reason for going from one step to another in solving a math problem, you can answer any problem requiring that property.

Checking your homework answers should be a part of your homework process because it improves your learning and helps you prepare for tests. Check the answers of the problems for which you do not have the solutions. This may be the even-numbered or odd-numbered problems or the problems not answered in the solutions manual. You can also check your answers by substituting the answer back into the equation or doing the opposite function required to answer the question.

Step Six — *If you do not understand how to do a problem, refer to these points:*

1. Review the textbook material that re-lates to the problem.

2. Review the lecture notes that relate to the problem.

3. Review any similar problems, diagrams, examples or rules that explain the misunderstood material.

4. Refer to another math textbook, solutions guide, math computer program software or videotape to obtain a better understanding of the material.

5. Call your study buddy.

6. Skip the problem and contact your tutor or math instructor as soon as possible for help.

Step Seven — *Always finish your homework by successfully completing problems.* Even if you get stuck, go back and successfully complete previous problems before quitting. You want to end your homework assignment with feelings of success.

Step Eight — *After finishing your homework assignment, recall to yourself or write down the most important learned concepts.* Recalling this information will increase your ability to learn these new concepts. This information can be placed in your textbook notes, glossary, or lecture notes, whichever you choose.

Step Nine — *Make up notecards containing hard-to-remember problems or concepts.* Notecards are an excellent way to review material for a test. More information on the use of notecards as learning tools is presented later in this chapter.

Step Ten — *Getting behind in math homework is academic suicide.* As mentioned in Chapter 1, math is a sequential learning process. If you get behind, it is difficult to catch up because each topic builds on the next. It would be like going to Spanish class without learning the last set of vocabulary words. The teacher would be talking to you using the new vocabulary, but you would not understand what was being said.

Do Not Fall Behind and Watch Out for Shortcuts!

To keep up with your homework, it is necessary to complete the homework every schoolday and even on weekends. Doing your homework one-half hour each day for two days in a row is better than one hour every other day. If you have to get behind in one of your courses, make sure it is not math. After using the 10 Steps to Doing Your Homework, you may be able to combine two steps into one. Find your best combination of homework steps and use them. Before moving on, take a breath. This study process seems very involved. However, if you adapt this process to work for you, this is what could happen:

- You will actually learn the math. This will help not only immediately but also in your future math courses.

- You will work with the math so much that it will land in your long-term memory, and you will not have to cram the night before the test.

- Imagine knowing how to do everything on the test the night before. Very little stress. A good night's sleep.

Watch Out for Shortcuts

When doing your math homework, you may get help from a friend or tutor. This friend or tutor wants to help you and should show you every step in working the problem. However, if you ever hear the statement "Let me show you a shortcut to solving this problem," BEWARE! Many students have told me that they were shown shortcuts to working problems and followed the steps. However, later on, they could not use the shortcuts to solve homework problems or test problems. Learning shortcuts can lead to over confidence and poorer grades. Some major problems with shortcuts are:

1. Shortcuts may require math knowledge above your math level.

2. Shortcuts may not be able to be used on similar problems.

3. Instructors may not want the shortcuts used on a test.

4. Shortcuts may not have a reference in the text to "fall back on."

5. Shortcuts are usually shown once and not remembered.

6. Shortcuts may be used by tutors or friends because they do not know how to work the problem step-by-step, and neither will you.

Not all shortcuts are bad, but you need to know the reasoning behind a shortcut. If a friend or tutor wants to show you a shortcut for solving a math problem, ask them for the rules or properties that support the shortcut. Once you understand the rule or property you can then apply the shortcut. Shortcuts are not bad when you understand the reasons behind them.

How to Solve Word Problems

The most difficult homework assignment for most math students is working story/word problems. Solving word problems is like solving a mini-mystery. It requires excellent reading comprehension and translating skills. Students often have difficulty substituting English terms for algebraic symbols and equations, but once an equation is written, it is usually easy to solve. To help you solve word problems follow these 10 steps:

Step One — *Read the problem three times.* Read the problem quickly the first time as a scanning procedure. As you are reading the problem the second time, answer these three questions:

1. What is the problem asking me? (Usually at the end of the problem.)
2. What is the problem telling me that is useful? (Cross out unnecessary information).
3. What is the problem implying? (Usually something you have been told to remember).

Read the problem a third time to check that you fully understand its meaning.

Step Two — *Draw a simple picture of the problem to make it more real to you.* (e.g., a circle with an arrow can represent travel in any form — by train, by boat, by plane, by car, or by foot).

Step Three — *Make a table of information and leave a blank space for the information you are not told.*

Step Four — *Use as few unknowns in your table as possible.* If you can represent all the unknown information in terms of a single

letter, do so! When using more than one unknown, use a letter that reminds you of that unknown. Then write down what your unknowns represent. This eliminates the problem of assigning the right answer to the wrong unknown. Remember you have to create as many separate equations as you have unknowns.

Step Five — *Translate the English terms into an algebraic equation.* To do this, use the list of terms in the Translating English Terms into Algebraic Symbols and Translating English Words into Algebraic Expressions figures on the next page.

Step Six — *Immediately retranslate the equation, as you now have it, back into English.* The translation will not sound like a normal English phrase, but the meaning should be the same as the original problem. If the meaning is not the same, the equation is incorrect and needs to be rewritten. Rewrite the equation until it means the same as the English phrase.

Step Seven—*Review the equation to see if it is similar to equations from your homework and if it makes sense.* Some formulas dealing with specific word problems may need to be rewritten. Distance problems, for example, may need to be written solving for each of the other variables in the formula. Distance = Rate x Time; therefore, Time = Distance/Rate, and Rate = Distance/Time. Usually, a distance problem will identify the specific variable to be solved.

Step Eight—*Solve the equation using the rules of algebra.* Remember, whatever is done to one side of the equation must be done to the other side of the equation. The unknown must end up on one side of the equation, by itself. If you have more than one unknown, then use the substitution or elimination method to solve the system of equations.

Step Nine—*Look at your answer to see if it makes common sense.* This is more important than you might think. If something seems wrong, it usually is. If your answer is way off the mark, you'll usually know it.

Step Ten—*Put your answer back into the original equation to see if it is correct.* If one side of the equation equals the other side of the equation, then you have the correct answer. If you do not have the correct answer, go back to Step 5.

The most difficult part of solving word problems is translating part of a sentence into algebraic symbols and then into algebraic expressions. To better understand the unique language of word problems, read over the chart in the right-hand column of this page. You'll notice that many different words are used to suggest the very same function.

Memorize this list, choose a set of homework problems from your text and practice translating the words into algebraic symbols and expressions.

Translating English Terms into Algebraic Symbols

Sum	+
In addition	+
More than	+
Increased	+
In excess	+
Greater	+
Decreased by	-
Less than	-
Difference	-
Diminished	-
Reduce	-
Remainder	-
Times as much	x
Percent of	x
Product	x
Interest on	x
Per	/
Divide	/
Quotient	/
Quantity	( )
Is	=
Was	=
Will be	=
Results	=
Greater than	>
Greater than or equal to	$\geq$
Less than	<
Less than or equal to	$\leq$

Examples of Algebraic Expressions

Ten more than x	$10 + x$
A number increased by 13	$x + 13$
A number decreased by 7	$x - 7$
Difference between 3 and x	$3 - x$
Ten percent of x	$10x$
Quotient of x and 3	$3/x$
Five times the difference of a number and 4	$5 (x - 4)$
Ten subtracted from 10 times a number is that number plus 5	$10x - 10$ $= x + 5$

Using Metacognitive Techniques

Metacognition was discussed in the Understanding and Improving the Memory Process chapter and can be applied to textbook and online homework. It is what students are thinking about when solving math problems. This is a self-monitoring process used to develop problem solving steps to find the solution to the problem. Memorization of problem steps instead of understanding the rules and principles to solve the problems leads to passive learning and unsuccessful problem solving. You need a model to follow when solving math problems.

The model of plan, monitor and evaluate is the framework for solving math problems. This model involves asking yourself questions when solving problems. Planning consists of understanding what the problem wants, the strategies to solve the problem, potential obstacles, understanding what information is required, doing the calculations and predicting the outcome. Monitoring is putting the steps in order, keeping one's place, identifying and finding errors, understanding when additional information is needed, knowing when to use another strategy and knowing when you have part of the answer. Evaluating includes knowing if the answer seems right (number sense), putting the answer back into the equation or doing the opposite of the function to see if the answer is correct and measuring the efficiency of the plan and monitoring.

Now that we know the theory about metacognition, let's apply it to solving some math problems. Let's look at the process for solving linear equations.

Solve: $-3(x-6) + 2 = 2(4x-1)$

The first step is making a plan by asking yourself questions about solving linear equations. Some example questions to solve this equation are:

1. Question: What is a linear equation?

Answer: It must have at least one variable and some numerals or variables and an = sign but no exponents greater than one.

Example: $-3(x-6) + 2 = 2(4x-1)$

2. Question: Are there any ( ) ?

Answer: Yes. Then multiply the number or variable in front times everything inside the ( ).

Example: $-3(x-6) + 2 = 2(4x-1)$
$$-3x + 18 + 2 = 8x - 2$$

3. Question: Are there like terms on the same side of the equation?

Answer: Yes. Then combine the like terms on the same side only.

Example: $-3x + 18 + 2 = 8x - 2$
$$-3x + 20 = 8x - 2$$

4. Question: Are there letters and/or numbers on both sides of the = ?

Answer: Yes. Then put the letters on one side and the numbers on the other side.

Example: $-3x + 20 = 8x - 2$
$$-3x + 20 + 2 = 8x - 2 + 2$$
$$-3x + 22 = 8x$$
$$3x - 3x + 22 = 8x + 3x$$
$$22 = 11x$$

5. Question: Is there a number attached to x?

Answer: Yes. Then divide both sides by the number that is attached to x.

Example: $\dfrac{22}{11} = \dfrac{11x}{11}$
$$2 = x$$

6. Question: Does this seem to be the right answer?

Answer: Yes. The answer is about right. It is not too large.

Question: How can you find out if it is right?

Answer: Substitute the answer back into the equations and see if one side equals the other side.

Example: $-3(x-6) + 2 = 2(4x-1)$
substitute 2 for x
$$-3(2-6) + 2 = 2(4(2)-1)$$
$$12 + 2 = 2(7)$$
$$14 = 14$$

Question 8: Is this the right answer?

Answer: Yes. One side equals the other side.

The metacongnitive process involves planing, monitoring and evaluating. Step one is part of the plan, steps two through five involve a combination of planning and monitoring. Step six is the evaluation. Use this as a model of asking yourself questions while solving linear equations. Ask your instructor about exceptions to these problems. Now let's look at the steps for solving quadratic equations. What are some of the questions you need to ask yourself to solve $x^2 + 6x = 16$. The first step to planning is to ask yourself questions about quadratic equations. Some example questions to solve this equation are:

1. Question: What is a quadratic equation?

Answer: It has a square term and has an = sign.

Example: $x^2 + 6x = 16$

2. Question: Does one side of the equation equal to 0?

Answer: No. Then move the term from the right side to the left side by using the opposite sign.

Example: $x^2 + 6x = 16$
$$x^2 + 6x - 16 = 16 - 16$$
$$x^2 + 6x - 16 = 0$$

3. Question: Can you factor the left side of the equation

Answer: Yes.

Example: $(x + 8)(x - 2) = 0$

4. Question: Do we have two factors?

Answer: Yes.

5. Question: What are the factors?

Answer: $(x + 8)$ and $(x - 2)$

6. Question: Can you solve each equation?

Answer: Yes.

Example:
$$x + 8 = 0 \qquad x - 2 = 0$$
$$x + 8 - 8 = 0 - 8 \qquad x - 2 + 2 = 0 + 2$$
$$x = -8 \qquad x = 2$$

7. Question: You should have two solutions. Do you?

Answer: Yes. They are -8 and 2.

8. Question A: Does this seem to be the right answer?

Answer: Yes. They are two answers and they are not too large.

Question B: How can you find out if it is right?

Answer: Put the answers back.

Example:
$$x^2 + 6x = 16; \text{ Solution one is } x = -8$$
$$64 - 48 = 16$$
$$16 = 16$$

or

$$x^2 + 6x = 16; \text{ Solution two is } x = 2$$
$$4 + 12 = 16$$
$$16 = 16$$

Question C: Are these the right answers?

Answer: Yes. One side equals the other side.

Like the previous problem, step one is part of the plan, steps two and three are a combination of planning and monitoring, while step four is monitoring. Steps five and six are a combination of planning and monitoring. Step seven is monitoring again, while step eight is evaluating. This is a model you can use to help ask yourself questions while solving problems.

You can ask your instructor about exceptions to these problems. Using metacognition to solve math problems will increase your homework and test-taking success. You may ask yourself different questions based on the different types of problems.

These questions may come slowly at first, but they will speed up and become almost automatic, just like your basic multiplication tables. Your math instructors have already achieved this goal and can solve linear and quadratic equations almost at the speed of light. Don't be intimidated. It has taken them many years to accomplish these skills. With practice, some day you can be just as effective.

Metacognition in Class

Practice these metacognitive strategies in the classroom or when watching math support videos. When your instructor puts the problem on the board or you see it in a video, follow the model of plan, monitor and evaluate. Ask yourself questions such as:

- "Do I understand the problem?"
- "What is this problem asking me to do?
- "How can I solve it using planning?"

The next step is to figure out the first step to the problem and see if the instructor writes down that first step. After doing this, move to the monitoring stage and start writing down the first step and anticipating the next steps.

As for the evaluation part of the process, pretend to check the instructor's steps to make sure they are done correctly (sometimes instructors do make mistakes). If you get confused with some of the steps, ask your instructor to clarify. By doing this, you are practicing metacognitive strategies in the classroom the same way you might while doing your homework.

Activity 7.4 Metacognitive Homework

Many students do not assess their thinking process for solving homework problems. This self-assessment will help you understand what you are thinking while working problems. This will allow you to use metacogntive strategies to solve similar problems.

1. Take one of your homework problems and write it down in the space below:

2. In the space below, write down what you are thinking as you solve the problem. In other words, describe your general approach to finding the correct answer:

3. Now write down a second similar homework problem and record what you are thinking while using the metacognitive model of plan, monitor and evaluate.

Homework problem:

Plan:

Model:

Evaluate:

Distance Learning, Emporium Model and Online Homework

Community colleges and universities are shifting more and more courses to the online and Emporium models. Both of these models require students to become self-learners and self-motivators. Emporium model classrooms require students to complete online homework without listening to lectures, and online courses require students to do just about everything on their own.

Many distance learning students have difficulty in communicating with their instructors and classmates. These students have told me that they do not know how or when to communicate with their instructor. Also, these students did not know that they could communicate with other students for support and help. As a result of this lack of communication, some of these students withdrew from their courses or made a lower grade than they'd intended.

Students in math classroom courses and distance learning math courses are having difficulty developing strategies for completing their required online homework assignments and learning the material. Students are used to doing homework with paper and pencil, not on the computer. Many of these students have told me that they completed the online homework and submitted it, only to realize later on that they have no homework to review for tests. Also, they had no homework to compare with other students or to use as a basis for in-class questions. In short, they did not know how to use online homework to improve their grades and learning. This is something that must be overcome.

These students need a system built specifically for doing online homework. This system needs to be just as detailed, perhaps even more so, than systems built for traditional, classroom-based math courses. With this in mind, over the next few sections, you'll learn:

- How to communicate with your professors and classmates.

- 10 Steps to Doing Your Online Math Homework

- Where to find additional learning resources online.

Communicating with Your Instructor and Classmates

Communicating with your instructor and classmates from a distance can be a challenge. The syllabus should have the email address and telephone number of your instructor. The first chance you get, send a "test" email to your instructor to make sure your have the correct address. Some students feel that it is an inconvenience to email their instructors questions. This is not so. The instructor expects your emails and will answer them. However, it is best not to start your email with, "I hate to bother you but…."or "I know this sounds like a stupid question but..." These types of introductions show that you are a novice distance learner and sometimes irritate the instructor. Start your email off with a direct question and you will get a direct answer.

Other students assume that their instructors are on the computer 24 hours a day, seven days a week. This is not true. These students expect the instructors to answer their questions immediately even if it is 1:00 a.m. Usually your instructors have set times of day that they answer email questions. You may want to email your instructor and ask when he or she usually answers the questions and how long it usually takes.

Don't forget about the phone. If you have detailed questions, it might be better to have them answered over the phone. Email your instructor and set up a time to call. Make sure you have the questions ready and can record the answers.

Remember: Your time and the instructor's time is valuable. Even with the best time management, you may not be able to finish the course on time. How do you communicate to your instructor that you may not finish the course on time? DON'T WAIT! Instructors hate to see an email the last week of class saying that you will not finish. As soon as you know you may not finish, let the instructor know about your difficulties.

Ask the instructor, "What do I need to do to complete the course," but also deal with the situation that has occurred. The instructor may be able to make suggestions and can give you the consequences of not finishing before it becomes a crisis. The later you wait, the less flexible the instructor will be.

Many distance-learning courses have group chat rooms. These chat rooms are live or the messages can be posted. The instant message capability of many email systems can set the stage for study groups. Ask your instructor if a time is set up for a group chat or study group. Also ask if your instructor will join the chat group and at what times. You may also get the email address of some of the other students so you can keep up with assignments and help each other with difficult problems. Communicating with your instructor can solve many problems students face in distance learning classes. Just don't wait too long to start the process.

10 Steps to Doing Your Online Math Homework

In some courses, all or part of your homework may be assigned to be done online. This is usually the case if you are taking a distance-learning course, a hybrid or blended course, an Emporium model course, or a course where the computer is an integral part of the learning process. In addition, some lecture instructors may assign homework to be done online as an alternative to homework done from the textbook. Whatever the case may be, you will need to develop study skills that can help you improve your online homework success and learning.

Doing your homework online can be a rewarding and enriching experience, but it can also be frustrating if you run into technical problems. Before you take a course that requires you to do homework online, you should ask yourself these questions:

1. Do I have easy access to computer equipment and software, including high-speed Internet access, to run the homework program?
2. Do I have the necessary computer skills to use the computer and software?
3. Am I comfortable doing my homework on the computer?

If you answered yes to all the questions, then you are ready to begin doing homework online! The 10 Steps to Doing Your Homework are still valid, but we will adapt the steps to online homework.

Step One — *Review the textbook material that relates to the homework.* This step is still essential when doing online homework. However, the software you are using may have an online textbook that has additional resources to help you learn concepts. Some programs provide you with lecture videos, animations, audio clips, and interactive exercises that you can practice working as you read through the examples in the multimedia textbook. Take advantage of these resources to help you learn the material.

Step Two — *Review your video lecture notes that relate to the homework.* If you are taking a course where your instructor does not lecture, you need to develop your own set of notes. Many software programs provide you with lecture videos. Watch these lectures and create your own notes as the presenter goes through the material. One big advantage of watching a video lecture is the ability to pause at crucial points and watch a segment over again if you need further review. In a live lecture, this is obviously not possible, and some students find it difficult to take good notes when the instructor moves too fast.

Step Three — *Do your homework as neatly as possible.* Although you will be doing your homework online, it remains important to do your work on paper and keep it in a notebook. Then, if you have a question about the homework, or if you disagree with the answer given by the program, you will be able to refer to your notes when discussing the homework with your instructor.

Step Four — *When doing your homework, write down every step of the problem.* First, write down the problem statement. This is especially important when doing online homework since many programs generate different problems for each student.

If you do not write down the problem, it can be difficult for you or your instructor to figure out what the original problem was. Next, solve the problem and show each and every step. Finally, enter the answer into the program. It is essential that you enter the answer in the correct wording and format. For example, if the program asks you to enter the answer as a fraction, and you enter the answer as a decimal, your answer may be marked wrong.

Step Five — *Understand the reasons for each problem step and check your answers.* Software programs check your answers and give you immediate feedback. This is one of the major advantages of doing homework online. If you get an answer incorrect, use the feedback along with your notes to try and figure out where you made the mistake. The program may also give you another opportunity to work the problem, perhaps with different numbers, and you should take advantage of this option. These programs also reinforce you for trying the problems by giving you positive statements when you get them correct. This makes many students feel good. However, you are not given positive statements for reading the text or watching a video. You can reinforce yourself for completing these tasks by learning more math and making better grades.

Step Six — *If you do not understand how to work the problem, use the resources provided by the software to learn how to do the problem correctly.* For example, you can ask the

program to guide you through the solution one step at a time. Use this approach to learn how to solve the problem. You may also be able to view an example that is similar to the problem you are trying to solve. You may also want to review the video lectures, multimedia textbook, or other online resources to help you understand the concepts.

Step Seven — *Always finish your homework by successfully completing problems.* With online homework, it's easier to end your homework session with feelings of success, since you can usually redo problems until you get the correct solution. Many students find that online homework not only helps them understand the concepts more readily, but it also gives them a boost in morale because of the immediate and positive feedback.

Step Eight — *After finishing your homework assignment, recall to yourself or write down the most important learned concepts.* This is still an important step when doing online homework, so resist the temptation to skip this step.

Step Nine — *Make up notecards containing hard-to-remember problems or concepts.* Some programs will provide students with ready-made notecards, and you can print these out and use them as starting points for your own notecards.

Step Ten — *Stay on schedule.* In a distance-learning, hybrid, or computer-aided course, there may not be fixed deadlines for each homework assignment, and students may be allowed to work at a flexible pace. However, if the course must be completed by the end of the term, it is better to pace yourself and complete the work in a timely manner rather than rushing to complete the bulk of the work just before the end of the term. Be sure to complete the online homework assignments in order. Math is still a sequential learning process regardless of how you do your homework!

Additional Learning Resources for In-Class and Distance Learning

For many students, additional outside resources are a necessity for doing well in a course. These outside resources supplement the online instruction and in some cases may become the primary instruction. The learning resources can be in the traditional sense and in the nontraditional sense. Traditional learning resources include the textbook, private tutoring, tutor centers, adult education centers, libraries, study skills training, DVDs, and commercial math computer programs. Non-traditional resources include call-in tutor centers, online tutor centers (comes with some textbooks), commercial online tutor centers and self-help websites. These resources often enhance your learning.

Learning resources can also be categorized based on location. There are campus-based, community-based and personal resources. Campus-based resources are becoming very important because of the unexpected number of students who take both distance-learning courses and regular classroom courses. Students who are distance learners and cannot visit the campus look for local community resources to support their learning. Personal resources, such as the computer, have tremendously expanded because of the need to support distance-learning students. Taking advantage of these resources, especially early in the term, can increase your learning and grades. Try to find out what academic resources are available before enrolling in a distance-learning course in math. It doesn't have to be just you and the course. You can always get additional help. Distance-learning students who have access to their campus resources may want to go to the college or university website. This website should give you the resource information you need to make further contacts. You may want to contact the math lab, learning center, assessment center, library, returning adult center or any other place that may be able to assist in your learning. You want to ask them the following questions:

1. Is tutoring by appointment or is it drop-in?
2. When is the best time to get tutoring?
3. Do you have evening hours for tutoring?

4. Do you have any computer programs to assess my study skills and learning styles?

5. Can math DVDs, resource books or computer programs be checked out?

6. Do you have a homework hotline?

7. What other learning resources do you have?

8. Do you have any locations that have these resources in my area?

Asking these questions will give you a good idea of the additional support that you can use on your campus. In many cases, it is too far to visit the campus to obtain this additional help. Look in your community to see if there are resources. Some of the places you can look are:

1. The local community, junior or technical college

2. The adult high school center

3. Goodwill learning centers

4. County libraries

5. Commercial tutor centers such as Sylvan Learning Center or Hunting Learning Center

6. Private tutoring

Once a resource is located, you can ask them some of the same questions that you would ask the on-campus resources. Personal resources are accessible from your home and can supplement your learning.

Personal resources have greatly expanded over the last several years to include all sorts of help aids and materials. Some of the personal resources include:

1. Private in home tutoring

2. Educational TV

3. Live telephone tutoring

4. Online book ordering

5. YouTube videos

6. Online mini-lessons, algebra models and worksheets

7. Online automated algebra problem solving

8. Live online tutoring.

Tutoring with trained tutors can be a great benefit to your learning. Some of these tutors will come to your home. You can find tutors in the phonebook by calling high school and college math departments or by asking your online instructor.

Make sure that the tutors are trained or they have references that you can call. Tutors can be a great help in improving your learning, but most students wait too long to use them. As soon as you are in trouble, or if you anticipate the need for assistance, find it immediately. Don't wait until you are failing.

There are many educational programs on television. Your local PBS station may have programs on mathematics. Also, some other colleges may have broadcast shows on how to do algebra, statistics or even calculus. Call your local cable company or PBS station to see if they have any programs on mathematics. It does not matter when the shows are broadcast because you can record them and play them back at your own convenience.

The college/university where you are taking the course may have live telephone tutoring. Also, some college textbook companies offer limited live tutoring if your college/university is using their text. Some high schools or community service groups may also have telephone or Internet tutoring.

Contact these sources to see if live telephone tutoring is an option for you. If tutoring exists, then call with specific questions about a problem. Don't just tell them, "I don't know how to do the problem." Give them the problems and tell them where you got stuck.

Sometimes your book does not give a good description on how to work certain problems. Math instructors know that some books give better explanations on how to work certain problems than other books. In this case, it would be a good idea to obtain another book on how to solve the problems.

Different self-help books or high school books may have a better explanation on how to work the problems. Now, if you are in college taking a developmental pre-algebra course, then the text you want is a combination of arithmetic and beginning algebra. If you are in a college developmental algebra course, you would want an algebra I book. If you are in college taking an intermediate algebra course, you may want Algebra II and Algebra III books. If you are in college algebra, then you want a college algebra book. You can get these books at your local bookstore, or you can go online at Amazon.com and order the books.

One extra book may make the difference in a letter grade in your course. With this in mind, another great resource for used and inexpensive text books is the Goodwill store. In fact, some cities have Goodwill stores that are just for books. These books usually only cost a few dollars and may explain math in a different way or a simpler language that works better for you.

Also, remember to ask your instructor or the math lab/learning support center director for the names of good software options like Algeblaster. Make sure this software is for adults instead of children and matches the area that you need to study.

Internet Resources

Online mini-lessons, algebra models, worksheets, virtual algebra solutions, and sites that solve math problems are on certain websites. Some websites are free. Others require a registration fee. Some of these sites have advertisements that pay for the site. You might want to review the sites under Student Math Practice and Learning Sites at AcademicSuccess.com—Student Resources. The sites are arranged by math course name with supplemental learning in calculator skills, virtual flash cards and video lessons.

Using these online sources can improve your math learning and skills. Distance learning students can also find free sites that will solve their submitted math problems.

Additional learning resources can make the difference in being successful in a distance-learning course. Explore the different resources to see which ones meet your learning style and time constraints. If you are not sure which learning resource meets your needs, then try several of the different learning resources to discover which one best improves your learning.

Using Google and YouTube to Solve Problems

Another way to use the Internet to solve homework problems is to Google the type of homework problem or to look for that type of problem on YouTube.

To Google the problem, you need to define the type of problem. Do this by turning to the textbook or homework section you are working on and looking for the heading. For example, if the section is titled "Dividing a Polynomial by a Monomial," enter the phrase exactly in the search bar. Doing this usually brings up numerous helpful websites. You may have to click on serveral before you find the best resource for your particular learning style, so do not focus on the first link you find unless it is immediately useful.

YouTube is also a great option. The website features thousands of math videos, which usually show the step-by-step processes required to solve specific types of math problems. For many visual and auditory learners, this is the best way to learn. Watching an expert solve a problem and listening to him or her describe the steps allows these students to grasp concepts much more quickly. If you are one of these students, don't hesitate to facilitate your reading sessions with any of the resources described above.

Once you discover which resources or videos work best for you, make sure to save them to your bookmarks. This will make it extremely easy to return to them in the future. This way, these Internet resources will become a part of your textbook reading process.

How to Recall What You Have Learned

After completing your homework problems, a good visual learning technique is to make notecards. Notecards are 3x5 index cards on which you place information that is difficult to learn or material you think will be on the test.

On the front of the notecard, write a math problem or information that you need to know. Color code important information in red or blue. On the back of the notecard, write how to work the problem or give an explanation of important information. Make notecards on important information you might forget. Every time you have five spare minutes, pull out your notecards and review them. Glance at the front of the card, repeat to yourself the answer and check yourself with the back of the card. If you are correct and know the information on a card, do not put it back in the deck. Mix up the cards you do not know and pick another card to test yourself. Keep doing this until there are no cards left that you do not know.

If you are an auditory learner, use a digital audio recorder just like the notecards. Record important information like you would on the front of a notecard, then leave a blank space on the recording. Record the answer. Play the audio file back. When you hear the silence, pause the recording, then say the answer out loud to yourself. Un-pause the recording and see if you were correct. You can use this technique in the car while driving to college or work.

Review What You Have Learned

After finishing your homework, close the textbook and try to remember what you have learned. Ask yourself these questions, "What major concepts did I learn tonight?" or "What test questions might the instructor ask on this material?"

Recall for about three to four minutes the major points of the assignment, especially the areas you had difficulty understanding. Write down questions for the instructor or tutor. Since most forgetting occurs right after learning the material, this short review will help you retain the new material.

Another great time to review your notes is right after completing an online homework assignment. Make sure you know what section you finish to keep track of your progress. Look at the key words and repeat them to yourself or write them down on flash cards. Review the flash cards as often as you can, and write down any websites that you find helpful, including links to YouTube videos.

When you go home, open up these sites on your computer for a second review, then bookmark them so you can use them in the future. This is an especially good strategy if you do not have a math textbook or your textbook is online. In this scenario, your online bookmarks work the same way a real bookmark would in a tradtional text.

Working with a Study Buddy

You need to have a study buddy in case you miss class or have questions when doing your homework. Group learners can especially benefit from a study buddy. A study buddy is a friend or classmate who is taking the same course. You can find a study buddy by talking to your classmates or making friends in the math lab.

Try to find a study buddy who knows more about math than you do. Tell the class instructor that you are trying to find a study buddy and ask which students might work well with you. Meet with your study buddy several times a week to work on problems and to discuss math. If you miss class, get the notes from your study buddy, so you will not get behind.

Call your study buddy when you get stuck on your homework. You can solve math problems over the phone. Do not sit for half an hour or an hour trying to work one problem; that will destroy your confidence, waste valuable time and possibly alienate your study buddy. Think how much you could have learned by trying the problem for 15 minutes and then calling your study buddy for help. Spend, at the maximum, 15 minutes on one problem before going on to the next problem or calling your study buddy. Remember that you are part of the study buddy team. If you adapt the study system that you are reading about to meet your needs, you will be an excellent study buddy.

Communicating Through Online Applications

Thanks to programs such as Skype and Apple's Facetime, it is now possible for students to conduct face-to-face study sessions from anywhere in the world. These programs are particularly useful for online students, as they are rarely in the same place at the same time as their classmates.

When setting up a video-based study session, come just as prepared as you would for a traditional meeting. Make sure to have your textbook, notes and other materials within reach. This is not a phone situation. Your study buddy can see you and everything you are doing. They will know if you are ill-prepared, so if you want a continued collegiate relationship with this person, it is important to treat the situation with respect.

Another important feature of these applications is how they allow you to share the contents of your computer screen. While this feature works differently in each program, all major video-call services allow you to show your study buddy your notes, PowerPoint slides and other materials.

Before conducting an online study session, make sure you know how these features work. This will save you a lot of time, as you won't have to constantly hold your notes up to the screen. In many cases, you won't even have to read them aloud.

Chapter 7: Summary

- Reading a math textbook is more difficult than reading texts for other courses.

- Students who learn how to correctly read a math text will be able to improve their math learning and understanding of the lecture material.

- Using the "10 Steps to Understanding Reading Material" is an excellent way to comprehend your math text.

- After using and understanding these steps, you may be able to customize your own reading steps to make reading easier and more efficient.

- Establishing study period goals is an excellent way to successfully manage homework time.

- Make sure to set a goal of either completing a given number of problems or working on problems for a set amount of time.

- Setting up short-term goals and accomplishing them is one of the best ways to gain control over math.

- Make sure you finish every homework session by working problems you can do.

- Using the "10 Steps to Better Understand What You Read" is a way to do your homework and learn math at the same time.

- These steps will decrease the chances of doing the homework one day and two days later forgetting how to work the problems.

- Follow these 10 steps until you are comfortable using them and until they become a part of your normal study routine. Then you may want to adjust the 10 steps to make your own efficient homework system.

- Applying the "10 Steps for Doing Online Homework" to distance learning courses or required online homework can increase your math learning.

- Use Google or YouTube to help solve difficult problems and bookmark these sites for future use.

- Take time after completing your homework to recall what you have learned. This will help you retain new information in your long-term memory and abstract memory.

- Make sure to find a classroom or online study buddy to help you learn math.

Name: _____   Date: _____

Assignment for Chapter 7

1. List and describe three reasons you need to read and understand your course syllabus.

> Reason One:

> Reason Two:

> Reason Three:

2. How is reading a math textbook different than reading another textbook?

3. List and describe the ten steps to reading a math textbook or online math textbook:

> Step One:

> Step Two:

> Step Three:

> Step Four:

> Step Five:

> Step Six:

> Step Seven:

> Step Eight:

> Step Nine:

> Step Ten:

4. Explain how taking notes while reading your textbook and developing a math glossary can help you learn math.

5. What do you need to do before starting your math homework?

6. What are the reasons for writing down every problem step while doing the homework?

7. List and describe the 10 Steps for Doing Your Math Homework or Online Homework:

   Step One:

   Step Two:

   Step Three:

   Step Four:

   Step Five:

   Step Six:

   Step Seven:

   Step Eight:

   Step Nine:

   Step Ten:

8. List five additional resources that you use to improve your learning.

   Resource One:

   Resource Two:

   Resource Three:

   Resource Four:

   Resource Five:

9. List and describe three strategies to help you recall what you have learned:

   Strategy one

   Strategy two

   Strategy three

10. In the space below, describe how you plan to work with your classroom or online study buddy:

How to Improve Your Math Test-Taking Skills

8

In Chapter 8
You will learn these concepts:

✓ Reasons why just attending class may not be enough to pass tests

✓ The general rules to follow before a test

✓ Ten steps to better test-taking

✓ How to take online or Emporium model tests

Why Doing Your Homework and Attending Class May Not Be Enough to Pass

Taking a math test is different from taking tests in other subjects. First, math tests not only require you to recall information, but apply it as well. Second, math tests build on each other, requiring students to know and recall material from previous units. Third, most math tests are speed tests. Fourth, Emporium model and online tests have strict time restraints and in most cases you cannot go back and review the problems.

During a test, your working memory pulls information from your long-term memory and/or fluid reasoning areas. It then puts this information together in order to answer questions. At the same time you are reading the problems, your brain is also deciding how to progress through the test, calculating answers and performing other functions. All this work requires working memory space, so you need to develop test-taking strategies and use accommodations if appropriate to free up enough working memory to correctly solve problems. Remember, math test preparation and test-taking skills are different from those needed for tests in other subjects. You need to have a test-taking plan to demonstrate your total knowledge. Students with these plans make better grades than their peers.

Most students and some instructors believe that attending class and completing every homework assignment ensures an "A" or "B" on tests. This is far from true. Listening in class and understanding how to solve problems at home is very different from actually solving the problems on a test.

Here are the reasons why:

1. In class, instructors can ask you questions to lead you to the next step.

2. In class, instructors can give you hints to help solve problems.

3. In class, you can ask helpful questions.

4. In class, instructors can do all the problem steps for you.

5. In class, you can refer to your textbook or solution manual.

6. In small groups, other students can help you solve problems.

7. There is less anxiety solving problems in class than during a test.

8. If you do not learn how to solve a problem in class, you can go to the instructor or tutor afterwards.

9. While in an Emporium model classroom, the homework management system refers you to helpful textbook sections and videos.

10. While in an online class, you can email the instructor for help.

Many students get a false sense of security because they know how to do the math problems while in class or when doing online homework. Then, when the test comes around, they have difficulty solving the same problems. Don't let this happen to you! I have worked with hundreds of students who falsely assume that they understand how to solve math problems because they got all the homework problems correct weeks before taking a test. These students guessed their way into failure, because they did not truly understand important math concepts. They did not take any notes on the problems they missed to review before the test. This reviewing could have moved the information from working memory to long-term memory or fluid reasoning. Correctly answering homework problems is very different from taking tests:

1. While doing homework there is little anxiety.

2. You are not under a time constraint while doing your homework.

3. If you get stuck on a homework problem, you have your textbook and notes.

4. Once you learn how to do several problems in a homework assignment, the rest are similar.

5. In doing homework, you have the answers to at least half the problems in the back of the text and answers to all the problems online.

6. While doing homework, you have time to figure out how to correctly use your calculator.

7. When doing homework, you can call your study buddy or ask a tutor for help.

8. When doing your homework, you can go to the Web and find online tutoring.

9. While in a Emporium model classroom, the homework management program gives you hints, examples and answers.

10. While in an online class, you can access online live tutor support programs, such as Smart Thinking.

General Pre-Test Rules

1. *Get a good night's sleep before taking a test.* If you cram all night and imagine you will perform well on your test with three to four hours of sleep, you are wrong. It is better to get seven or eight hours sleep and be fresh enough to use your memory to recall information needed to answer the questions.

2. *Start studying for the test at least three days ahead of time.* Make sure you take a practice test to find out what you do not know. Review and work the problems in your problem log. If you did not do a problem log, use the chapter review test to find out what you don't know. An even better way is to work with classmates to make up test questions. Review the concept errors you made on the last test. Meet with your instructor or tutor for help on those questions you cannot solve.

3. *Only review already-learned material the night before a test.* This prevents you from forgetting information. Studying new material sometimes forces learned concepts out of your memory.

4. *Make sure you know all the information on your mental cheat sheet.* Review your notebook to make sure you understand the concepts. Work a few problems and recall the information on your mental cheat sheet right before you go to bed. Go directly to bed; do not watch television, listen to the radio or visit Facebook. While you are asleep, your mind works on and remembers the last thing you did before going to bed.

5. *Get up in the morning at your usual time and review your notes and problem log.* Do not do any new problems. Make sure your calculator is working.

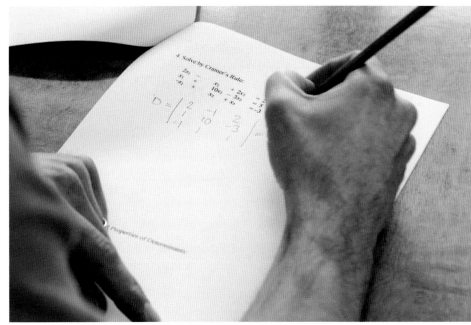

Ten Steps to Better Classroom Math Test Taking

Most students know how to take a multiple choice test, but have no clue about the best way to take a math test. When taking any test, you are being measured in two areas: the content of the material and how well you take a test. To take a math test you need a plan. This plan will make you more efficient and confident. The plan needs to be developed before you take the test and needs to be followed during the test. I have known hundreds of students who have lost tests points because they did not have a test plan and did not practice that plan before taking the test. Make sure you develop and memorize your mental cheat sheet so you can write down the information on the test (don't use the sheet during the test). Finally, make sure to practice the test-taking steps printed below.

10 Steps to Taking a Math Test (in class)

The following few pages describe a math test-taking method that has help thousands of students thrive in their math courses. Before reading the steps, however, you need to assess your current test taking method. To do this, complete activity 8.1, which is located on page 197. If you are currently taking an online math course, fill out the same form and move on to the "10 Steps to Better Online Test-Taking" section in this chapter.

Step One — *Use a memory data dump.* When you get your test, turn it over and write down the information that you put on your mental cheat sheet. Your mental cheat sheet has now turned into a mental list and writing down this information is not cheating. Do not put your name on the test, do not skim it, just turn it over and write down those facts, figures and formulas from your mental cheat sheet or other information you might not remember during the test. This is called your first memory data dump. The data dump provides memory cues for test questions.

Step Two — *Preview the test.* Put your name on the test and start previewing. Look through the entire test to find different types of problems and their point values.

Put a mark by the questions that you can do without thinking. These are the questions that you will solve first.

Step Three — *Do a second memory data dump.*

The second data dump is for writing down material that was jarred from your memory while previewing the test. Write this information on the back of the test.

Step Four — *Develop a test progress schedule.*

When you begin setting up a test schedule, determine the point value for each question. You might have some test questions that are worth more points than others. In some tests, word problems are worth five points and other questions might be worth two or three points. Just like in a video game, you must decide the best way to get the most points in the least amount of time. This might mean working the questions worth two to three points first and leaving the more difficult word problems for last. Decide how many problems should be completed halfway through the test. You should have more than half the problems completed by that time.

Step Five — *Answer the easiest problems first.*

Solve, in order, the problems you marked while previewing the test. Then, review the answers to see if they make sense. Start working through the test as fast as you can while being accurate. Answers should be reasonable. For example, the answer to a problem of trying to find the area of a rectangle cannot be negative, and the answer to a land-rate-distance problem cannot be 1,000 miles per hour. Clearly write down each step to get partial credit, even if you end up missing the problem. In most math tests, the easier problems are near the beginning of the first page; you need to answer them efficiently and quickly. Completing several easy problems first boosts your confidence, decreases anxiety and guarantees test points.

Step Six — *Complete the difficult problems you know how to do.*

These are the problems that have quite a few steps and take some time to complete, but are also problems you can complete without any real trouble. These problems are usually worth more points than the rest of the test, so it is important to finish them before you attempt problems that you don't know how to do. By finishing these problems early on in your test time, you can relax, knowing that you already have quite a few points in the bag. This will boost your confidence as you head into the problems you might not know how to do.

Step Seven — *Tackle the toughest problems.*

These are the problems that you might remember a few things about, but you don't know enough to complete them. You might remember the first step, but then draw a blank on what to do next. It is important to begin the problem, even if you know that you cannot complete it. By starting the problem and writing down what you know, you are warming up your brain, which might trigger the "Ah ha!" response. The "Ah ha!" response is when your brain suddenly remembers how to complete a problem. A memory from your homework or a lecture sometimes will pop back into your head right when you need it most. Take some time on these problems, but move on if you are completely stuck.

Step Eight — *Guess at the remaining problems.*

Do as much work as you can on each problem, even if it is just writing down the first step. If you cannot write down the first step, rewrite the problem. Also remember that the way you learned how to solve a problem was by writing, not just looking at the problem. Sometimes rewriting the problem jars your memory enough to do the first step or the entire problem. If you leave the problem blank, you will get a zero. You MUST put something down, even if it doesn't make sense. Your instructor may give you points just for the attempt.

Step Nine — *Review the test.*

Look for careless errors or other errors you may have

made. Students usually lose two to five test points on errors that could have been caught in review. Do not talk yourself out of an answer just because it may not look right. This often happens when an answer does not come out even. It is possible for the answer to be a fraction or a decimal. Remember, answers to math problems do not have "dress codes." Research shows that the odds of changing a right answer to a wrong one are much greater than the odds of changing a wrong answer to a right one.

Step Ten — *Use all of your alloted test time.* Review each problem by substituting the answer back into the equation or doing the opposite function required to answer the question. If you cannot check the problem in these ways, rework the problem on a separate sheet of paper and compare the answers. Do not leave the classroom unless you have reviewed each problem two times or until the bell rings.

Even though we encourage students to work until the end of the test period, most students leave the classroom before the end of the period. These students state that even though they know they should use all their test time, they cannot stay in the room until the end of the test time. After talking to hundreds of these students, I discovered two different themes for leaving the classroom early. First, test anxiety gets so overwhelming that they cannot stay in the room. The relief from the test anxiety (leaving the room) is worth more than getting a better grade. The other reason for leaving the test early is that they do not want to be the last or one of the last few students to turn in their tests. They still believe that students who turn their tests in last are "dumb and stupid." These students also believe that students who turn their tests in first make "A's" and "B's" and those students who turn their tests in last make "D's" and "F's."

These students need a new strategy for the middle or last part of a test. This involves performing a second relaxation technique either in the middle of the test or before reviewing the problems. Students who do a short-term relaxation technique, such as visual imagery, prevent their anxiety from getting so high that they have to leave the room. Other students may do a cognitive technique, such as telling themselves to calm down, stay in the room and finish checking their answers. Students who have extremely high test anxiety can do these techniques during the middle of the test and at the end of the test to take control of their anxiety.

If you are one of these students, you don't need to care about what other students think about you (it's usually wrong anyway). YOU need to fight the urge to leave early and use all the test time.

Remember, passing mathematics is the best way to get a high paying job and support yourself or your family. Do not worry about what others think. DO IT NOW!

Benefits to Turning in Your Scratch Paper

Stapling your scratch paper to a math test when handing it in has several advantages. First, if you incorrectly copy the answer from the scratch paper, you might still get partial credit for your answers.

Second, if you get the answer incorrect due to a careless error, your work on the scratch paper may salvage you a few points.

Third, if you do get the problem wrong, it will be easier to locate errors when the instructor reviews the test. This prevents you from making the same mistakes on your next math test.

Fourth, showing your work shows your instructor that you put in the effort to solve a problem and did not just guess or leave it blank. Many college professors are more generous than you might think. If they can tell that you put in the work, they may give you enough points to pass a test you might have otherwise failed. The important thing is to put in the effort. Even if you occasionally come up short, you'll never embarrass yourself if put in the right amount of work.

Activity 8.1   Assessing Your Test-Taking Methods

By reviewing how you took your last math test we can determine what changes you can make to improve your test-taking skills. In the space below, list your typical test-taking steps and explain them. Some students may have less than six steps and others may have more than six steps. If you have more than six steps, add them in the blank space at the bottom of this page.

Step One:

Step Two:

Step Three:

Step Four:

Step Five:

Step Six:

How to Become a Better Computer-Based Test Taker

Taking a computer-based math test differs in many ways from taking tests in traditional classrooms. Whether a part of an online math course or an Emporium classroom, computer-based tests usually measure two areas: the content of the material and how well you take a test. The second measure is more important for online tests than classroom tests and requires different test-taking skills.

First of all, depending on the rules and setup of the software you are using, you may have to vary your plan of attack. Different tests allow you different amounts of time to complete problems. Also, some tests allow you to revisit previous questions and some don't. I've worked with many students who have lost test points because a test was turned off after 55 minutes, and they were still working on problems. I've seen others lose points because the software prevented them from going back and checking their answers.

Before deciding which of the Ten Steps to Computer Test-Taking you want to use, ask your instructor these questions:

1. How much time do I have for the quiz or test?

2. How many problems are on the quiz or test?

3. Will the quiz or test automatically terminate after a certain period of time?

4. Can I have extra test time if I did not finish a problem?

5. Can I go back and review the problems that I do not finish?

6. Can I go back and review the problems that I finish?

7. Can I turn in my scratch paper for partial credit?

8. What additional resources, if any, can I have for the test?

9. Once the tests starts, can I use a blank sheet of paper for my memory data dump (mental cheat sheet)? Or will my teacher assume I am cheating?

10. After the test is graded, can I go over the test to review my mistakes?

Each instructor in a distance-learning class or Emporium model class may set up the testing process differently. Emporium tests may or may not occur during class time. It is important that you understand how this process works the first week to avoid any surprises. It is possible that you may not be able to take the tests in the way that they are set up. Math tests in distance-learning classes have been particularly problematic. Review the syllabus to see how and where you will be tested. In most cases, you may take practice tests and quizzes online, but the major tests will probably be in a secure test center, usually on a college campus. In some cases you may have to go to the local community college or university and pay to take the test in their testing centers. Make sure you are able to do this if it is the way the test administration is set up. If you can't, talk to the instructor immediately during the first week of classes. This way, if there are no alternative ways to take the tests, you are still allowed to drop or change sections of the math class.

Getting ready to take the test also involves knowing what aids you can use on the test. Check the syllabus to see if any test aids, such as calculators or index cards, can be used. If you are not sure about what you can use, email or call your instructor and ask. If you are allowed to use a calculator, make sure you know what type is permitted. When you practice taking a test, practice using the aids you are allowed to use.

Sometimes students feel a little more stressed when they have to go to a new testing center that they have never visited. First, some people get nervous about even finding the testing center. It is wise to call the testing center and get directions. If you think you are one of these people, practice getting there on a day before the test.

You will know how much time to allow for travel. Second, some students just get nervous in new environments, so when you make the "practice run" to the test center, stop in and talk to the staff just to say hi. Then if you need to call them for some reason, you can ask for particular staff who will remember who you are. Ask to see the room where you will be taking the test. Your early visit might also make the staff double check to see if they have your test scheduled. Third, if you are used to taking tests with others around you, it might be that the testing administration is set up for students to come in within certain time limitations that could be certain hours on one day or over a period of several days. You may be taking the test by yourself. Just be mentally prepared. Finally, unless you have met with several students in a study group, it will be easy to get distracted with meeting all the students with whom you have conversed over the internet or during video conferences. Stay focused and review after the test.

Remember, make sure you develop and memorize a mental cheat sheet before your test. This way, you can write down the information on a sheet of paper when the test starts.

10 Steps to Taking a Computer-Based Math Test

Before taking your test, practice the steps printed below. This test-taking plan will make you more efficient and confident. It will also lower your test anxiety.

Step One—*When you get your test, use the blank sheet of paper you showed to your instructor, and write down the information from your mental cheat sheet.* Your mental cheat sheet has now turned into a mental list, and writing down this information is not cheating. Do not wait until you get stuck on a problem before writting down the memory data dump. By that time, you may have forgotten some of the information you tried to memorize. Write down those facts, figures and formulas from your mental cheat sheet or other information you might not remember during the test. This is called your first memory data dump. The data dump provides memory cues for test questions.

Example: You have been having difficulty

multiplying two binomials, and it may take you a while to remember the rule. Write down the FOIL method, and explain each step.

Step Two — *Develop a test progress schedule.* When you begin setting up your test schedule, determine how much time you have for each question. You should already know how many questions are on the quiz or test. Then, figure out how many minutes you have to complete each problem. For example, if you have 25 test problems to complete in 60 minutes, then you have about two minutes per problem. Decide how many problems should be completed halfway through the test. You should have more than half the problems completed by that time.

If your quiz or test has a time limit, write down the time the test will end. Some students take their watch off and put it on the desk so they can keep track of time. If you cannot review test questions, use all your time working the problems. If you get ahead of your schedule, you may have extra time to check your answers on the last problems, which usually are the most difficult.

Step Three — *Start by answering the problems in proper order, unless your program allows you to skip and return to problems.* Solve the problems quickly and accurately. Then, review the answers to see if they make sense. On most computer math tests, the easier problems are near the beginning; you need to answer them efficiently and quickly. This will give you more time for the harder problems and time to review the whole test (if the software allows). If you can choose the order you answer questions, always do the easiest problems first.

Step Four — *Start working through the rest of the test as fast as you can while remaining accurate and thoughtful.* Answers should be reasonable. Make sure you are using scratch paper to work the problems. Clearly write down each step because if you are allowed to turn in your scratch paper, you may get

partial credit even if you end up missing the problem. Also, if you cannot turn in the scratch paper with the test, you can still use the scratch paper when reviewing. This allows you to discover your mistakes and correct them. Resist the idea of doing the problems in your head like you may have done while completing your computer-based homework. If you made a mental mistake during your homework, you can correct it. This is not true on the test.

Example: The answer to an equation is $x = 100$. In most cases, answers to equations are not three digits. In reviewing the problem, a mistake is found. The true answer is $x = 10$.

Step Five — *Second memory data dump.* The second data dump is for writing down material that was forgotten or jarred while working on other problems. If you are working on a problem and remember something you forgot to write on your memory data dump, write it down now. If you wait to finish the problem, you may forget it.

Step Six — *Try difficult problems.* As you are working through your test, you may encounter a difficult problem. These are the problems that you might remember something about, but you don't know enough to solve them. You might remember the first step, but then draw a blank on what to do next. It is important to begin the problem, even if you know that you cannot complete it. By starting the problem and writing down what you know, you are warming up your brain, which may lead to the solution. Take some time on these problems. If you get stuck and are able to return to unsolved problems, write down the problem number and move on. If you work too long on the problem, you waste time and increase anxiety, which reduces your ability to solve the next problem. **If your software does not allow you to review problems, then guess and move on to Step 10.**

Step Seven — *Review skipped problems.* While you are working problems, certain information may trigger an "Ah ha!" response. The "Ah ha!" response is when your brain suddenly remembers how to complete a problem. A memory from your homework or a lecture sometimes pops back into your head in the middle of a test. When this happens, immediately go back to the skipped problem and solve it. If you wait, your response may revert to: "Oh no I forgot the answer!" If you did not have an "Ah ha!" response while finishing other problems, then go back and review the skipped problems and try to solve them anyway.

Step Eight — *Guess at the remaining problems.* If you cannot write down the first step, rewrite the problem. Also, remember that the way you learned how to solve a problem was by writing — not just looking at the problem. Sometimes, rewriting a problem jars your memory enough to complete the first step or the entire problem. Also, review your memory data dump to see if any of that information leads to writing the first step.

If you are taking a multiple choice test, take the answers and put them back into the equation to see which one is correct. Do the opposite of the function to see if you can work backwards to get the correct answer. For example, if you are asked to simplify $5(x + 2)$, then take the answer and do the opposite of the function to see if your answer is correct. The answer is $5x + 10$. The opposite of the function involves factoring $5x + 10$, which is $5(x + 2)$. This is the correct answer because it matches the problem you started with. Based on the time you are given, you may only solve a few problems using this strategy. However, even if you only solve a few problems you will still gain test points. If you cannot review your answers, then this strategy should be used at the end of the test so you don't run out of time. Always put down an answer. If you leave the problem blank, or if you don't select an answer, you will get a zero.

Step Nine — *Review the test.* Review each problem by substituting the answer back into the equation or doing the opposite function required to answer the question. If you cannot check the problem in these ways, rework the problem on a separate sheet of paper and compare the answers. Look for careless errors or other errors you may have made. Students usually lose two to five test points on errors that could have been caught in review. Do not talk yourself out of an answer just because it was easy to solve.

Step Ten — *Use all your alloted test time.* Do not leave the classroom unless you have reviewed each problem twice, or if you can't review problems, until you have finished all the test. When working on the last problems, don't rush. This is an excellent time to make sure you get problems correct.

Even though we encourage students to use all of their test time, most don't. These students state that even though they know better, they cannot stay in the room until the end of the period. They also know that their grades would probably improve if they'd just check their answers or focus more on working the last problems. After talking to hundreds of these students, I have discovered two different themes for leaving the classroom early. First, test anxiety gets so overwhelming that they cannot continue the test. The only way to lessen this anxiety is to finish the test before time is up — even though they may get a lower grade. Don't let test anxiety control your grades! In the Emporium model, the other reason for completing a test early is that students do not want to be one of the last ones to finish. They still believe that students who finish last are considered "dumb and stupid." These students also believe that students who hand their tests in first make "A's" and "B's," and those students who finish their tests last make "D's" and "F's." If you are one of these students, you don't need to care about what other students think about you (it's usually wrong anyway). YOU need to fight the urge to finish early. Use all your alloted test time. Remember, passing mathematics is the best way to get the career you most want.

Activity 8.2 Assessing Your Test-Review Methods

Before you can learn how to turn your old tests into handy study guides, you need to determine what you are currently doing with your tests and how well this method is working for you. Below, put a check by what you tend to do with your graded tests (you can mark more than one):

_____ Throw the test away

_____ Look at the grade and put the test in your book

_____ Review the test without working out the missed problems

_____ Review the test and work out the missed problems

_____ Compare the problems you missed with another student's problems

_____ Work problems that are similar to the ones that you missed

_____ Go over the missed problems with your tutor

_____ Go over the missed problems with your instructor

_____ Use the test review to develop new test-taking strategies

Other:

The Six Types of Test-Taking Errors

When students get their tests back they usually don't look at them. Some throw them away or stick them in their books and forget about them. In most cases it does not matter if the students make a good grade on the test or a poor grade. They do not like reviewing the tests. Some instructors make the students review the tests by going over them in class, but rarely do the students analyze the tests on their own. This leads to repeating mistakes.

As a comparison, imagine what would happen if your doctor gave you a blood test to see why you were sick and you decided to just throw away the results and just pick some medicine off the shelf to see if it would cure you. The doctor would be sued for malpractice, and you may pick the wrong medicine and die. Perhaps the analogy exaggerates, but it makes the point. The real question is, "What do you do with your returned tests?"

Analyzing your math test will not kill you, but not doing it may kill your grades. Many students make the same mistakes over and over again, which causes them to fail too many tests. Students who analyze their tests are at a great advantage to determine how to improve on their next tests. These students find out the types of mistakes they made and now can change them. They develop better test-taking strategies for the next test and in most cases make higher scores. To improve future test scores, you must conduct a test analysis of previous tests.

In analyzing your tests, look for the following kinds of errors:

1. Misread-direction errors
2. Careless errors
3. Concept errors
4. Application errors
5. Test-taking errors
6. Study errors

Look at your last test to determine how many points you lost in the six types of test-taking errors. Analyze any previous tests to determine if there is a pattern of test errors. The type of errors is very important to determine how you can improve your studying and test-taking. For more information, visit the sample test printed at the back of this chapter.

Misread-Direction Errors

Now look at your last test. See how many points you lost to misread-direction errors. Misread-direction errors occur when you skip or misunderstand directions and do the problem incorrectly. If you do not understand if a problem you missed was a result of misread directions, ask the instructor for clarification.

Example 1: You have this type of problem to solve: (x + 1) (x + 1). Some students will try to solve for x, but the problem only calls for multiplication. You would solve for x only if you have an equation such as (x+1)(x+1) = 0.

Example 2: Another common mistake is not reading the directions before doing several word problems or statistical problems. All too often, when a test is returned, you find only three out of the five problems had to be completed. Even if you did get all five of them correct, it costs you valuable time, which could have been used obtaining additional test points.

To avoid misread-direction errors, carefully read and interpret all the directions. Look for anything that is unusual, or if the directions have two parts. If you do not understand the directions, ask the instructor for clarification. If you feel uneasy about asking the instructor for interpretation of the question, remember the instructor in most cases does not want to test you on the interpretation of the question but how you answer it. Also, you don't want to make the mistake of assuming that the instructor will not interpret the question. Let the instructor make the decision to interpret the question, not you.

Careless Errors

Careless errors are mistakes made because students lose complete focus on the question. If a student is nervous or in a hurry, little mistakes like switching signs mess up the entire problem. Sometimes, simple problems turn into nearly impossible problems if a student makes a careless error. This can really waste precious test time. Careless errors can be caught automatically when reviewing the test. Both good and poor math students make careless errors. Such errors can cost a student the difference of a letter grade on a test. Many students want all their errors to be careless errors when they analyze their

tests because it is easier to admit carelessness than admitting that they just didn't know the material. In such cases, I ask the student to solve the problem immediately while I watch. If the student can solve the problem or point out his/her mistake in a few seconds, it is a careless error. If the student cannot solve the problem immediately, it is not a careless error and is probably a concept error.

Careless Error Examples

1. Dropping the sign: -3(2x) = 6x, instead of -6x, which is the correct answer.

2. Not simplifying your answer: Leaving (3x -12)/3 as your answer instead of simplifying it to x - 4.

3. Adding fractions: 5/16 + 7/16 = 12/16 instead of 3/4.

4. Word problems: X = 15 instead of the "student had 15 tickets."

When working with students who make careless errors, I ask them two questions: First, "How many points did you lose due to careless errors?" Then I follow with, "How much time was left in the class period after you handed in your test?" Students who lose test points to careless errors are giving away points if they hand in their test papers before the test period ends. To reduce careless errors, you must realize the types of careless errors made and recognize them when reviewing your test. If you cannot solve the missed problem immediately, it is not a careless error. If your major error is not simplifying the answer, review each answer as if it were a new problem and try to reduce it.

Concept Errors

Concept errors are mistakes made when you do not understand the properties or principles required to work the problem. Concept errors, if not corrected, will follow you from test to test, causing you to lose a lot of points.

Some common concept errors are not knowing:

- (-)(-)x = x, not -x
- -1(2) > x(-1) implies 2<x, not 2>x
- 5/0 is undefined, not "0"
- (a+x)/x is not simplified to "a"
- The order of operations
- 2 + 3 x 5 = 17, not 25
- 1/2 + 1/3 = 5/6, not 2/5

Concept errors must be corrected to improve your next math test score. Students who have numerous concept errors will fail the next test since each chapter builds on the previous ones. Just going back to rework the concept error problems is not good enough. You must go back to the textbook or notes and learn why you missed those types of problems, not just the one problem itself.

The best way to learn how to work those types of problems is to set up a concept-problem error page in the back of your notebook. Label the first page "Test One Concept errors." Write down all your concept errors and how to solve them. Then, work five more problems, which use the same concept. Now, in your own words, write the reasons that you can solve these problems.

If you cannot write the concept in your own words, you do not understand it. Get assistance from your instructor if you need help finding similar problems using the same concept or cannot understand the concept. Do this for every test. For example, when preparing for your second test, review the concept errors on the first test. Continue the process all the way into the final. This is a proven system to improve your test scores.

Application Errors

Application errors occur when you know the concept but cannot apply it to the problem. Application errors usually are found in word problems, deducing formulas (such as the quadratic equation) and graphing. Even some better students become frustrated

with application errors; they understand the material but cannot apply it to the problem.

To reduce application errors, you must predict the type of application problems that will be on the test, then think through and practice solving those types of problems using the concepts.

Example: If you must derive the quadratic formula, you should practice doing that backward and forward while telling yourself the concept used to move from one step to the next.

Application errors are common with word problems. When solving word problems, look for the key phrases displayed in the "Translating English Words into Algebraic Expressions" figure to help you set up the problem. After completing the word problem, reread the question to make sure you have applied the answer to the intended question.

Application errors can be avoided with appropriate practice and insight. However, if all else fails, memorize a word problem or a graphing problem and use it as part of your memory data dump. Write it down on your test and use it as an example to solve the problems on the test.

Test-Taking Errors

Test-taking errors apply to the specific way you take tests. Some students consistently make the same types of test-taking errors. Through recognition, these bad test-taking habits can be replaced by good test-taking habits. The result will be higher test scores. The list that follows includes the test-taking errors, which can cause you to lose many points on an exam.

Error 1— *Missing more questions in the first third, second third or last third part of a test.* Divide your test in thirds. For example, if your test had 20 problems, look at the number of points missed from problems 1 through 6. How many points were missed from problems 7 through 13? How many points were missed from problems 14 to 20? Missing more questions in the first third of a test could be caused by carelessness when doing easy problems or from test anxiety. Missing questions in the last part of the test could be due to the fact that the last problems are more difficult than the earlier questions or due to increasing your test speed to finish the test.

If you consistently miss more questions in a certain part of the test, use your remaining test time to review that section of the test first. This means you may review the last part of your test first.

Error 2 — *Not completing a problem to its last step.* If you have this bad habit, review the last step of the test problem first before doing an in-depth test review.

Error 3 — *Changing correct answers to incorrect answers.* Look for erased answers on your test. I have seen students erase the correct way to solve the problem, and thus the correct answer, and then change it to an incorrect answer. I have asked these students why they erased the correct answer. In almost every case the student said that the answer was too easy to solve, so they thought it was wrong. These students need to build their test-taking confidence and know how to check their answers. If this is you, make sure you learn how to check your answers and have confidence in them.

On multiple choice tests, most students indicate that they are bad answer changers. That is because they only remember changing answers from right to wrong. They usually do not remember the times they change answers from wrong to right.

Now, let's see if you are a good, bad or neutral answer changer.

On multiple choice problems, you can change your answer three ways: from right to wrong, wrong to right and wrong to wrong. Look at the eraser marks on your answer sheet that represent the number of answers that you changed. You may want to do this on several of your tests. Count the number

of changes that represent the three categories and change them into percents.

If you have a pattern of changing over 50 percent of your answers from wrong to right then keep changing your answers. If over 50 percent of your answers are changed from right to wrong then stop changing answers. If the three categories of changing answers are about the same, then do what makes you feel the best because it is not affecting your grade.

If you don't have previous tests to measure the effectiveness of your answer changing, then wait to review several tests before you make your decision. If you are indeed a bad answer changer, then on test day use a pencil without an eraser to mark your multiple choice tests. This should stop you from changing your answers.

Error 4 — *Getting stuck on one problem and spending too much time on it.* You need to set a time limit on each problem before moving to the next problem. Working too long on a problem without success will increase your test anxiety and waste valuable time that could be used in solving other problems or in reviewing your test. For example, if your test has twenty problems that must be completed in one hour, how long should you spend on each problem? You should spend the maximum of three minutes on each problem. Of course this depends on the complexity of the problems. Spending more than three minutes, unless it is the last problem you are working on, can cost you test points.

Error 5 — *Rushing through the easiest part of the test and making careless errors.* This happens even to the best students. If you have the bad habit of getting more points taken off for the easy problems than for the hard problems, first review the easy problems and then the hard ones.

Error 6 — *Incorrectly copying an answer from your scratch paper to your test.* To avoid these kinds of errors, systematically compare your last problem step on scratch paper with the answer written on the test. In addition, always hand in your scratch work with your test.

Error 7 — *Leaving answers blank.* If you look at a problem and cannot figure out how to solve it, do not leave it blank. Write down some information about the problem, rewrite the problem or try to do at least the first step.

Error 8 — *Answering only the first step in a two-step problem.* These students get so excited when answering the first step of the problem that they forget about the second step. This is especially true on two-step word problems. To correct this test-taking error, write "two" in the margin of the problem. That will remind you that there are two steps or two answers to this problem.

Error 9 — *Not understanding all of the functions of your calculator.* Some students barely learn how to use the critical calculator functions. Then they forget or have to relearn how to use their calculator during the test, which costs test points and time. Do not wait to learn how to use your calculator on the test. Over-learn the use of your calculator *before* the test.

Error 10 — *Completing the test early without checking all of your answers.* Do not worry about the first person who finishes the test and leaves. Many students get nervous when other students start to leave early. This can lead to test anxiety, mental blocks and loss of recall. According to research, the first students to finish a test do not always get the best grades. It sometimes is the exact opposite. Ignore those students who leave and use the full time allowed.

Error 11 — *Trying to complete problems in your head.* This is especially common among distance learners and students in Emporium model courses. These student get into this habit while doing online homework. Doing problems in your head causes you to lose

points. Make sure to write down your steps so that you are able to check your work.

Error 12 — *When taking a timed test on a computer, many students do not use the last few minutes effectively.* If students cannot review their test answers, they do not slow down and check all the last questions to make sure the problems are correct. If they can check their answers, then they do not go back and do it because they think it is a waste of time. Both types of students are wasting time and losing test points.

Study Errors

Study errors, the last type of mistake to look for in a test analysis, occur when you study the wrong type of material or do not spend enough time on pertinent material. Review your test to find out if you missed problems because you did not practice that type of problem or because you did practice it but forgot how to do it during the test. Study errors will take some time to track down, but correcting study errors will help you on future tests.

Most students, after analyzing one or several tests, will recognize at least one major, common test-taking error. Understanding the effects of this test-taking error should change your study techniques or test-taking strategy.

Example: If there are seven minutes left in the test, should you review for careless errors or try to answer those two problems you could not totally solve? This is a trick question. The real question is, "Do you miss more points due to careless errors or concept errors, or are the missed points about even?" The answer to this question should determine how you will spend the last minutes of the test. If you missed more points due to careless errors or missed about the same number of points due to careless/concept errors, review for careless errors.

How to Prepare
for a Final Exam

The first day of class is when you start preparing for the final exam. Look at the syllabus or ask the instructor if the final exam is cumulative. A cumulative exam covers everything from the first chapter to the last chapter. Most math final exams are cumulative. The second question you should ask is if the final exam is a departmental exam or if your instructor makes it up. In most cases, departmental exams are more difficult and need a little different preparation. If you have a departmental final, you need to ask for last year's test and ask other students what their instructors say will be on the test.

The third question is, how much will the final exam count? Does it carry the same weight as a regular test or, as in some cases, will it count for a third of your grade? If the latter is true, the final exam will usually make a letter grade difference on your final course grade. The final exam could also determine if you pass or fail the course. Knowing this information before the final exam will help you prepare.

The fourth question pertains to a new concept in developmental education called the exit exam. Some states like Florida have an exit exam for developmental math.

Ask your instructor if you must pass an exit exam (usually the final exam) to pass the course even if you are making an "A." If this is true then ask if there is a required grade in the course such as a "C" to be eligible to take the exit test. Knowing all this information before taking the final exam will help you prepare.

Preparing for the final exam is similar to preparing for each chapter test. You must create a pretest to discover what you have forgotten. You can use questions from the textbook chapter tests or questions from your study group. Review the concept errors that you recorded in the back of your notebook labeled "Test One," "Test Two," etc. Review your problem log for questions you consistently miss. Even review material that you knew for the first and second test but which was not used on any other tests. Students forget how to work some of these problems.

If you do not have a concept error page for each chapter and did not keep a problems log you need to develop a pre-test before taking the final exam. If you are individually preparing for the final, then copy each chapter test and do every fourth problem to see what errors you may make. However, it is better to have a study group where each of the four members brings in ten problems with the answers worked out on a separate page. Then each group member can take the 30-question test to find out what they need to study. You can refer to the answers to help you solve the problems that you miss. For an example of how to analyze a previous test, review the boxes printed on the next page.

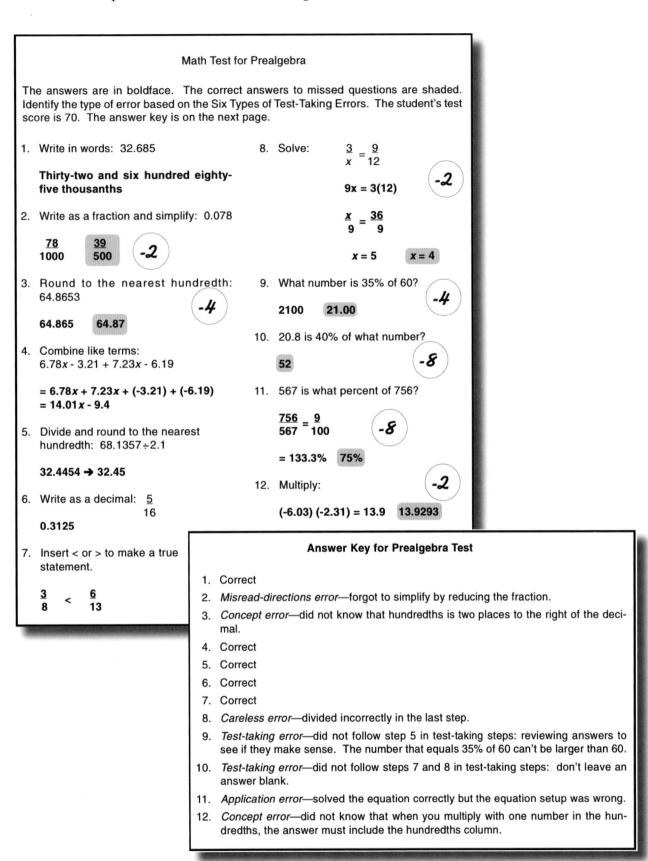

Math Test for Prealgebra

The answers are in boldface. The correct answers to missed questions are shaded. Identify the type of error based on the Six Types of Test-Taking Errors. The student's test score is 70. The answer key is on the next page.

1. Write in words: 32.685

   Thirty-two and six hundred eighty-five thousanths

2. Write as a fraction and simplify: 0.078

   $\frac{78}{1000}$ **$\frac{39}{500}$**   *-2*

3. Round to the nearest hundredth: 64.8653

   64.865   **64.87**   *-4*

4. Combine like terms:
   $6.78x - 3.21 + 7.23x - 6.19$

   $= 6.78x + 7.23x + (-3.21) + (-6.19)$
   $= 14.01x - 9.4$

5. Divide and round to the nearest hundredth: $68.1357 \div 2.1$

   32.4454 → 32.45

6. Write as a decimal: $\frac{5}{16}$

   0.3125

7. Insert < or > to make a true statement.

   $\frac{3}{8}$ < **$\frac{6}{13}$**

8. Solve: $\frac{3}{x} = \frac{9}{12}$

   $9x = 3(12)$ *-2*

   $\frac{x}{9} = \frac{36}{9}$

   $x = 5$ **$x = 4$**

9. What number is 35% of 60?

   2100   **21.00**   *-4*

10. 20.8 is 40% of what number?

    52   *-8*

11. 567 is what percent of 756?

    $\frac{756}{567} = \frac{9}{100}$ *-8*

    $= 133.3\%$ **75%**

12. Multiply: *-2*

    $(-6.03)(-2.31) = 13.9$ **13.9293**

Answer Key for Prealgebra Test

1. Correct
2. *Misread-directions error*—forgot to simplify by reducing the fraction.
3. *Concept error*—did not know that hundredths is two places to the right of the decimal.
4. Correct
5. Correct
6. Correct
7. Correct
8. *Careless error*—divided incorrectly in the last step.
9. *Test-taking error*—did not follow step 5 in test-taking steps: reviewing answers to see if they make sense. The number that equals 35% of 60 can't be larger than 60.
10. *Test-taking error*—did not follow steps 7 and 8 in test-taking steps: don't leave an answer blank.
11. *Application error*—solved the equation correctly but the equation setup was wrong.
12. *Concept error*—did not know that when you multiply with one number in the hundredths, the answer must include the hundredths column.

Chapter 8 Summary

- Just completing your homework and attending class does not guarantee that you will pass math.

- Do not cram for your math tests.

- Improving your math test-taking skills begins with completing a practice math test several days before the actual exam. This pretest can help you locate math areas that need improvement.

- Follow the general principles of good test-taking before each math test.

- Weakness can be corrected by reviewing homework or obtaining help from your instructor or tutor.

- Follow the 10 steps to better test-taking to obtain the greatest number of test points in the least amount of time.

- Make sure you develop a mental cheat sheet before each test for your memory data dump.

- After your first major test, you need to complete a test analysis to learn from your mistakes and to increase test points on the next exam.

- Decide before each test if you are going to spend the last few minutes of each test checking for careless errors or finishing problems you left incomplete.

- Without conducting a test analysis, you will probably continue to make the same old test errors and lose valuable test points.

- You need to start preparing for the final exam the first day of class.

- Ask if the final exam is going to be made up by the instructor or if it is a departmental exam. Find out how much the final exam counts for the final grade and if it is cumulative.

- When preparing for the final exam, make sure to take a pretest developed by either the instructor or yourself. This pretest must be taken under the same timed conditions as the final exam.

- You must have enough time after taking the pretest to learn how to solve the missed problems before the final exam.

- Review the 10 steps for taking a computer test to prepare for your online tests. Make sure to use the correct sequence of steps depending on your ability to return to previous questions.

Name: _____   Date: _____

Assignment for Chapter 8

1. List four reasons for why you can understand how to do the math problems in class but can still miss them on the test.

   Reason One:

   Reason Two:

   Reason Three:

2. List four reasons how you can correctly complete all the homework assignments and still not score highly on math tests.

   Reason One:

   Reason Two:

   Reason Three:

   Reason Four:

3. List two ways you can use a study group to prepare for a math test.

   One:

   Two:

4. List and discuss two general pretest rules that can help you become more successful in taking your math test.

   One:

   Two:

5. List three reasons you make a plan before taking a math test.

    One:

    Two:

    Three:

6. List the Ten Steps for Better Test-Taking (either online or in-class):

1	6
2	7
3	8
4	9
5	10

7. List the Six Types of Test-Taking errors:

1	4
2	5
3	6

8. Complete a test analysis on your last test. List two types of errors you made and how you can correct them.

    Error Type One:

    Correction:

    Error Type Two:

    Correction:

9. What are the answers to the three questions you need to ask your instructor about the final exam?

    One:

    Two:

    Three:

10. How should you run a study group to prepare for tests and the final exam?

TAKING CONTROL OF YOUR MOTIVATION AND DEVELOPING A MATH SUCCESS PLAN

9

IN CHAPTER 9
YOU WILL LEARN THESE CONCEPTS:

- ✓ Strategies to develop an internal locus of control
- ✓ Way to avoid or overcome learned helplessness
- ✓ Process to improve self-esteem and self-efficacy
- ✓ How to communicate with your math instructor
- ✓ Developing "My Math Success Plan"

Understanding Your Learning Strengths

You can take control and learn math by understanding your learning strengths, by improving your weaknesses, and by making a commitment to change your behaviors. Many students who have problems with math want to improve their learning, but no one has shown them how to change. It is not your fault that you have not been taught how to study math. Even students taking general study skills courses are often not taught how to study and learn it.

You need to take on the responsibility to improve your math learning skills and to use these new learning strengths. Students with an internal locus of control take the responsibility to change their learning behaviors and do not blame the teacher or the math department for their poor grades. Such students believe that they can change their lives and become successful math students. Students with an internal locus of control are also aware that, even without knowing it, some part of them may try to sabotage their math learning. This sabotage often comes in the form of procrastination that is meant to protect their self-esteem. This is one of the leading causes of learned helplessness.

Due to previous math failures, students with learned helplessness have learned to not even try to pass math. By better understanding themselves, such students can guard against the effects of procrastination through the use of successful math study skills.

Another key to an internal locus of control is the ability to set goals. Developing short and long-term goals decreases procrastination and prevents learned helplessness. Short-term goals can be accomplished in a few days while long-term goals may take a month or a semester. Both play a role in your math success plan.

You must also learn how to communicate with your professors. Many students are intimidated by the thought of approaching their teacher, which causes problems in overall learning, as well as poor grades. It is important for students to know that it is possible to build a communication line with a professor, and that in doing so, they can improve their grades. We will discuss this at length later in this chapter.

The last step in taking control of your math success is completing and following through with your "My Math Success Plan." This plan is a personal prescription for success.

You may have been working on your success plan while reading this text. If you have not partially completed your plan, then you will have an opportunity to complete the plan at the end of this chapter. This plan should be placed in a visible area and shared with your math instructor or advisor/counselor.

How to Develop an Internal Locus of Control and Self-Efficacy

The ways you can take control over math are by developing an internal locus of control, avoiding learned helplessness, and eliminating (or at least decreasing) procrastination. This is first accomplished by setting short-term goals and accomplishing them, in order to see the relationship between changing learning behavior and mathematics success. Then you can develop long-term goals such as making an "A" or "B" in your math class and graduating.

Defining Locus of Control and Self-Efficacy

Locus of control has to do with the locus, or location, in which a student places the control over his/her life; in other words, who or what the student feels controls his/her behavior and grades. Reviewing the information on your learning strengths in Chapter Two will help you use this chapter to your full benefit. Using this chapter can help external students to become internal and also help internal students to remain that way.

Students who feel that conditions beyond their control prevent them from getting good grades have an external locus of control. These students blame instructors, home conditions and money problems for their poor grades, and they can do nothing about their problems. In essence, external students feel their lives are controlled by outside forces, such as fate or the power of other people.

Other students feel they have the power to control their situation, and this power comes from within. These internal students take responsibility for their success, while most external students reject responsibility. Internal students believe that they can overcome most situations, since results depend on their behavior or personal characteristics. Internal students accept the responsibility for their behavior and realize that studying today will help them pass the math test scheduled for next week. Internal students can delay immediate rewards; instead of going to a party, they study for tomorrow's test. Internal students also know when to postpone putting in extra hours at their workplace in order to study for a math test.

Generally, locus of control means that students who are internal will work harder to meet their educational goals than will external students. The internal student can relate today's behavior (e.g., studying, textbook reading) to obtaining a college degree and gainful employment.

On the other hand, external students cannot connect the behavior of studying today with getting passing grades and obtaining future career opportunities. Thus, internals are more oriented toward making high math grades than are externals.

Self-Efficacy

Self-efficacy is another term that is being used in colleges and universities. This term is related to locus of control but is more specific to certain tasks. Locus of control is an overall belief that you can be successful. Self-efficacy is more specific to the belief that you have the abilities or skills to complete certain tasks (Bandura, 1982).

To determine self-efficacy, ask yourself this question by filling in the blank, "Do I have the skills and ability to succeed at _____." The blank could include tasks such as employment, an English course, history course, math course or graduating from college.

Just like in locus of control, education research has found out that self-efficacy is an important success predictor of student motivation and self-management behavior (Schunk, 1991). Students with high efficacy are more likely than students with low efficacy to complete difficult tasks, to put in more effort, to show persistence, to have used different learning strategies, and to have less fear about completing a task. In short, these students believe they can complete tasks such as taking notes, reading the textbook, completing their homework and managing their time. They persist at these skills until proficient.

Before reading this text you may not have had these skills and may have suffered from low self-efficacy. Now, you can use these learning and test-taking skills to improve your self-efficacy in math, which will lead to more motivation to becoming successful in math.

Productive Persistence

Productive persistence is the newest term associated with math success. The Carnegie Foundation defines productive persistence as the tenacity and good strategies students need to use to become successful. According to the Carnegie Foundation's research, the combination of tenacity and good study strategies is a formula for math success.

Tenacious students work hard, study the appropriate amount of hours, put a priority on learning and postpone immediate self-gratification for long-term success in math. These student remain in math classes and do not withdraw at the first sign of difficulty. They also develop short-term and long-term goals. This allows them to see the progress they make even when they hit a stumbling block. You can improve your tenacity by applying the motivational and goal setting suggestions in this chapter.

The good strategies part of this successful formula involves learning and using math study skills. Those students who use general study skills often study 15 to 20 hours a week on math without any success. I call these students "wheel spinners." By not learning math-specific study skills, these students are in effect riding a stationary bike. They are putting in a whole lot of work, but they aren't going anywhere.

The math study skills you have learned in this text have been proven to improve math success. Using these skills as part of your My Math Success Plan allows you to fulfill the Carnegie Foundation's formula. At the end of this chapter, you will complete this plan. For now, take note of all of the upcoming sections.

Based on the research you now understand that using productive persistence strategies can improve your learning and grades.

Developing Short and Long-Term Goals

External students can change into internals by taking more responsibility for their lives and completing their education. You can take more responsibility by developing and accomplishing both short-term and long-term goals. Some of your short-term goals can include the learning techniques presented in this text.

Short-term goals are goals developed and accomplished within a day or a week. The steps to obtaining your short-term or long-term goals must be thought out and written down. Keep the written goals in a place where you will see them many times each day. This will help to frequently remind you of the goals that you have set for yourself.

> **Example:** A short-term goal could be a goal of studying math today between 7:00 p.m. and 9:00 p.m. A long-term goal, for example, could be earning an "A" or "B" in the math course for the semester.

Some students need a more precise process to set up goals. It is more difficult to develop short-term goals than long-term goals. In a previous chapter, you should have developed long-term goals for your GPA and math course grade. By using the following information, it will make it easier to learn how to set up short-term goals and to evaluate your progress.

Successfully completing goals is based on the relationship of the strategy to exact study behaviors—in other words, how soon you can reach the goal and the goal's difficulty level. Goals that can be easily measured and accomplished in a short period of time have a good chance at being met. These specific goals help determine how much effort is needed and how it feels when accomplished. Students now believe they have the ability to complete the strategy, which leads to meeting their goal. This sounds a lot like internal locus of control, self-efficacy and productive persistence. The overall result is improving motivation!

New learning and test taking skills are excellent learning tasks to use for short-term goals. These skills have been proven to increase math success. If you have not done so already it is now time to set up goals to use these skills. Use the SMART goals (Smith, 1994) system for goal setting, which stands for: Specific, Measurable, Action-oriented, Realistic, and Timely.

Specific means that you want to be exact about what you want to complete. You need to describe a certain behavior to be accomplished or an outcome that you can see. Describe the specific outcome to be obtained and avoid general terms such a "satisfied", "good", "understood"and "accomplished".

General Statement: I want to do my homework

Specific statement: I will use the "Ten Steps for Doing Your Homework" and complete the 25 assigned problems.

Measurable means that you can easily see if you completed the goal. You need to determine how to measure the results or you will not know if the goal is accomplished. Establish a maximum level of goal attainment, and if need be, a minimum level.

General Statement: I am going to read my math textbook.

Specific Statement: I will read all the pages in sections 2.1 to 2.8.

Action-Oriented means that the goal includes the action that is required to accomplish that task. You need to know what skill or behavior is required to best accomplish that task.

General Statement: I am going to read my math text.

Specific statement: I will use the Ten Steps for Reading a Math Text to read all the pages in sections 2.1 to 2.8.

Realistic means that you can really accomplish the goal during the specified time.

Make sure the goal is not too challenging to be accomplished. It is better to set two short-term goals that can be accomplished than one unrealistic goal.

General Statement: I will study Sunday night for Monday's math test so I can make an A.

Specific statement: I will study Friday afternoon, Saturday afternoon and Sunday night for the Monday math test and want at least a B.

Timely means that you are breaking down a long-term goal into several short-term-goals with a specific date of completion. Breaking down a goal that can be accomplished by shorter goals can improve motivation.

General Statement: "I want to make an A in my math class."

Specific statement: "I want to make an A or B on my next math test."

The preceding were examples of each aspect of the SMART goal system. The following are some short-term goals that use the SMART system:

- I will practice two short-term relaxation techniques each day for the next two weeks.
- Two days before my next test on March 16, I will develop my "memory data dump" with at least five items.
- For every homework assignment, I will review my textbook and notes before starting the problems.
- I will develop my weekly time management schedule with eight hours a week for studying math.
- I will review my math notes the same day as the class using Six Steps to Reworking Your Notes.
- I will review my online homework problem notes two days before the online test and the day before my online test.

- I will do all my online homework using the Ten Steps for Doing Online Homework before the next class meeting.
- I will develop and practice my memory data dump (mental cheat sheet) two days before the next test. I will write it down from memory three different times.
- I will set up a study group online or at the campus three days before the test. Each group member will be assigned to bring in five questions with the written answers.

Advice on Goal Setting

These are some examples of appropriate short-term goals to improve math success. On the next page, you are going to write down three appropriate short-term goals. Think about short-term goals that will have an immediate impact on your learning and grades. As you'll soon read, it is important to immediately feel the pride-boost associated with completing a goal.

I suggest that you select one easy to accomplish goal, one medium-difficult goal and one difficult goal. These goals should be attainable in the next two weeks. The goals can have different completion dates; however, the completion date must be written down. Keep a list of these accomplished goals and review them as a motivational strategy. The more goals you accomplish, the better you will feel about succeeding in math. Also, remember that meeting short-term goals leads to greater success in meeting long-term goals. In time, meeting a goal becomes a reward in and of itself.

The ultimate success is passing your math courses and graduating. Make sure to write this goal down with your short and long-term goals. This particular goal represents the finish line to your college experience. It is easier to stay upbeat when this line is in clear view. Stay focused, stay positive and take note of each of your successes.

Activity 9.1 Setting Short-Term Goals

Rewarding yourself after meeting short-term goals increases your internal locus of control by making a strong mental connection between your behavior and the desired reward. To get started with your short-term goals, fill out the form below.

Think about three other short-term goals that will help you in math. Use the SMART system to write them in the space given below:

Goal One:

Goal Two:

Goal Three:

Now that you have developed your goals, use the information in this text and on the website to help you obtain these goals. After one week (it may be shorter for some goals) you need to evaluate the progress on obtaining your goals. In some cases, you may have to alter or rewrite your goals. Put a check by the correct response for each goal and answer the questions that apply to the goal.

Goal One
Accomplished _____
Partially accomplished _____
Not accomplished _____
This is a continuous goal _____
What was the evidence of accomplishing the goal_____
The goal needs to be rewritten Yes _____ No _____

Goal Two
Accomplished _____
Partially accomplished _____
Not accomplished _____
This is a continuous goal _____
What was the evidence of accomplishing the goal_____
The goal needs to be rewritten Yes _____ No _____

Goal Three
Accomplished _____
Partially accomplished _____
Not accomplished _____
This is a continuous goal _____
What was the evidence of accomplishing the goal_____
The goal needs to be rewritten Yes _____ No _____

How to Avoid Learned Helplessness and Procrastination

As students become more external, they develop learned helplessness. Learned helplessness means believing that other people or influences from such things as instructors, poverty or "the system" control what happens to them. Students who have failed math several times may develop learned helplessness.

A good example of learned helplessness is the total lack of motivation to complete assignments. In the past, students may have completed math assignments but did not get the grade they had hoped for. This led to the attitude of "Why try?" because they tried several times to be successful in math and still failed. The problem with this thinking is the way these students actually "tried" to pass the math course. Their ineffective learning processes, lack of anxiety reduction and poor test-taking techniques proved to be their demise. For them, it was like trying to remove a flat tire with a pair of pliers instead of using a tire iron. This text is your "tire iron." The question is, are you motivated enough to put forth the effort to use the tire iron in order to learn more and make a good grade?

Fear of Failure

Some students who fear failure procrastinate to avoid any real assessment of their true ability. By waiting too long to begin work on a paper or studying for a test, real ability is never measured — the rushed paper or the lack of preparation for a test does not reflect what you are really capable of accomplishing. Thus, you never learn the degree of "goodness" or "badness" of your academic ability. It does not feel as bad if you only study for a test for two hours and fail it compared to studying for a test for ten hours and failing.

Example: A math student who was failing a course at midterm decided to drop it and retake it the next semester. She set a goal to make an "A" when the next semester began. After making a "C" on the first major test, she became frustrated at not reaching her goal, and she started procrastinating in her studies. She fully expected to fail the course. This student believed that it was preferable not to try to pass the course if she could not make an "A."

Fear of Success

Fear of success means not making an all-out effort toward becoming successful. This is due to the student's fear that someone might be hurt or offended by the student's success. Some students believe becoming too successful will lose them friends, loved ones or spouses. They feel overwhelmingly guilty for being more successful than their family or close friends. This "fear of success" can be generalized as "fear of competition" in making good grades. These students do not fear the chance of making low grades when competing, but they fear that others will not like them if they make high grades.

> **Example:** A math student may fear that by studying too much she will make the highest test grade and set the grading curve. She has more fear that students will not like her due to her high grades than the fear of just making average grades. Such students need to take pride in their learning ability and let the other students take responsibility for their own grades.

Some of my female students have told me that this is not an unrealistic fear. According to them, if a girl does better than a boy, he often wants nothing to do with her. Sometimes they have to act dumb in order to get dates. Unfortunately, this still happens in colleges and universities.

Rebellion Against Authority

The third cause of procrastination is the desire to rebel against authority. Some students believe that by handing in their homework late or by missing the test they can "get back" at the instructor (whom they may not personally like and whom they may hold responsible for their poor math performance). These external students usually lack self-esteem and would rather blame the instructor for their poor grades than take responsibility for completing their homework on time. Rebelling against the instructor gives them a false sense of control over their lives. However, rebellious students are fulfilling the exact expectations their instructors place on them by becoming academic failures. These students discover, often too late, that they are hurting only themselves.

Perfectionism

Another group of students that are prone to procrastination are the perfectionists. This is an unusual group because they usually set goals higher than they can realistically meet. If they cannot meet the high goal of making A's on all their math tests, they want to quit. Another example of perfectionism occurs when students attend college after working or being out of school for several years. These students feel they have to make up for lost time by making perfect grades and by graduating faster than younger students. These students look at "B's" as a failure, since their goal is to make 100's on all their tests. For the older perfectionist, making a "B" on their math test means they are a failure and they want to quit college. Sometimes these goals are so unrealistic — even a genius would fail. Their motto is, "If I can't be perfect, I don't want to try at all."

These students need help to realize that, with their family and/or work responsibilities, making a B is all right. They must also learn that finishing a degree later than planned is better than not finishing at all. Being a perfectionist is not related to how high you set the goal; rather, it is the unrealistic nature of the goal itself. Extreme perfectionists are more fearful of making a "B" than an "F." These students, who are usually returning students, not only want but need to make "A's" on all their math tests to feel worth while. These students usually are making "A's" in the rest of their courses but are making "C's" and "B's" in their math classes. Even though being a perfectionist may cause some educational problems, being an extreme perfectionist causes problems in learning and testing, and can even cause psychological problems in life.

In a learning situation, extreme perfectionists want to learn math by doing homework and getting most of the problems correct on the first try. They may attempt a second try but if the problems become more difficult, they may give up in disgust and stop doing their homework all together. In other words, they tell themselves that if I cannot get it right the first time why should I try? In most cases, they have little tolerance for frustration.

Some of these students study hard (25 hours a week, just for math) and thus expect to benefit from that studying by making all "A's." This process is fine, until the extreme perfectionist student starts calculating during the test how many problems they can miss to make an "A." They have the skills to do this calculation, but during the test when they missed enough questions to drop from an "A" to a "B" sometimes they give up. Then they tell themselves, "If I cannot make an 'A,' then why should I try on the rest of the test?" They get depressed and stop trying. They will finish the test but will not give 100% on the last set of problems because they know they have made a "B" or lower. This may sound funny to students who will do anything just to make a "C," but it is the truth. The extreme perfectionists need to get help from the counseling department and from their math instructors to be successful in math. Instead of throwing away their college career, these students need to learn how to cope with making "B's" and then move on and graduate.

Determining Your Personal Habits

There are four main causes of procrastination. All students use some of these reasons for delaying studying and doing homework. Some students may use more than one reason to procrastinate. Mark in order from 1 to 4 (one being the most often used and 4 the least often used) which procrastination strategies that you are using. Use N/A if you never use these procrastination strategies.

Fear of failure _____

Fear of success _____

Rebellion _____

Perfectionism _____

Now that you have selected your reason(s) for procrastination, how much does it affect your learning? BE HONEST!

All the time _____

Most of the time _____

Some of the time _____

Not at all _____

Now you know your type(s) of procrastination and how much it affects your learning. Procrastination is not a simple issue. Students procrastinate for various reasons. Procrastination is mainly a defense mechanism that protects self-esteem. Most students who procrastinate have poor grades. By understanding the reasons for procrastination, you can avoid it and become a better math student. Another way to avoid procrastination is developing and successfully fulfilling your short-term goals. However, if you answered that procrastination affects your grades all the time or most of the time, talk to your instructor, advisor or counselor about additional strategies to reduce procrastination.

Remember, a little procrastination is normal; however, if you have determined that procrastination is a major issue for you, then advisors and instructors may not have the skills to help you. Don't wait to see a counselor or psychologist for help. They can help you to understand the reasons for your procrastination. They can also help you build a plan to decrease procrastination, which will help you complete your homework on time and allow ample time to prepare for tests. This also helps you deal with your fear of failure. You may want to include seeing a counselor or advisor as part of your math success plan. For many students learning math is not a calculation issue but a psychological issue. Don't wait to get help. DO IT NOW.

How to Improve Your Self-Esteem

Many students experience problems in both their academic and personal lives because they lack self-esteem. Self-esteem is the part of our personality which allows us to feel good about ourselves and enjoy our accomplishments. Having self-esteem means that you respect others and have a sense of peace within yourself. Students who have self-esteem also have a "can do" attitude about accomplishing their goals.

Students with poor self-esteem may not put forth as much effort to accomplish their goals. These students can improve their self-esteem by taking responsibility for their feelings, thoughts, abilities and behaviors. Students with poor self-esteem need to change their negative emotional reactions into positive emotional reactions.

Improving self-esteem can be accomplished by changing the negative emotional statements you are telling yourself and by changing the behaviors that can result in poor self-esteem. By developing positive short-term goals, you change the behaviors that are associated with poor self-esteem. You have already developed some of these short-term goals. Now you can change negative emotional self-statements, which are called self-talk, to positive statements. Follow the procedure developed by Butler (1981) and Dembo (2000) — Activity 9.2 — to help understand how to change negative self-talk to positive self-talk.

10 Ways to Improve Your Self-Esteem

Improving your self-esteem is an important step to improving your success in mathematics. Use the following positive statements to replace any negative thoughts you have during math class.

1. When I do well at something, I am going to congratulate myself.
2. I am going to stop procrastinating and blaming others for my problems.
3. When I fail at something, I am not going to blame myself but find out how to be more successful the next time.
4. I will not worry about what others think of me.
5. I will do something I like to do at least one day per week.
6. I will keep a "To Do" list, and I will feel good about myself when marking off each completed item.
7. I will set up short-term and long-term personal/educational goals.
8. I will like myself and have the courage to take risks to change.
9. I will ask for help without feeling guilty.
10. I will put five positive statements about myself on a 3x5 card, and I will read them to myself when I feel bad.

Activity 9.2 Procedures for Improving Self-Talk

The Procedures for Improving Self-Talk help change negative self-talk to positive self-talk. The importance of this process cannot be understated. To get started, follow the directions below.

1. Write down your self-talk statements. You cannot change self-talk unless you understand what you are telling yourself.

2. Review your self-talk statements to see if they are helpful or harmful. How do the statements affect your motivation, locus of control, emotions and behavior? Keep the statements that are helpful and change those that are harmful.

3. Keep the self-talk statements that are helping you become successful. Replace your negative self-talk with positive self-talk. Allow yourself to try another strategy to be successful in the task relating to the negative self-statement. Identify one of your positive characteristics (e.g. study skills, motivation, homework skills) that will help you with that task, and use that knowledge to replace your negative self-talk.

4. Develop a plan: Decide what strategies you need in order to support positive self-talk. Decide which behaviors or attitudes that need to be changed. Explain this new behavior.

How to Communicate with Your Professor

Communicating with your math instructor can help you gain control over math. However, many students have difficulty communicating with their instructor in and out of class. Some students fear talking to their instructors, while other students simply don't see the need to communicate with them at all.

Most of this fear is based on past experiences. Students often indicate that going to their math instructor is like going to the principal's office. Even if you had a poor experience attempting to communicate with an instructor in the past, that does not mean you will have the same experience with your current instructor. In fact, most math instructors want you to learn the material and want to see you succeed. Why else would they have chosen teaching as a profession? One of the biggest complaints among math instructors is that students do not ask questions in class and do not take advantage of office hours to receive additional help. If you are one of these students, then you need to take control and realize that communicating with your math instructor is essential to your success.

You should begin communicating with your math instructor in class immediately. Be sure to ask any questions you may have about the syllabus early in the course. If you have any questions about the math concepts as they are being presented, ask them.

Remember, if you have a question about something, chances are other students in the class have the same question but are afraid to ask it.

Also, be sure to communicate with your professor outside of class early in the semester. At the very least, you should make an effort to reach out to your professor before the first major exam. Use this time to ensure that you understand what material will be covered on the first exam and to work with the instructor to clarify any concepts you do not understand. Your first exam sets the tone for the rest of the class, so it is important to take it very seriously.

You can reach out to your math professor outside of class in several ways:

1. Call the math department office and make an appointment.

2. Visit the instructor during his/her office hours. Usually the office hours and syllabus are posted on their door.

3. Call the instructor at his/her office and speak on the phone.

4. Email the instructor to his/her college email address.

5. If your course has an online component or is fully online, use any available chat rooms, discussion boards, or other communication tools.

Now that you have decided to speak with your instructor, what do you want to discuss?

Don't feel that you have to wait until you are having major problems to communicate with your instructor. In fact, it is much better to start communication if you are having only minor issues with the material or simply need more information about the course. Here are some suggested topics for discussion:

1. The course syllabus (grading policy, attendance policy, etc.).

2. Your math background. Don't be afraid to tell him/her that you've had math problems in the past.

3. How to solve some math problems you are struggling with. Bring a short list of specific problems.

4. Additional resources that might be available such as tutoring, videos, etc

5. Any class meetings you know that you might miss and/or how to inform the instructor in the case of absence.

6. Questions you may have about the online homework system, the calculator, or any other course materials as applicable.

Do not ask questions or make statements like these:

1. How many classes can I miss before being withdrawn?

2. Will you be giving us any extra credit in this course?

3. Are you an easy instructor?

4. When will I ever use this stuff?

5. How many times have you taught this class before?

6. Why do I have to do my homework online?

7. You explain things differently than my last instructor.

8. I looked you up on Rate My Professor.

9. This is my second time taking this class. I really need to pass this time.

10. I'm taking this class online because I thought it would be easier.

These types of questions and statements may give the instructor a bad impression of you and put him/her on the defensive. If you ensure that your questions are positive and represent you as a dedicated and involved student who is serious about succeeding in the course, then communicating with your instructor can have many benefits. Here are just a few of them:

1. Instructors know who you are among their many other students.

2. In class, you feel more open to asking questions.

3. The instructor often answers your questions more quickly and more thoroughly than those from other students, and it becomes easier to meet with the instructor if more difficult questions or serious issues arise.

4. Your instructor is able to identify your problem areas faster and target his/her explanations to your needs.

5. The instructor is often able to teach to your preferred learning style.

6. If you have a borderline grade, the instructor may have a reason to give you the higher of the two grades based on your level of dedication.

7. The instructor may recognize your genuine desire to succeed and take longer answering your questions, particularly in an online class or in e-mail responses.

8. Your instructor may become someone you can visit in the future for additional help in other courses or to write you letters of recommendation.

The bottom line is that positive, ongoing communication with your instructor improves math learning and even math grades. DO NOT BE AFRAID! Use your internal locus of control and self-efficacy to reach out to your instructor and communicate early and often. Your instructor wants you to succeed just as much as you do!

Completing Your "My Math Success Plan"

It is now time to complete your "My Math Success Plan." By now, you should have filled out sections A-C. If you haven't, return to Chapter 2 and reread the section titled "Creating an Individual College Success Plan for Math." For a good example of what your plan should look like, review the My Math Success Plan figure in Chapter 2, which shows a completed college plan for a fall semester. As you can see, there is a blank form for you to fill out on page 216. For additional blank forms, go to the "Winning at Math Student Resources" section at AcademicSuccess.com and click on "Student Resources."

Of all of the resources available in this book, your "My Math Success Plan" is the most important. It collects your academic strengths, weaknesses, study strategies and semester goals on one single form.

Section D

Section D is where you should write down the semester goals mentioned earlier in this chapter. If you want, transfer the goals you wrote down in Activity 9.1. You may need a second meeting with your counselor to establish the rest of your goals. Remember, these goals should relate to your expected grades, study skills improvement, study schedule and, if applicable, services offered by the disability support service office.

Section E

Section E is perhaps the most important section of this activity. It is where you put together everything you have learned in this book. If you need to work on your note-taking skills, use this space to write down your intention to use the "Seven Steps to Math Note-Taking." If you need to work on your test-taking skills, write down what you learned in Chapter 8.

What you write should be completely personalized. No two students share the exact same strengths and weaknesses. Be truthful and accurate.

As you complete this section, remember that you do not need to go into too much detail. Just write down the exact strategies you are going to use from this text, and make sure you remember where to find them. In fact, it is a good idea to write down page numbers next to each strategy.

Section F

Section F is where you log all of the motivational strategies you have learned about in this chapter. For example, if you have a problem with procrastination, you would write something like, "I will figure out the reasons for my procrastination and overcome them." This is also where you list the positive statements you have created to replace any negative talk.

My Math Success Plan

Semester:

A: Student Information
Name:
Year in College:

B: Course

C: Learning Information

D: Semester Goals

1.

2.

3.

4.

5.

6.

E: Math Study Strategies

F: Motivation Strategies

Chapter 9 Summary

- Taking control over math means becoming more internal, avoiding learned helplessness and decreasing procrastination.

- You can start internalizing your locus of control by taking the responsibility for practicing the learning suggestions in this text, while setting and accomplishing realistic short-term academic goals.

- You can reduce your fear of failure by telling yourself that previous math failures were due to poor study skills, not your lack of ability.

- You can avoid learned helplessness by not giving up on making a good grade in math and, if needed, getting help from your instructor and counselor.

- If you have high test anxiety, following the suggestions given in this text can start decreasing procrastination, which should relieve some of it.

- If you have a math study procrastination problem, you can immediately set up a time management schedule and plan your study time. If you need help setting up this schedule see your counselor.

- Improve your self-esteem by making positive statements to yourself.

- In order to succeed in math, you must replace negative thoughts with positive thoughts.

- Do not believe other students when they tell you that "you can't do math."

- Productive persistence involves developing a tenacious attitude and developing math-specific study strategies.

- Using general study skills as opposed to math-specific study skills is like riding a stationary bike. You put in a great deal of effort, but don't really get anywhere.

- Communicating with your math instructor can improve your learning and grades.

- Creating a detailed math success plan is extremely important for students who want to improve in math.

- This plan involves figuring out your learning style, applying study strategies based on this learning style and then setting semester goals.

- Tell yourself that you now have the math learning strategies, test-taking strategies, motivation and persistence to become successful in math.

Name: _____   Date: _____

Assignment for Chapter 9

1. Meet with your math instructor at least three times during the semester to get feedback on your course progress and suggestions to improve your learning.

2. Meet with the math lab staff (or an LRC staff member) for your current math course at least once to discuss what you can do to improve your math grades.

3. Define Productive Persistence and how you obtain this characteristic:

4. Describe five of your short and long-term goals.

     Goal One:

     Goal Two:

     Goal Three:

     Goal Four:

5. Describe learned helplessness and how you can avoid it:

6. Explain the concept of fear of failure in your own words:

7. Explain the concept of fear of success in your own words:

8. Explain the concept of perfectionism in your own words:

9. On a separate sheet, write an analysis of your reasons for procrastination in math and decide how you are going to overcome them. Keep these posted in an area where you will frequently see them.

10. Complete "My Math Success Plan" and hand it in to your instructor or counselor/advisor. Record their comments about the plan.

APPENDIX

Scoring the Test Attitude Inventory

Test Attitude Inventory Total Score (T)

To score the Test Attitude Inventory, add the circled items 2 to 20. The maximum score will be 86, and the minimum score will be 19. On question one, reverse the values: i.e., "almost never" is a 4 instead of a 1, "sometimes" is 3 instead of 2, "often" is 2 instead of 3, and "always" is a 1 instead of a 4. NOTE THAT ONLY THE VALUES OF RESPONSES TO ITEM 1 ARE REVERSED. Add both scores for the total raw score.

Score for items 2-20   _____

Score for item 1   _____

Total Raw Score   _____

Now that you have your score, we need to find the percentile norm. Look at the chart below and select university/college or community college student. Find your raw score on the left side. Go over to the F (female) or M (male) column and circle that score. That is the percentile score to be put on your graph.

University/College

Raw score	M	F
80	100	100
79	100	100
78	100	100
77	100	99
76	100	99
75	100	98
74	99	98
73	99	97
72	99	97
71	98	96
70	98	96
69	97	96

Community College

Raw score	M	F
80	100	100
79	100	100
78	100	100
77	100	99
76	100	99
75	100	98
74	99	98
73	99	97
72	100	97
71	99	97
70	99	96
69	99	96

Raw score	M	F	Raw score	M	F
68	97	95	68	99	95
67	96	94	67	98	95
66	96	94	66	98	94
65	96	93	65	96	92
64	96	92	64	96	92
63	95	92	63	93	91
62	95	91	62	93	89
61	94	90	61	93	88
60	94	88	60	93	87
59	93	87	59	93	87
58	92	85	58	93	87
57	92	84	57	92	86
56	91	83	56	91	86
55	89	81	55	90	84
54	89	79	54	89	82
53	87	77	53	88	79
52	86	75	52	88	76
51	85	72	51	85	75
50	84	70	50	84	73
49	82	68	49	82	70
48	79	67	48	81	67
47	78	65	47	80	66
46	75	63	46	78	62
45	73	61	45	77	59
44	71	58	44	72	57
43	68	57	43	71	54
42	65	54	42	69	52
41	63	52	41	68	52
40	60	50	40	65	48
39	57	47	39	61	44
38	55	44	38	54	41
37	53	42	37	50	39
36	51	40	36	46	34
35	48	38	35	40	33
34	44	34	34	40	28
33	42	31	33	38	27
32	39	27	32	35	22
31	38	25	31	33	20
30	32	21	30	31	17

Raw score	M	F
29	29	19
28	26	16
27	23	13
26	17	10
25	15	9
24	12	6
23	10	5
22	7	4
21	4	2
20	2	1

Raw score	M	F
29	26	15
28	22	13
27	19	11
26	16	9
25	11	8
24	6	5
23	4	3
22	2	1
21	1	1
20	1	1

Test Attitude Inventory Worry Score (W)

To score the Test Attitude Inventory Worry Subscale (W), add the circled values (1,2,3,4) marked for items # 3,4,5,6,7,14,17, and 20. Enter the sum on the following line _____. This is your raw score. The maximum score is 32 and the minimum score is 8. Now that you have your raw score, we need to find the percentile norm. Look at the chart below and select university/college or community college student. Find your raw score on the left side. Go over to the F (female) or M (male) column and circle that score. That is the percentile score for the Worry Subscale (W).

University/College

Raw score	M	F
32	100	100
31	100	100
30	100	100
29	99	98
28	99	97
27	98	96
26	97	95
25	96	94
24	95	93
23	94	91
22	93	90
21	92	87
20	90	85
19	88	81
18	85	76
17	80	71
16	76	66
15	70	61

Community College

Raw score	M	F
32	100	100
31	100	100
30	100	100
29	97	100
28	96	98
27	96	96
26	96	96
25	95	95
24	94	94
23	94	94
22	91	91
21	91	91
20	85	85
19	83	83
18	81	81
17	78	78
16	74	74
15	65	65

Raw score	M	F
14	65	56
13	57	50
12	51	43
11	43	33
10	35	24
9	25	16
8	14	9

Raw score	M	F
14	57	57
13	53	53
12	44	44
11	35	35
10	28	28
9	19	19
8	10	10

Test Attitude Inventory Emotionality Subscale (E)

To score the Test Attitude Inventory Emotionality Subscale (E) add the circled values (1, 2, 3, 4) marked for items # 2, 8, 9, 10, 11, 15, 16, and 18. Enter the sum on the following line _____. This is your raw score. The maximum score is 32 and the minimum score is 8.

Now that you have your raw score, we need to find the percentile norm. Look at the chart below and select university/college or community college student. Find your raw score on the left side. Go over to the F (female) or M (male) column and circle that score. That is the percentile score for the Emotionality Subscale (E).

University/College

Raw score	M	F
32	100	100
31	99	99
30	98	95
29	97	93
28	96	91
27	94	88
26	93	86
25	91	82
24	89	77
23	87	73
22	84	69
21	78	64
20	74	61
19	70	56
18	65	51
17	59	47
16	52	42
15	46	36
14	38	29
13	32	24
12	25	18
11	20	13
10	14	8
9	8	4
8	4	2

Community College

Raw score	M	F
32	100	100
31	100	100
30	100	100
29	99	97
28	97	94
27	97	94
26	96	88
25	94	85
24	93	82
23	90	79
22	88	75
21	87	70
20	84	65
19	79	60
18	72	53
17	62	47
16	55	39
15	44	32
14	39	26
13	30	20
12	26	17
11	19	12
10	10	9
9	4	5
8	2	3

B

Learning Modality Inventory for Math Students

The following survey can help you discover how you best learn math. Answer the questions based on what you are like. There are no right or wrong answers. The more you answer truthfully, the more you will be able to use the results to improve studying math. "1" means the statement is hardly like you. "4" means the statement is really like you. Then, if you think the statement is somewhere in between, decide if it is a "2" or a "3."

Questions	Least like me		Most like me	
1. Reading a math problem out loud helps me learn better when I am studying.	1	2	3	4
2. I learn math better if I can talk about it.	1	2	3	4
3. I select certain problems and memorize what they look like so I can use them to help me remember on a math test.	1	2	3	4
4. Making things with my hands helps me learn better.	1	2	3	4
5. Drawing a picture of the word problem helps me understand how to do it on a test.	1	2	3	4
6. Math makes more sense when I see it worked out on the board.	1	2	3	4
7. Moving around while studying helps me concentrate and learn more.	1	2	3	4
8. I understand written instructions better than ones told to me.	1	2	3	4
9. I memorize what a problem looks like so I can remember it better on a test or quiz.	1	2	3	4

Questions	Least like me			Most like me
10. I repeat steps to a problem out loud or to myself in order to remember what I am supposed to do.	1	2	3	4
11. Watching someone complete a math problem helps me understand more than listening to someone tell me how to do it.	1	2	3	4
12. Talking about a math problem while learning in class helps me understand it better.	1	2	3	4
13. I learn math better when I watch someone do it.	1	2	3	4
14. When I take a test, I read the problems to myself softly.	1	2	3	4
15. When I solve a math problem on a test, I picture my notes in my head to help me remember how to solve it.	1	2	3	4
16. I enjoy making things with my hands for a hobby.	1	2	3	4
17. Math makes more sense when someone talks about it while doing it on the board rather than just doing it on the board.	1	2	3	4
18. Explaining a math problem to someone else helps me learn better when I am studying.	1	2	3	4
19. Looking at a picture from my notes or math book helps me understand a math problem.	1	2	3	4
20. Making study aids with my hands helps me learn better.	1	2	3	4
21. I understand instructions better when someone tells me what they are.	1	2	3	4
22. I memorize sentences or words I can say to myself to help me remember how to do problems on a test.	1	2	3	4
23. Pictures and charts help me see how all the parts of a word problem work together.	1	2	3	4
24. I enjoy putting things together.	1	2	3	4
25. When I solve a problem on a math test, I talk my way through it in my head or softly to myself.	1	2	3	4

Scoring Your Results

Step One: Fill in each answer score in the appropriate question number. Add the column totals. Divide Column Totals A and B by 2. Those numbers will be your final column totals. Leave Column C total as is.

Column A	Column B	Column C
1. _____	3. _____	4. _____
2. _____	5. _____	7. _____
10. _____	6. _____	16. _____
12. _____	8. _____	20. _____
14. _____	9. _____	24. _____
17. _____	11. _____	
18. _____	13. _____	
21. _____	15. _____	
22. _____	19. _____	
25. _____	23. _____	
A total _____ /2 =_____ Column Total	B total _____ /2 =_____ Column Total	C Total _____ (Do not divide).

Step Two: Fill in the number of squares to represent each column total. Any total greater than 12 indicates that modality style as a strength when you learn math. You can be strong in more than one modality. If none of the totals equal 12 squares, your highest score is your strongest modality. If you have a tie, pick the first one that comes to mind as your strongest.

	Least Like Me															Most Like Me				
Modality	1			5				10				15				20
A = Auditory																
B = Visual																
C = Kinesthetic																

Bibliography

Bloom, B. (1976). *Human Characteristics and School Learning*. New York: McGraw-Hill Book Company. (p. 35)

Brown, J. & Copper, R. (1978). *Learning Styles Inventory*. Kirkwood, MO: Educational Activities Software. (p. 46)

Butler, P. (1981). *Talking to Yourself. Learning the Language of Self-Report*. San Francisco: Harper & Row. (p. 219)

Dembo, H. (200) *Motivation and Learning Strategies for College Success*. Mahway, New Jersey: Lawrence Erlbaum Associates, Inc. (p. 219)

Farr, M & Ludden (2013) *Best Jobs for the 21st Century*. Indianapolis, IN: JIST Works pp 84-87 (p. 25)

Nolting, K. (2008). *Learning Modality Inventory for Math Students*. Bradenton, FL: Academic Success Press, Inc. (p. 46)

Nolting, P. (1987). *How to Reduce Test Anxiety, a CD*. Bradenton, FL: Academic Success Press, Inc. (p.40)

Nolting, P. D. (2014). *My Math Success Plan, a Student Workbook*. Bradenton, FL: Academic Success Press, Inc. (p. 40)

Richardson. F, and Suinn, R. (1973). "A comparison of traditional systematic desensitization , accelerated mass desensitization, and mathematics anxiety." Behavior Therapy . No. 4, pp. 212-218. (p. 57)

Spielberger, C. (1980). *Test Attitude Inventory*. Redwood, California: Mind Garden.

Tobias, S (1970). "Who's Afraid of Math and Why?" Atlantic Monthly, September, pp. 63-65. (p. 57)

About the Author

Over the past 30 years, Dr. Paul Nolting and Kimberly Nolting have helped thousands of students improve their math learning and obtain better grades. Dr. Nolting is a national expert in assessing math learning problems, developing effective student learning strategies and assessing institutional variables that affect math success. He has been an undergraduate and graduate instructor, a learning specialist, an institutional test administrator, a director of Title III, a Student Support Services director, and math lab and disability coordinator.

Copyright 2014 Randy Kennedy

His expertise ranges from designing math study skills curriculum to redesigning math courses. He is also an expert in disabilities as they relate to mathematics learning and how to set up effective accommodations. Since his dissertation in 1986 on improving math success for developmental math students with math study skills intervention, he has continued to conduct mathematics research, consult, serve as an interview subject for journal articles, write journal articles and conduct national training.

Dr. Hunter Boylan interviewed Dr. Nolting as a national math expert for the 2011 Spring edition of the Journal of Developmental Education. The article was titled, "Improving Success in Developmental Mathematics: An Interview with Paul Nolting." Dr. Nolting also coordinated the first National Math Summit held in conjunction with the American Mathematical Association of Two-Year Colleges annual conference in 2013. The summit was in response to a nationwide need for mathematic course redesigns. The summit featured two panels of national experts along with workshops that helped college faculty develop their own "Math Success Plan for College Innovation."

Dr. Nolting is also a nationally recognized consultant and trainer of math study skills, math faculty training, tutor/learning assistance training and improving classroom success. He has also consulted with colleges/universities on their Quality Enhancement Plans (QEP). One of the QEP consultations, which focused on improving the success of the school's Intermediate Algebra program, resulted in the institution receiving a national award for QEP of the Year.

He is also well-regarded for his ability to teach faculty and tutors about learning styles. This process includes assisting administrators as they develop affective math and study skills programs. He also assists colleges/

universities in providing teaching strategies and appropriate learning and testing accommodations for wounded warriors and students with disabilities.

He has written books, authored websites and conducted PBS workshops on math study skills and learning styles.

His text, *Winning at Math: Your Guide To Learning Mathematics Through Successful Study Skills*, is used throughout the United States, Canada and the rest of the world as the definitive text for math study skills. This text was selected Book of the Year by the National Association of Independent Publishers.

"The strength of the book is the way the writer leads a reluctant student through a course from choosing a teacher to preparing for the final examination," says Mathematics Teacher, a publication of the National Council of Teachers of Mathematics.

Winning at Math is the only math study skills text that features extensive research on how to improve students' success with mathematics.

Dr. Nolting has conducted numerous national conference workshops on math learning and disability issues at the American Math Association of Two Year Colleges, American Mathematics Association, National Developmental Education Association and the Association on Higher Education and Disabilities. He was a consultant for the American College Test (ACT) and the Texas Higher Education Coordinating Board.

Dr. Nolting has been widely acclaimed for his ability to communicate with faculty and students on the subject of improving math learning.

Over the last 30 years, Dr. Nolting has consulted with over 100 colleges, universities and high school campuses, including the University of Massachusetts, Florida State University, New Jersey City University, Rucker University, University of Colorado-Bolder, Texas Tech University, Black Hills State University, Tennessee Tech University, Austin Pea University, Clemson University, Colorado State University and the University of Connecticut.

Other colleges with which he has consulted include San Antonio College, St. Louis Community College, J. Sargeant Reynolds College, Montgomery College, Broward College, Miami-Dade College, Northeast State Technical Community College, Landmark College, Denver Community College, Valencia College, Mesa Community College, Glendale Community College, and Austin Community College.

He also has written seven other books, three DVDs, two CDs and authored three websites. His latest two books are *My Math Success Plan* and *Mathematics and Disability Handbook*.

My Math Success Plan is a workbook for wounded warriors and students with disabilities, which combines math study skills and educational information on how disabilities affect math learning.

The Mathematics and Disability Handbook serves as a reference text for math instructors and disability/veteran coordinators.

The three DVDs and CDs feature step-by-step guides to improving math note-taking, reducing text anxiety and improving test-taking. The websites are custom-built to improve online and Emporium model learning.

Dr. Nolting holds a Ph.D. degree in Education in Curriculum Instruction from the University of South Florida. His Ph.D. dissertation was "The Effects of Counseling and Study Skills Training on Mathematics Academic Achievement."

In recent years, he has served as an adjunct instructor for the University of South Florida and Florida Gulf Coast University. He currently serves as a visiting professor at New Jersey City University in Jersey City, New Jersey.

He conducts workshops on improving academic achievement for faculty and students with and without disabilities. He also reviews students' disability files to suggest appropriate accommodations and consults universities about the President's Taskforce on Retention and Graduation.

Index

Figures Index